Banking Pillars

How Banks of All Sizes Can Achieve Excellence under Basel III

Banking Pillars

How Banks of All Sizes Can Achieve
Excellence under Basel III

Peter W. Buerger

RMA is a member-driven professional association whose sole purpose is to advance sound risk principles in the financial services industry.

RMA helps our members use sound risk principles to improve institutional perform-ance and financial stability, and enhance the risk competency of individuals through in-formation, peer sharing, and networking.

Edited by Frank Devlin
Cover design by Arielle Morris
Text design and composition by Stephen Druding
Front and back cover photos by Shutterstock, Inc.

RMA Product Number: 0640838

ISBN: 978-1-57070-324-9

Library of Congress Control Number: 2015 930 432

Printed in the United States of America.

Contents

Introduction:
Why I Wrote This Book

The history of banking begins with merchants of the ancient world who made grain loans to farmers, and traders who carried goods between cities. This began around 2000 B.C. in Assyria and Babylonia. Historians may cite many causes for this development; I would simply call it "risk management."

Later, in ancient Greece and during the Roman Empire, lenders based in temples made loans and added two important innovations: They accepted deposits and changed money. Banking, in the modern sense of the word—with its strong focus on credit and risk insurance—can be traced to medieval and early Renaissance Italy, in particular to the rich cities in the north, such as Florence, Venice, and Genoa. Families dominated banking in 14th century Florence, establishing branches in other parts of Europe; probably the most famous Italian bank was the Medici bank, established by Giovanni de' Medici in 1397. The development of banking then spread from northern Italy throughout the Holy Roman Empire, and in the 15th and 16th centuries to northern Europe. This was followed by a number of important innovations that took place in Amsterdam during the Dutch Republic in the 17th century and in London in the 18th century.[1]

Banks have always had credit functions to minimize the potential that a bank borrower will fail to meet its obligations in accordance with agreed terms. During the 20th century, developments in telecommunications and computing caused major changes to banks' operations and let institutions dramatically increase in size and geographic spread. The use of derivatives as instruments to manage risk began in the 1970s, and developed significantly over the next decades. In the 1980s, institutions began to consider financial risk management in a portfolio or even enterprise context; firms intensified their credit and market risk management activities. Operational risk emerged in the 1990s when a rogue trader brought down a prestigious British bank.

International regulation of risk, in particular the Basel Accord, also began in the late 1980s. Financial institutions allocated significant human and monetary resources and developed proprietary risk management models and capital calculation formulas to protect themselves from unanticipated risks and reduce regulatory capital. At the same time, governance of risk management became essential, integrated risk management was introduced, and the first enterprise risk manager positions were created.

I consider myself fortunate because, after finishing my academic education, I was recruited by a large international banking organization as a junior analyst in its newly established risk management unit, and therefore experienced the development of modern enterprise risk management—from its early days when risk tools had to be developed from scratch, to the peak expansion phases in capital market divisions in the 1990s and 2000s, to the global financial crisis of the late 2000s.

The financial crisis caused many banks, including some of the world's largest, to fail, and provoked much debate about bank regulation and risk management. In particular, the crisis has demonstrated numerous weaknesses in the global regulatory framework

---

[1]Source of banking history: Wikipedia

viii Introduction: *Why I Wrote This Book*

and in banks' risk management practices. The Financial Crisis Inquiry Report in the U.S. clearly concluded[2] (a) that the crisis was avoidable, i.e., it was a result of human action and inaction; and (b) dramatic failures of corporate governance and risk management at many systemically important financial institutions (SIFIs) were a key cause. Indisputably, many institutions acted recklessly, took on too much risk, did not have enough loss-absorption capacity (capital), had too much dependence on short-term funding, and reduced their lending standards to astonishingly low levels.

However, it would be wrong to simply blame risk management divisions of banks or financial institutions. The causes of the crisis were quite diverse and complex. They are described in Chapter 1 in more detail.

Central banks / regulatory authorities and financial institutions world-wide have responded to the crisis. The Basel Accord, a set of agreements set by the Basel Committee on Bank Supervision (BCBS), which provides recommendations on banking regulations globally, has been amended under what is called Basel III to ensure that financial institutions have enough capital on account to meet obligations and absorb unexpected losses, and subsequently, avoid systemic risk through the entire global financial system. Due to various reasons, mainly the differences in the economic environment of the respective nations, it was a tremendous challenge for the international regulatory community to comprehend the Basel III document. I have a tremendous respect for the document—which was written in a relatively short period of time—and all the efforts by the experts involved. The integration of Basel III into the regulations of the various member countries—i.e., the signing of its guidelines into national laws—is another major challenge that has led to many debates on a large number of issues.

In addition, certain countries developed their own banking reforms, which are typically aligned with Basel III in core concepts but show many differences in detail, e.g., the Dodd-Frank Act in the United States, the Banking Reform in the United Kingdom, and the Swiss Finish in Switzerland. While the different banking reforms vary in depth and breadth, they share a common focus with respect to the following expectations:

1. Ensure adequate levels of capital (quality and quantity), including buffers / loss- absorption capacity for unexpected losses and periods of stress;
2. Structure asset quality in line with loss-absorption capacity and avoid large concentrations;
3. Improve risk assessment, both coverage and methodology / ensure adequacy of risk-weighted assets;
4. Ensure adequate liquidity buffers, especially in periods of stress;
5. Ensure appropriate funding profiles with limited dependence on wholesale markets;
6. Ensure the adequate handling and risk management of complex capital markets transactions, in particular over-the-counter (OTC) derivatives and securitization;
7. Improve institutions' governance and risk management, including the alignment of revenues, risk, capital, compensation, and annual distributions;
8. Protect depositors, senior creditors, and, eventually, taxpayers;
9. Optimize the organization and effectiveness of supervisory authorities;
10. Minimize/mitigate systemic risk for the entire financial system.

---

[2]"The Financial Crisis Inquiry Report: Final Report of the National Commission on the Causes of the Financial and Economic Crisis in the United States," January 2011

Financial institutions, in particular banks and investment banks, have responded to the crisis as well, especially by upgrading their governance, risk management capabilities, and—most importantly—their risk-absorption capacity and liquidity levels.

Thousands of papers have been written by international organizations, central banks, regulators, bank lobby institutions, financial institutions, and other market participants—e.g., rating agencies, consultancies, auditing firms, and information technology providers—in many countries to address the points listed above. The Bank for International Settlements (BIS) alone lists on its website (www.bis.org) hundreds of excellent documents, typically describing subjects in great detail.

Further, financial institutions—banks, in particular—have significantly upgraded their disclosures, i.e., risk reports, as parts of their annual reports or quarterly earnings reports / presentations.

Banking Pillars is different from other books about the financial crisis, banking, and risk management, in three ways.

First of all, it is written by a risk management practitioner, whose work for nearly 25 years cuts across virtually all aspects of modern banking / risk management, including all relevant divisions such as consumer finance, corporate lending, commercial real estate, capital markets / investment banking, and asset management. For all these years, I have always been at the frontier of risk management issues, for example risk assessment in the key areas of credit risk, market risk, liquidity risk, operational risk, risk governance, risk capital management, and disclosure. I have worked in senior risk management roles in large financial institutions in both head office (corporate center) and foreign operations. My roles as secretary of a risk committee and member of a credit committee at group level helped me to sharpen my personal risk perspective beyond risk management. My international perspective on banking in general and risk in particular is globally diverse: After spending seven years in New York in the 1980s, I have worked in Frankfurt, Munich, and London. My responsibilities in former roles and in my current role as consultant and trainer to financial institutions and corporations have taken me to 35 countries around the world, including developed economies and emerging-market countries.

The second difference is that *Banking Pillars* provides a comprehensive view on key banking and risk issues. This book intends to summarize the most important issues, with a focus on the 10 items listed above concentrated into one comprehensive document to help financial services executives and other interested readers absorb the complex material in a simple way.

Thirdly, this book is about simple and prudent things in life that are important to most human beings all over the world. It is about having money (capital or solvency), having some cash in your pocket (liquidity), knowing your risks, operating with realistic and sustainable goals in mind, and acting as a prudent and honest businessperson with ethics and morals (known in Germany as an "Ehrbarer Hamburger Kaufmann"). In other words, acting like our fathers and forefathers who created/developed this fantastic and exciting business.

Finding fault with individuals or institutions is not my intention. My ultimate purpose is to make a small contribution in the long-lasting process to sharpen banks' professionalism and effectiveness and to improve banks' fractured relationship with society. All in all, we need strong and efficient banks, as they play an important role in supporting economic growth, in both developed and emerging-market economies.

Acknowledgments

I would first like to acknowledge The Risk Management Association (RMA)—in particular Frank Devlin, Francis Garritt, and Edward DeMarco in Philadelphia, and Steve Shaw in London—who supported me in writing this book and with other matters. It is an honor and privilege to be associated with RMA, which has been serving the financial services industry since 1914 to advance the use of sound risk principles.

Since my first day in the business in 1990, I have met and worked with a large number of individuals; I am grateful to everyone, as they all contributed to some extent to the experience and know-how in this book.

Thanks finally to my family for putting up with me, especially during the writing process.

Peter Buerger
December 2014

P A R T

Introduction

The Financial Crisis – a Review

The global financial crisis of the late 2000s has demonstrated numerous weaknesses in the global regulatory framework and in banks' risk management practices. The crisis is considered by many economists the worst financial crisis since the Great Depression of the 1930s. It resulted in the threat of total collapse of large financial institutions, the bailout of banks by national governments, and downturns in stock markets around the world. In many areas, the housing market also suffered, resulting in evictions, foreclosures, and prolonged unemployment. The crisis played a significant role in the failure of key businesses, declines in consumer wealth estimated in the trillions of U.S. dollars, and a downturn in economic activity leading to the 2008–2012 global recession and contributing to the European sovereign-debt crisis.

The bursting of the U.S. housing bubble, which peaked in 2006, caused the values of securities tied to U.S. real estate pricing to plummet, damaging financial institutions globally. The interconnectedness of large financial conglomerates had heightened systemic risks significantly and led to a domino effect that shook all market participants and eventually taxpayers in a number of countries. Major market players were forced to exit the business and were eventually taken over by other large institutions; other highly reputed institutions only survived through government support, i.e., capital/liquidity injections or guarantees. And even those institutions that were able to steer through the crisis without any major mishaps saw their profitability fall significantly short.

Even today, more than seven years after the financial crisis began, the financial services industry remains deeply unpopular. In fact, the banking industry in particular has a seriously fractured relationship with society; customers' trust in banks has eroded notably and is far from being intact. The blame for the crisis is actually shared by many, most notably:

- Bankers—both from commercial and investment banks;
- Central bankers and regulators;
- Fund managers;
- Investors and their advisors;
- Credit rating agencies; and
- Homebuyers and mortgage brokers.

3

In the words of *The Final Report of the National Commission on the Causes of the Financial and Economic Crisis in the United States:*[3]

> "We conclude this financial crisis was avoidable. The crisis was the result of human action and inaction, not of Mother Nature or computer models gone haywire."[3]

Main Causes of the Financial Crisis

1. The Economy/Monetary Policy in the United States

Low interest rates in the United States encouraged borrowing. From May 2000 to June 2003, the Federal Reserve lowered the federal funds rate target from 6.5 percent to 1.0 percent.[4] This was done to soften the effects of the collapse of the Internet bubble and the September 2001 terrorist attacks, as well as to combat a perceived risk of deflation. Further, the U.S. trade deficit had increased by $650 billion in the time period from 1996 to 2004, or from 1.5 percent to 5.8 percent of GDP.[5] Financing these deficits required the country to borrow large sums from abroad, much of it from countries running trade surpluses. These were mainly the emerging economies in Asia and oil-exporting nations.

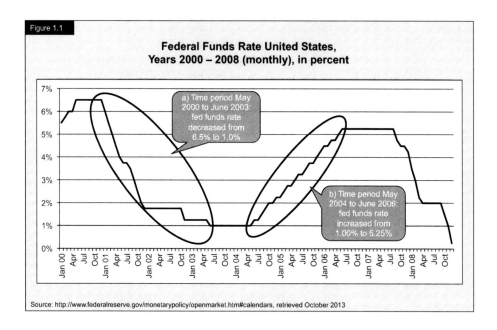

Figure 1.1

Federal Funds Rate United States, Years 2000 – 2008 (monthly), in percent

a) Time period May 2000 to June 2003: fed funds rate decreased from 6.5% to 1.0%

b) Time period May 2004 to June 2006: fed funds rate increased from 1.00% to 5.25%

Source: http://www.federalreserve.gov/monetarypolicy/openmarket.htm#calendars, retrieved October 2013

---

[3]"The Financial Crisis Inquiry Report, Final Report of the National Commission on the Causes of the Financial and Economic Crisis in the United States," January 2011

[4]http://www.federalreserve.gov/monetarypolicy/openmarket.htm#calendars. Retrieved October 14, 2013.

[5]Wikipedia

Impact and Effect of the Low Interest Rate Environment:

- Substantial borrowing leading to excessive credit growth.
- Consumer price index significantly up.
- Inflation massively up.
- Massive foreign funds invested in the United States. Low rates and the weakening dollar created a monumental carry trade (borrow dollars, buy anything). This transmitted the Fed's monetary excess abroad and into commodities. Eventually, global bonds bubbled (prices rose, yields fell), contributing to the global housing boom.
- Commodities booming.
- Liquidity flowing into real estate markets / prices significantly up, later creating a bubble.

2. Widespread Failures in Financial Regulation and Supervision

The financial crisis report notes:

- The sentries were not at their posts.
- More than 30 years of deregulation (in the U.S.) and reliance on self-regulation by financial institutions.
- The U.S. government permitted financial firms to pick their preferred regulators in what became a race for the weakest supervisor.

There are a number of other subjects to mention, some of them also relevant for banking supervisors in other major economies:

- Basel II had not yet been fully implemented, especially the most advanced methodologies for credit risk (advanced internal ratings-based approach) and operational risk (advanced measurement approach).
- Significant gaps in risk measurement for trading products between regulatory requirements (such as risk-weighted assets) and bank-internal methodologies, i.e., internal models for counterparty risk measurement or economic capital.
- Organizational separation between central banks / monetary policy and banking supervision.
- No stress testing for loss-absorption capacity / capital adequacy was monitored on the basis of unexpected losses at a high confidence level.
- No adequate supervisory approach for liquidity risk.

3. The Shadow Banking System

The market environment as described earlier created a demand for various types of financial assets with higher yields than government paper. U.S. banks created a series of new products, including collateralized debt obligations (CDOs), asset-backed securities (ABS), residential mortgage-backed securities (RMBS), and commercial mortgage-backed securities (CMBS). These products were seen as low risk, often stamped AAA by credit rating agencies, and allowed risk to be transferred from one investor to the next without the original investor retaining a share of the risk (just like in a pyramid scheme, that needs new investors to keep the system going). As a consequence, tremendous volumes of toxic mortgages were transferred from neighborhoods across America to investors around the globe.

These innovative forms of refinancing helped make for a more complex environment that featured:

- A tremendous increase in volume in the CDO, ABS, RMBS, and CMBS securitization markets, as illustrated in Figure 1.2.
- Significant volume in over-the-counter derivatives, e.g., credit default swaps (CDS).
- High complexity in the products, e.g., collateralized debt obligations
- Partial lack of understanding of products and strategies amongst top managers and non-executive directors.
- Hunt for return by many investors, including private individuals. Surprisingly, no one seemed to bother with the question of why these new securities paid a premium in yield over U.S. government paper.

Many market participants profited from the low-interest rate environment and the resulting innovations for a number of years: banks, investment banks, mortgage brokers, broker/dealers, funds, and other investors.

4. Excessive Borrowing and Risky Investments

In the years leading to the crisis, financial institutions and households borrowed too aggressively. In 2007, the five major U.S. investment banks—Bear Stearns, Goldman Sachs, Lehman Brothers, Merrill Lynch, and Morgan Stanley—were operating with extraordinarily thin capital and leverage ratios as high as 40 to 1 (for every $40 in assets, there was only $1 in capital to cover losses.) Further, leverage was often hidden in OTC derivatives positions.

In addition, investment banks were, and still are, lacking stable funding sources, especially retail depositors. Much of their borrowing was short term with a high dependency on other interbank market players / wholesale lenders.

5. Other Failures in Risk Management

For many years, banks had been upgrading their risk management infrastructures. In fact, since the emergence of derivatives in the 1980s, banks and other financial institutions world-wide invested huge amounts in both human resources and information technology. Yet risk management clearly failed in many institutions, even in a number of firms with the highest reputations in terms of risk management.

So, why did these failures occur? First of all, one needs to answer the question of what risk management actually constitutes. Banks are often organized in silos where the interrelationship between operational units is far from being optimized. Often, risk management has been set up as a separate silo, too far from the business and its strategies and, therefore, in a sub-optimal position. Further, the interrelationship between risk and finance divisions was far from optimal.

Risk management is not an organizational unit that should be detached from the rest of the organization. Of course, there must be an organizational entity called "risk management," typically headed by the head of risk or chief risk officer (CRO). But risk management's function must be present through the entire organization, starting with senior management and including the firm's culture, governance, policies, and strategy. Business divisions must have clear incentives in their scorecards, to grow/manage the balance sheet in a risk-sensitive way.

Leading up to the crisis, risk management failed in the following areas:

- Financial institutions focused somewhat on one-sided data collection and model development rather than applying a bilateral approach of using best practice methodology on one side and experience and common sense on the other side.
- Weak and even fraudulent underwriting practices: In fact, many mortgage lenders set the bars, i.e., loan-to-value ratios or documentation standards, at incredibly low or risky levels (for example, in the case of subprime mortgages).
- Home ownership in the United States increased significantly in the time period 1997 to 2004.
- Predatory lending by many institutions increased. The share of subprime lending increased in the time period from 1997 to 2006 from about 7 percent to nearly 70 percent of total mortgage originations.[6]
- Incorrect pricing of risk: In many asset classes, risk was not adequately covered in the price, especially in corporate lending.
- In the Basel II implementation period, risk management in many institutions focused significant resources on credit risk issues from the commercial loan book and on trading-related risk issues, i.e., counterparty credit risk, market risk, and operational risk. Obviously, especially regarding risk assessment for the capital markets business, not all measures and projects fulfilled their goals and objectives. And, equally important, some financial institutions failed to develop best practice infrastructures to measure, monitor, and manage liquidity risk, and eventually failed.
- A number of banks had weak risk management infrastructures; top management did not focus enough on risk.

One BIS document noted: "Some institutions in the financial system appeared to be resilient and ready to absorb also enormous market shocks. Other institutions, even with similar capital levels, appeared to be unable to protect themselves. The crucial differences between the two were found in: the quality and the level of the capital base, the availability of the capital base, liquidity management, and the effectiveness of their internal and corporate governance."[7]

6. Failures in Credit-Rating Agencies

The credit-rating agencies play a major role in the global financial markets. A credit rating is an evaluation of the creditworthiness of a debtor, especially a company or a government. The evaluation is made by a credit-rating agency of the debtor's ability to pay back the debt and the likelihood of default. The credit-rating agencies' tremendous

---

[6]Wikipedia
[7]"Capital Requirements – CRD IV/CRR – Frequently Asked Questions," Bank for International Settlements, July 16, -2013

wealth in default data and their experience and intimate know-how of institutions have placed them into an authoritative position that has largely been unchallenged.

Investors relied on the agencies' assessment or "'seal of approval,'" often blindly. In addition, credit-rating agencies were volume driven, generating huge revenues by signing large amounts of single securities. From 2000 to 2007, Moody's rated nearly 45,000 mortgage-related securities as triple-A. In 2006 alone, Moody's put its triple-A stamp of approval on 30 mortgage-related securities every working day.[8] Meanwhile, other issues added to the failure, e.g., lack of independence, lack of resources, and too much emphasis on computer models.

7. Accountability and Ethics

An ethical and sustainable bank is a bank concerned with the social and environmental impacts of its investments and loans. Ethical banks are part of a larger societal movement toward more social and environmental responsibility in the financial sector. Such movements include ethical investment, socially responsible investment, corporate social responsibility, and fair trade. Some institutions claimed to be ethical and sustainable but in reality were completely different.

Key priorities for most institutions were revenues and growth and, consequently, pay-outs to shareholders in forms of dividends and to executive management in bonuses and corporate stocks. In addition, allegations of unethical behavior proliferated in the news and books.[9]

Federal Reserve Action from 2004 to 2006 and its Consequences

To fight rising inflation, the Fed increased the federal funds rate between May 2004 and July 2006 from 1.00 percent to 5.25 percent, as illustrated in Figure 1.1 (comment b). This contributed to an increase in one-year and five-year adjustable-rate mortgage (ARM) rates, making ARM resets more expensive for homeowners. This may have also contributed to the deflating of the housing bubble, as asset prices generally move inversely to interest rates, and it became riskier to speculate in housing. U.S. housing and financial assets dramatically declined in value after the housing bubble burst.[10]

Consequences for the market:

- Adjustable-rate mortgage rates significantly up, following the increases in the benchmark rate.

---

[8]"The Financial Crisis Inquiry Report: Final Report of the National Commission on the Causes of the Financial and Economic Crisis in the United States," January 2011
[9]Greg Smith, *Why I left Goldman Sachs – A Wall Street Story*
[10]Wikipedia

- Drastic decline in demand for houses / sequential drop in markets.
- Deep recession in the housing market.
- Default rates massively up.
- Foreclosures dramatically up.
- Special purpose vehicles (SPVs) / structured products / securitization not performing.
- Asset prices falling.
- Banks and other capital markets players taking a massive hit.

Impact on Financial Markets

1. Financial Institutions

The first notable event signaling a possible financial crisis occurred in the United Kingdom on August 9, 2007, when BNP Paribas, citing "a complete evaporation of liquidity," blocked withdrawals from three hedge funds. The significance of this event was not immediately recognized but soon led to a panic as investors and savers attempted to liquidate assets deposited in highly leveraged financial institutions. The International Monetary Fund (IMF) estimated that large U.S. and European banks lost more than $1 trillion on toxic assets and from bad loans from January 2007 to September 2009. Losses of U.S. and European banks were in the trillions.[11]

Initially, the companies affected were those directly involved in home construction and mortgage lending, as they could no longer obtain financing through the credit markets. Over 100 U.S. mortgage lenders went bankrupt during 2007 and 2008. Concerns that investment bank Bear Stearns would collapse in March 2008 resulted in its fire sale to JPMorgan Chase. The financial institution crisis hit its peak in September and October 2008.

Several major institutions failed, were acquired under duress, or were subject to government takeover. In Europe, many banks had significant write-downs in assets and some were eventually rescued by their respective governments. In many cases, the failed banks did not have appropriate levels of loss-absorption capacity, i.e., capital.

However, a number of institutions failed because of a liquidity squeeze. One of the most prominent examples is Northern Rock, the fifth-largest bank in the United Kingdom in 2007. Northern Rock is most famous for its bank run in September 2007. Along with its aggressive growth strategy, the bank's funding mix in 2007 was the main contributor to the liquidity squeeze and, hence, the start to the end of operations. Northern Rock's funding distribution was heavily capital-markets driven and consisted of securitization (50 percent), interbank borrowings (25 percent), and retail deposits (25 percent). Problems were accelerated when BNP Paribas seized its hedge funds / securitized businesses. As a consequence, investors' appetite for securitized products disappeared overnight. Even though Northern Rock's securities were not backed by subprime assets, investors simply stopped buying.

---

[11]Wikipedia

Further, interbank market players closed their windows to Northern Rock in the wholesale markets, as credit analysts immediately recognized upcoming difficulties for the institution. Shortly behind them were retail depositors, who started the famous bank run that made headlines around the world. In a rather short period of time, the United Kingdom's No. 5 bank was forced out of business. Liquidity was back on the main radar screens of bank CEOs and, of course, regulators, around the globe.

The collapse of a major financial institution led to a collapse of the shadow banking system and to a contagion in the money markets. Investors world-wide started to protect their investments by withdrawing money from banks, i.e., money market mutual funds. This had a major effect on banks' ability to borrow short-term money. The global financial crisis had created a global liquidity crisis.

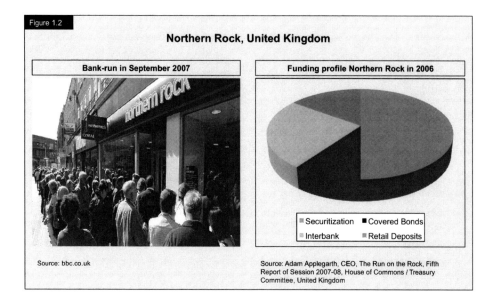

Figure 1.2

Northern Rock, United Kingdom

Bank-run in September 2007

Funding profile Northern Rock in 2006

Securitization ▪ Covered Bonds
Interbank ▦ Retail Deposits

Source: bbc.co.uk

Source: Adam Applegarth, CEO, The Run on the Rock, Fifth Report of Session 2007-08, House of Commons / Treasury Committee, United Kingdom

2. Wealth Effects[12]

The U.S. stock market peaked in October 2007, when the Dow Jones Industrial Average Index exceeded 14,000 points. It then entered a pronounced decline, which accelerated markedly in October 2008. By March 2009, the Dow Jones average had reached a low of around 6,600.

Between June 2007 and November 2008, Americans lost an estimated average of more than a quarter of their collective net worth. By early November 2008, the S&P 500 U.S. stock index was down 45 percent from its 2007 high.

Bond markets reacted accordingly, as there was an immediate flight-to-quality tendency with the expected results, such as lower yields and widening government spreads.

---

[12]Wikipedia

Housing prices had dropped 20 percent from their 2006 peak, with futures markets signaling a 30–35 percent potential drop. Total home equity in the United States, which was valued at $13 trillion at its peak in 2006, had dropped to $8.8 trillion by mid-2008 and was still falling in late 2008.

Total retirement assets, Americans' second-largest household asset, dropped by 22 percent, from $10.3 trillion in 2006 to $8 trillion in mid-2008. During the same period, savings and investment assets (apart from retirement savings) lost $1.2 trillion and pension assets lost $1.3 trillion. Taken together, these losses totaled a staggering $8.3 trillion.

Since peaking in the second quarter of 2007, household wealth was down $14 trillion.

Further, U.S. homeowners had extracted significant equity in their homes in the years leading up to the crisis, which they could no longer do once housing prices collapsed. Free cash used by consumers from home equity extraction doubled from $627 billion in 2001 to $1.428 trillion in 2005 as the housing bubble grew, for a total of nearly $5 trillion over that period. U.S. home mortgage debt relative to GDP increased from an average of 46 percent during the 1990s to 73 percent during 2008, when home mortgage debt hit $10.5 trillion.

3. Effects on the Global Economy

- Liquidity crisis.
- Recessions in many developed economies with significant impacts on the real economy, i.e., unemployment.
- European sovereign crisis, mainly in the GIIPS countries (Greece, Ireland, Italy, Portugal, and Spain).
- Economic slowdown in many emerging-market countries.
- Credit squeezes in many markets.

Government Responses

Governments and their central banks reacted quickly in various countries and provided or arranged rescue solutions. Government intervention included the following measures:

- Liquidity injections in the interbank markets.
- A lowering of the eligibility standards for refinancing with central banks.
- Capital injections into financial institutions. For example, the German government assisted the mortgage company Hypo Real Estate with a bailout through which German banks agreed to contribute €30 billion and the Bundesbank another €20 billion to a credit line.
- Control of banks with significant impact on the firms, such as management changes, compensation and dividend restrictions, review of strategy, and so on.
- Guarantees for financial institutions. For example, the Irish government introduced a blanket guarantee for its banking sector.

▪ Creation of specialized financial institutions—in other words, "bad banks"—for the transfer of non-performing assets or non-core portfolios. For example Erste Abwicklungsanstalt in Düsseldorf, Germany, was spun off from Westdeutsche Landesbank (WestLB) in 2009.

▪ Merger of financial institutions, or rather, integration of weaker firms into stronger firms. Examples include the integration of Merrill Lynch into Bank of America, the takeover of Washington Mutual by JPMorgan Chase, and the (partial) takeover of Lehman Brothers by Barclays, just to name a few.

▪ Central banks buying distressed assets and, as a consequence, increasing their balance sheets.

"We conclude the (U.S.) government was ill prepared for the crisis, and its inconsistent response added to the uncertainty and panic in the financial markets."[2]

Most notably, a number of governments quickly established deposit insurance, which followed in general the established Federal Deposit Insurance Corporation system in the United States. Explicit deposit insurance is a measure implemented in many countries to protect bank depositors, in full or in part, from losses caused by a bank's inability to pay its debts when due. Deposit insurance systems are one component of a financial system safety net that promotes financial stability. Today, deposit insurance exists in many countries, both developed and emerging.

Conclusion

The financial crisis was avoidable. Many causes have been suggested, with varying weight assigned by experts. It is important to understand these causes, as described above, in order to understand Basel III and other key banking reforms such as the Dodd-Frank Act in the United States or the Banking Reform in the United Kingdom. After all, all reforms were enacted to lessen the chance of a recurrence of another financial crisis.

The Regulators' Response to the Financial Crisis – Architecture and Timeline of Basel III[13]

Following the financial crisis of the late 2000s and the consequent government actions, the priority of governments and central banks has been first and foremost to make the financial system safe and to protect the prosperity of nations and their citizens.

Central bankers and regulators have been working hard and at high speed on new financial measures and reforms. After all, the crisis outlined weaknesses in many areas of the financial system. Experts from various countries worked with the Basel Committee on Banking Supervision (BCBS) on a new international banking reform, which eventually was discussed at the meeting of the G-20 heads of government in 2010. This, of course, was a major challenge. The suggested new reform, called Basel III, must be seen as a tremendous achievement, especially considering the breadth and depth of issues, the different economic conditions and interests in the member states, and the short period of time available.

The Basel Committee on Banking Supervision

- The Basel Committee on Banking Supervision has the task of developing international minimum standards on bank capital adequacy.
- Members come from Argentina, Australia, Belgium, Brazil, Canada, China, France, Germany, Hong Kong SAR, India, Indonesia, Italy, Japan, Luxembourg, Mexico, the Netherlands, Russia, Saudi Arabia, Singapore, South Africa, South Korea, Spain, Sweden, Switzerland, Turkey, the United Kingdom, and the United States.
- The European Commission, the European Banking Authority (EBA), and the European Central Bank are observers.
- The committee's secretariat is located at the Bank for International Settlements (BIS) in Basel, Switzerland. However, the BIS and the Basel Committee remain two distinct entities.

Endorsement by the G-20

In November 2010, the G-20 heads of government discussed the global financial system and the world economy at their meeting in Seoul, South Korea. The G-20 is the premier

13"Basel Committee on Banking Supervision Reforms – Basel III,"
http://www.bis.org/bcbs/basel3/b3summarytable.pdf, retrieved October 16, 2013

forum for discussing, planning, and monitoring international economic cooperation. The summit leaders addressed several mid- and long-term policy issues, including:

- Ensuring global economic recovery.
- Framework for strong, sustainable, and balanced global growth.
- Strengthening the international financial regulatory system.
- Modernizing the international financial institutions.
- Global financial safety nets.
- Development issues.
- The risk of a currency war.

At the Seoul meeting, the G-20 leaders endorsed the Basel III regulatory framework as follows:

"We endorsed the landmark agreement reached by the BCBS on the new bank capital and liquidity framework, which increases the resilience of the global banking system by raising the quality, quantity, and international consistency of bank capital and liquidity, constrains the build-up of leverage and maturity mismatches, and introduces capital buffers above the minimum requirements that can be drawn upon in bad times."[14]

November 2010 G-20 Seoul Summit Participants:

1. G-20 Members: Argentina, Australia, Brazil, Canada, China, France, Germany, India, Indonesia, Italy, Japan, Mexico, Russia, Saudi Arabia, South Africa, South Korea (host), Turkey, United Kingdom, United States, European Commission / European Council
2. Invited States: Singapore, Spain, Vietnam
3. International Organizations: African Union, Association of Southeast Asian Nations (ASEAN), Financial Stability Forum, International Labor Organization, International Monetary Fund, New Partnership for Africa's Development (NEPAD), Organization for Economic Co-operation and Development (OECD), United Nations, World Bank Group, World Trade Organization

In November 2011, the leaders, at their summit in Cannes, France, emphasized the importance of implementing Basel III:

"We are committed to improve banks' resilience to financial and economic shocks. Building on progress made to date, we call on jurisdictions to meet their commitment to implement fully and consistently the Basel II risk-based framework as well as the Basel II-5 additional requirements on market activities and securitization by end 2011 and the Basel III capital and liquidity standards, while respecting observation periods and review clauses, starting in 2013 and completing full implementation by 1-Jan-2019."

November 2011 G-20 Cannes Summit Participants:

1. G-20 Members: Argentina, Australia, Brazil, Canada, China, France (host), Germany, India, Indonesia, Italy, Japan, Mexico, Russia, Saudi Arabia, South Africa,

---

[14]"Report to G-20 Leaders on Basel III Implementation," BIS, June 2012, www.bis.org/publ/bcbs220.pdf

South Korea, Turkey, United Kingdom, United States, European Commission / European Council
2. Invited States: Ethiopia, Singapore, Spain, United Arab Emirates
3. International Organizations: African Union, Basel Committee on Banking Supervision, Cooperation Council for the Arab States of the Gulf (CCASG), European Central Bank, Financial Stability Forum, Global Governance Group, International Labor Organization, International Monetary Fund, NEPAD, OECD, United Nations, World Bank Group, World Trade Organization

Why Did Existing Rules (Basel II) Not Stop the Crisis From Happening?

The financial crisis unveiled a number of shortcomings of Basel II and necessitated unprecedented levels of public support in order to restore confidence and stability in the financial system. In particular, better regulation comprises the following key components:

- Better quality and quantity of regulatory capital, i.e., loss-absorption potential.
- Better liquidity management and supervision.
- Better risk management and supervision, including enhanced Pillar 2 guidelines.
- Enhanced Pillar 3 disclosures, promoting transparency.
- Enhanced governance.

International Implementation of Basel II

BCBS Member Countries and Other EU Countries

By participating in the drafting of Basel II, BCBS countries implemented the agreement, though in some cases partially. So far, only the United States has decided against full implementation—i.e., Basel II was only binding for large, internationally active U.S. banking organizations.

Non-BCBS Member Countries

Basel II was adopted by a large number of countries throughout the world.

Aims and Objectives of Basel III

Basel III is a comprehensive set of reform measures to strengthen the regulation, supervision, and risk management of the banking sector. These measures aim to:

- Improve the banking sector's ability to absorb shocks arising from financial and economic stress, whatever the source.
- Improve risk management and governance.
- Strengthen banks' transparency and disclosures.

The Main Architecture of Basel III

Basel III is not a completely new set of regulations. In fact, the new reform enhances the Basel II concept in its three main pillars, as Figure 2.1 illustrates:

- Pillar 1: Minimum capital and liquidity requirements.
- Pillar 2: Supervisory review process for firm-wide risk management and capital planning.
- Pillar 3: Risk disclosure and market discipline.

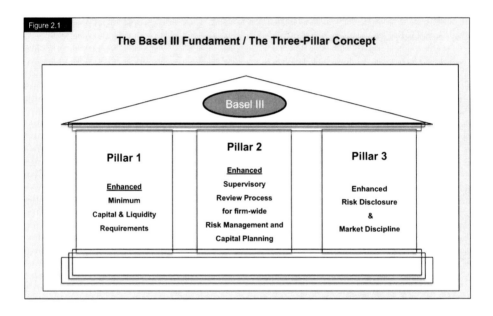

Figure 2.1

The Basel III Fundament / The Three-Pillar Concept

Pillar 1

Capital

Basel III introduces a new and stricter definition of capital and new capital buffers in order to increase the quality, consistency, and transparency of the capital base. The reform places significantly greater focus on common equity before buffers (see below). The minimum will be raised to 4.5 percent of risk-weighted assets (RWAs), after deductions.

Capital Loss Absorption at the Point of Non-Viability

Contractual terms of capital instruments will include a clause that allows—at the discretion of the relevant authority—write-off or conversion to common shares if the bank is judged to be non-viable. This principle increases the contribution of the private sector to resolving future banking crises and thereby reduces moral hazard.

Capital Conservation Buffer

The new buffer comprises common equity of 2.5 percent of risk-weighted assets, bringing the total common equity standard to 7 percent. Constraint on a bank's discretionary distributions will be imposed when banks fall into the buffer range, i.e., dividends or bonuses.

Countercyclical Buffer

When authorities determine that credit growth is resulting in an unacceptable build-up of systematic risk, an additional buffer, the countercyclical buffer, will be imposed within a range of 0-2.5 percent comprising common equity.

Risk Coverage / Risk-Weighted Assets

Moreover, Basel III increases capital requirements / risk-weighted assets for trading business, mainly counterparty credit risk arising from over-the-counter (OTC) derivatives, repurchase agreements (repos), and securities financing activities and securitization.

Securitizations

Basel III strengthens the capital treatment for certain complex securitizations. It requires banks to conduct more rigorous credit analyses of externally rated securitization exposures.

Trading Book / Market Risk

The reform charges significantly higher capital for trading and derivatives activities, as well as complex securitizations held in the trading book. It introduces a stressed value-at-risk (VaR) framework to help mitigate procyclicality. Further, a capital charge for incremental risk is introduced that estimates the default and migration risks of unsecuritized credit products and takes liquidity into account.

Counterparty Credit Risk (CCR)

Basel III closes the gap toward banks' internal measurement approaches and, therefore, substantially strengthens the framework for counterparty credit risk. This includes:

- More stringent requirements for measuring exposure.
- Capital incentives for banks to use central counterparties and utilize collateralization for OTC derivatives.
- Higher capital for inter-financial sector exposures.

Bank Exposures to Central Counterparties (CCPs)

The committee has proposed that trade exposures to a qualifying CCP will receive a 2 percent risk weight and default fund exposures to a qualifying CCP will be capitalized according to a risk-based method that consistently and simply estimates risk arising from such a default fund.

Leverage Ratio

The regulation introduces a non-risk-based leverage ratio that includes off-balance-sheet exposures that will serve as a backstop to the risk-based capital requirement. The ratio also helps to contain a system-wide build up of leverage.

More Balanced Liquidity

A major problem during the crisis was the lack of liquid assets and liquid funding—referred to as "the market dried up." Basel III requires bankers to manage their cash flows and liquidity much more intensely than before, to predict the liquidity flows resulting from creditors' claims better than before, and to be ready for stressed market conditions by having sufficient "cash" available, both in the short term and in the longer run.

Pillar 2

Risk Management and Supervision / Supplemental Pillar 2 Requirements

The requirements address firm-wide governance and risk management. Key areas of focus include:

- Capturing the risk of off-balance sheet exposures and securitization activities;
- Managing risk concentrations; i.e., from large credit exposures to individual borrowers or a specific industry, or from dependencies on certain funding sources;
- Providing incentives for banks to better manage risk and returns over the long term;
- Sound compensation practices;
- Valuation practices;
- Stress testing;
- Accounting standards for financial instruments; and
- Corporate governance.

Pillar 3

Market Discipline / Revised Pillar 3 Disclosure Requirements

The requirements introduced relate to securitization exposures and sponsorship of off-balance-sheet vehicles. Enhanced disclosures regarding the detail of the components of regulatory capital and their reconciliation to the reported accounts will be required, including a comprehensive explanation of how a bank calculates its regulatory capital ratios. All in all, banks have to disclose their key risk and performance indicators in a very transparent way.

Systemically Important Financial Institutions (SIFIs)

In addition to meeting the Basel III requirements, global systemically important financial institutions must have higher loss-absorbency capacity to reflect the greater risks that they pose to the financial system. The committee has developed a methodology that includes both quantitative indicators and qualitative elements to identify global systemically important banks (SIBs).

The additional loss-absorbency requirements are to be met with a progressive common equity tier 1 (CET1) capital requirement ranging from 1 percent to 3.5 percent, depending on a bank's systemic importance. For banks facing the highest SIB surcharge, an additional loss absorbency of 1 percent could be applied as a disincentive to increase materially their global systemic importance in the future.

SIFIs will have higher requirements regarding risk management and governance and disclosure. Hence, this issue addresses all three pillars.

Global Liquidity Standard

Liquidity Coverage Ratio (LCR)

The liquidity coverage ratio will require banks to have sufficient high-quality liquid assets (HQLA) to withstand a 30-day stressed funding scenario that is specified by supervisors.

Net Stable Funding Ratio (NSFR)

The net stable funding ratio is a longer-term structural ratio designed to address liquidity mismatches. It covers the entire balance sheet and provides incentives for banks to use stable sources of funding.

Principles for Sound Liquidity Risk Management and Supervision

The committee's 2008 guidance, *Principles for Sound Liquidity Risk Management and Supervision*, takes account of lessons learned during the crisis and is based on a fundamental review of sound practices for managing liquidity risk in banks.

Supervisory Monitoring

The liquidity framework includes a common set of monitoring metrics to assist supervisors in identifying and analyzing liquidity risk trends at both the bank and system-wide level.

Did you know?[15]

- G-20 members represent almost 90 percent of global GDP.
- G-20 members represent 80 percent of international global-trade.
- Two-thirds of the world's population lives in G-20 member countries.
- 84 percent of all fossil fuel emissions are produced by G-20 countries.

---

[15]G-20 Website, www.g20.org

Basel III Timetable / Phase-in Arrangements[16]
(effective dates are January 1 of each year)

	Phases	2013	2014	2015	2016	2017	2018	2019
Capital	Leverage ratio		Parallel run 1-Jan-2013 to 1-Jan-2017 Disclosure starts 1-Jan-2015				Migration to Pillar 1	
	Minimum Common Equity Capital Ratio	3.5%	4.0%	4.5%				4.5%
	Capital Conservation Buffer				0.625%	1.25%	1.875%	2.5%
	Minimum Common Equity Plus Capital Conservation Buffer	3.5%	4.0%	4.5%	5.125%	5.75%	6.375%	7.0%
	Phase-in of Deductions from CET1*		20%	40%	60%	80%	100%	100%
	Minimum Tier 1 Capital	4.5%	5.5%	6.0%				6.0%
	Minimum Total Capital	8.0%						8.0%
	Capital Instruments That No Longer Qualify As Non-Core Tier 1 Capital or Tier 2 Capital	Phased out over 10 year horizon beginning 2013						
Liquidity	Liquidity Coverage Ratio – Minimum			60%	70%	80%	90%	100%
	Net Stable Funding Ratio						Introduce minimum standard	

* including amounts exceeding the limit for deferred tax assets (DTAs), mortgage servicing rights (MSRs) and financials

A Final Comment

The task of fulfilling the new requirements is monumental for both regulators and banking organizations. Financial institutions face a significant challenge merely to achieve technical compliance with the new rules and ratios, let alone the need to be successful and profitable. Nor is the implementation challenge made much easier by the long transition periods pre-scribed by Basel III, with some rules not being implemented until 2019.

In a way, the time until 2019 seems both long and short, as follows:

- Short, because time of implementation is limited. Basel III has a major impact on business, strategy, organization, and information technology.
- Also short, because some stakeholders will not be patient and allow banks to achieve better capital and liquidity levels all the way until 2019. Investors, credit rating agencies, and other capital market participants will look at exactly the same key risk and performance indicators—capital and liquidity—right here and now. In reality, the game has started.
- Long, because regulators may change certain issues over time. This must even be expected, especially in the alignment process between Basel III and other major banking reforms around the world, for example the Dodd-Frank Act in the United States.

---

[16]Basel Phase-in Arrangements, http://www.bis.org/bcbs/basel3/basel3_phase_in_arrangeements.pdf. Retrieved October 16, 2013.

Capital Adequacy for Banks

Capital Definition / Components of Capital

Basel III contains various measures aimed at improving both the quantity and quality of capital, with the ultimate aim to improve loss-absorption capacity in both the going-concern and the liquidation (gone-concern) scenarios.

A key focus of the new regulation is to ensure that a bank's tier 1 capital—in other words, the loss-absorption capacity in the going-concern scenario—is mostly made up of ordinary shares termed "common equity tier 1" (CET1). Non-common equity tier 1 capital, also known as "additional tier 1 capital," is subject to strict conditions and must be capable of supporting a bank on a going-concern basis. Significant changes are also made to tier 2 capital while tier 3 capital is removed. In addition, all non-CET1 capital instruments must contain loss-absorbency characteristics in the form of conversion into equity or principal write-down mechanism.

> *Governor Daniel K. Tarullo, Member of the Board of Governors of the United States Federal Reserve Board:*[17]
>
> *"First, the basic prudential framework for banking organizations is being considerably strengthened, both internationally and domestically. Central to this effort are the Basel III changes to capital standards, which create a new requirement for a minimum common equity capital ratio. This new standard requires substantial increases in both the quality and quantity of the loss-absorbing capital that allows a firm to remain a viable financial intermediary."*

Going-Concern versus Gone-Concern Scenarios

The going-concern assumption is universally understood and accepted by financial services professionals. A going concern is a business that functions without the threat of liquidation for the foreseeable future, usually regarded as at least within 12 months.

Under Basel III, going-concern capital is equal to tier 1 capital and includes common shares, retained earnings, and additional tier 1 capital. It serves simply to absorb losses and should allow an institution to continue its activities and help prevent insol-

---

[17]Daniel K. Tarullo, "Evaluating Progress in Regulatory Reforms to Promote Financial Stability." Speech presented at Peterson Institute for International Economics, Washington, D.C., May 3, 2013.

vency. Under Basel III, losses in the going-concern scenario are fully covered by the institution's shareholders. The gone-concern capital consists of tier 2 capital, which serves to help ensure that depositors and senior creditors can be repaid if the institution fails. In any case, the new reform ensures that taxpayers will not have to pay the bill as in instances during the financial crisis. Figure 3.1 illustrates the going-concern and gone-concern capital elements.

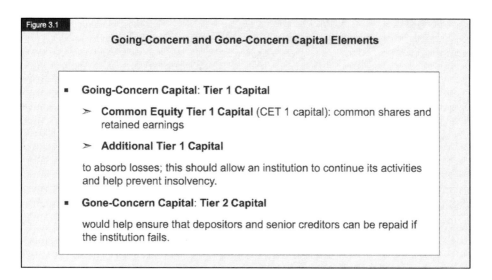

Figure 3.1

Going-Concern and Gone-Concern Capital Elements

- **Going-Concern Capital: Tier 1 Capital**
  - ➣ **Common Equity Tier 1 Capital** (CET 1 capital): common shares and retained earnings
  - ➣ **Additional Tier 1 Capital**

    to absorb losses; this should allow an institution to continue its activities and help prevent insolvency.
- **Gone-Concern Capital: Tier 2 Capital**

    would help ensure that depositors and senior creditors can be repaid if the institution fails.

Increased Quality and Consistency of Capital[18]

It is critical that banks' risk exposures are backed by a high-quality capital base. The predominant form of tier 1 capital must be common shares and retained earnings. This standard is reinforced through a set of principles that also can be tailored to the context of non-joint-stock companies to ensure they hold comparable levels of high-quality tier 1 capital. Deductions from capital and prudential filters have been harmonized internationally and generally applied at the level of common equity or its equivalent in the case of non-joint-stock companies. The remainder of the tier 1 capital base must be comprised of instruments that are subordinated, have fully discretionary noncumulative dividends or coupons, and have neither a maturity date nor an incentive to redeem. Innovative hybrid capital instruments with an incentive to redeem through features such as step-up clauses, currently limited to 15 percent of the tier 1 capital base, will be phased out. In addition, tier 2 capital instruments will be harmonized, and so-called tier 3 capital instruments, which were only available to cover market risks, eliminated. Finally, to improve market discipline, the transparency of the capital base will be improved, with all elements of capital required to be disclosed along with a detailed reconciliation to the reported accounts.

---

[18]BIS. Revised June 2011. http://www.bis.org/publ/bcbs189.pdf

Common Equity Tier 1 Capital

CET1 capital consists of the sum of the following elements:

- Common shares issued by the bank that meet the criteria for classification as common shares for regulatory purposes (or the equivalent for non-joint-stock companies);
- Stock surplus (share premium) resulting from the issue of instruments included in common equity tier 1;
- Retained earnings, including interim profit or loss;
- Accumulated other comprehensive income and other disclosed reserves;
- Common shares issued by consolidated subsidiaries of the bank and held by third parties (i.e., minority interest) that meet the criteria for inclusion in common equity tier 1 capital; and
- Regulatory adjustments applied in the calculation of common equity tier 1.

For an instrument to be included in common equity tier 1 capital it must meet all of the following criteria:

1. Represents the most subordinated claim in liquidation of the bank.
2. Entitled to a claim on the residual assets that is proportional with its share of issued capital, after all senior claims have been repaid in liquidation.
3. Principal is perpetual and never repaid outside of liquidation.
4. The bank does nothing to create an expectation at issuance that the instrument will be bought back, redeemed, or canceled, nor do the statutory or contractual terms provide any feature which might give rise to such an expectation.
5. Distributions are paid out of distributable items (retained earnings included). The level of distributions is not in any way tied or linked to the amount paid in at issuance and is not subject to a contractual cap (except to the extent that a bank is unable to pay distributions that exceed the level of distributable items).
6. There are no circumstances under which the distributions are obligatory. Non-payment is therefore not an event of default.
7. Distributions are paid only after all legal and contractual obligations have been met and payments on more senior capital instruments have been made. This means that there are no preferential distributions, including in respect of other elements classified as the highest-quality issued capital.
8. It is the issued capital that takes the first and proportionately greatest share of any losses as they occur. Within the highest-quality capital, each instrument absorbs losses on a going-concern basis proportionately and pari passu with all the others.
9. The paid-in amount is recognized as equity capital (i.e., not recognized as a liability) for determining balance sheet insolvency.
10. The paid-in amount is classified as equity under the relevant accounting standards.
11. It is directly issued and paid in and the bank cannot have directly or indirectly funded the purchase of the instrument.

Additional Tier 1 Capital

Additional tier 1 capital consists of the sum of the following elements:

- Instruments issued by the bank that meet the criteria for inclusion in additional tier 1 capital (and are not included in common equity tier 1);
- Stock surplus (share premium) resulting from the issue of instruments included in additional tier 1 capital;
- Instruments issued by consolidated subsidiaries of the bank and held by third parties that meet the criteria for inclusion in additional tier 1 capital and are not included in common equity tier 1; and
- Regulatory adjustments applied in the calculation of additional tier 1 capital.

For an instrument to be included in additional tier 1 capital it must meet all of the criteria as follows:

1. Issued and paid-in.
2. Subordinated to depositors, general creditors, and subordinated debt of the bank.
3. Is neither secured nor covered by a guarantee of the issuer or related entity or other arrangement that legally or economically enhances the seniority of the claim vis-à-vis bank creditors.
4. Is perpetual, i.e., there is no maturity date and there are no step-ups or other incentives to redeem.
5. May be callable at the initiative of the issuer only after a minimum of five years.
6. Any repayment of principal (e.g., through repurchase or redemption) must be with prior supervisory approval and banks should not assume or create market expectations that supervisory approval will be given.
7. Dividend/coupon discretion:
   a. The bank must have full discretion at all times to cancel distributions/payments.
   b. Cancellation of discretionary payments must not be an event of default.
   c. Banks must have full access to canceled payments to meet obligations as they fall due.
   d. Cancellation of distributions/payments must not impose restrictions on the bank except in relation to distributions to common stockholders.
8. Dividends/coupons must be paid out of distributable items.
9. The instrument cannot have a credit-sensitive dividend feature—that is, a dividend/coupon that is reset periodically based in whole or in part on the banking organization's credit standing.
10. The instrument cannot contribute to liabilities exceeding assets if such a balance sheet test forms part of national insolvency law.
11. Instruments classified as liabilities for accounting purposes must have principal loss absorption through either (i) conversion to common shares at an objective pre-specified trigger point or (ii) a write-down mechanism which allocates losses to the instrument at a pre-specified trigger point. The write-down will have the following effects:
    a. Reduce the claim of the instrument in liquidation;
    b. Reduce the amount repaid when a call is exercised; and
    c. Partially or fully reduce coupon/dividend payments on the instrument.

12. Neither the bank nor a related party over which the bank exercises control or significant influence can have purchased the instrument, nor can the bank directly or indirectly have funded the purchase of the instrument.
13. The instrument cannot have any features that hinder recapitalization, such as provisions that require the issuer to compensate investors if a new instrument is issued at a lower price during a specified time frame.
14. If the instrument is not issued out of an operating entity or the holding company in the consolidated group—e.g., a special purpose vehicle—proceeds must be immediately available without limitation to an operating entity or the holding company in the consolidated group in a form that meets or exceeds all of the other criteria for inclusion in additional tier 1 capital.

Tier 2 Capital

Tier 2 capital consists of the sum of the following elements:

- Instruments issued by the bank that meet the criteria for inclusion in tier 2 capital (and are not included in tier 1 capital);
- Stock surplus (share premium) resulting from the issue of instruments included in tier 2 capital;
- Instruments issued by consolidated subsidiaries of the bank and held by third parties that meet the criteria for inclusion in tier 2 capital and are not included in tier 1 capital;
- Certain loan loss provisions; and
- Regulatory adjustments applied in the calculation of tier 2 capital.

For an instrument to be included in tier 2 capital it must meet all of the criteria as follows:

1. Issued and paid-in.
2. Subordinated to depositors and general creditors of the bank.
3. Is neither secured nor covered by a guarantee of the issuer or related entity or other arrangement that legally or economically enhances the seniority of the claim vis-à-vis depositors and general bank creditors.
4. Maturity:
   a. Minimum original maturity of at least five years.
   b. Recognition in regulatory capital in the remaining five years before maturity will be amortized on a straight line basis.
   c. There are no step-ups or other incentives to redeem.
5. May be callable at the initiative of the issuer only after a minimum of five years:
   a. To exercise a call option a bank must receive prior supervisory approval;
   b. A bank must not do anything that creates an expectation that the call will be exercised; and
   c. Banks must not exercise a call unless:
      i. They replace the called instrument with capital of the same or better quality and the replacement of this capital is done at conditions which are sustainable for the income capacity of the bank; or

    ii. The bank demonstrates that its capital position is well above the minimum capital requirements after the call option is exercised.

6. The investor must have no rights to accelerate the repayment of future scheduled payments (coupon or principal), except in bankruptcy and liquidation.

7. The instrument cannot have a credit sensitive dividend feature—that is, a dividend/coupon that is reset periodically based in whole or in part on the banking organization's credit standing.

8. Neither the bank nor a related party over which the bank exercises control or significant influence can have purchased the instrument, nor can the bank directly or indirectly have funded the purchase of the instrument.

9. If the instrument is not issued out of an operating entity or the holding company in the consolidated group (e.g., a special purpose vehicle), proceeds must be immediately available without limitation to an operating entity or the holding company in the consolidated group in a form that meets or exceeds all of the other criteria for inclusion in tier 2 capital.

Capital Adequacy Ratio – The Formula

Figure 3.2 illustrates the capital adequacy ratio formula, a measure of the amount of a bank's capital expressed as a percentage of its risk-weighted assets.

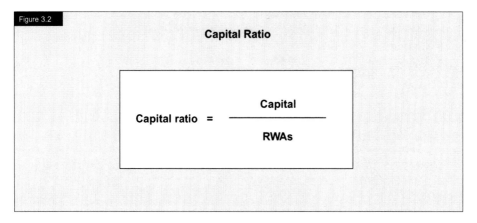

Figure 3.2

Capital Ratio

$$\text{Capital ratio} = \frac{\text{Capital}}{\text{RWAs}}$$

Increased Quantity of Capital

Basel III significantly enhances institutions' loss-absorption capacity; i.e., an institution's capital level compared to its risk-weighted assets (RWAs).

Common Equity Tier 1 Capital

- Common equity tier 1 ratio (CET1) has been increasing:
  - 3.5 percent from January 1, 2013;
  - 4.0 percent from January 1, 2014; and
  - 4.5 percent from January 1, 2015.

Tier 1 Capital

- Tier 1 capital ratio has increased from 4.0 percent to **6.0 percent**.
    - 4.5 percent from January 1, 2013;
    - 5.5 percent from January 1, 2014; and
    - 6.0 percent from January 1, 2015.

Before buffers, the minimum total capital ratio consisting of common equity tier 1 capital, additional tier 1 capital, and tier 2 capital remains unchanged at a level of **8.0 percent**, as Figure 3.3 illustrates. Tier 2 capital instruments will be harmonized while tier 3 capital will be phased out.

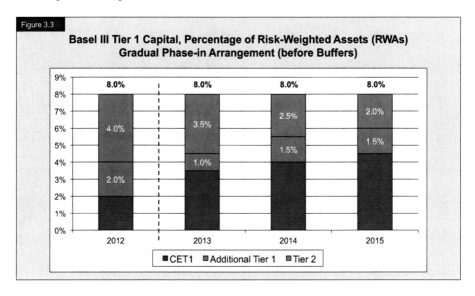

Figure 3.3

Basel III Tier 1 Capital, Percentage of Risk-Weighted Assets (RWAs) Gradual Phase-in Arrangement (before Buffers)

In addition, Basel III introduces the concept of buffers. Three buffers are introduced to enhance the minimum capital:

- The Basel Committee is introducing a framework to promote the conservation of capital and the build-up of adequate buffers above the minimum that can be drawn down in periods of stress. A **capital conservation buffer** is introduced to increase the level of CET1 capital by eventually 2.5 percent, from 4.5 percent to 7.0 percent. This buffer is relevant for all institutions that are governed by Basel III.
- A **countercyclical buffer** to address procyclicality will be set at the discretion of national authorities for their respective jurisdictions in order to better control aggressive lending by banks. The buffer will become effective in 2016 and will be set between 0 percent and 2.5 percent.
- The **systematically important financial institutions (SIFI) buffer** introduces an additional loss-absorbency requirement for systemically important banks, i.e., Bank of America Corporation in the United States, Deutsche Bank in Germany, and UBS in Switzerland. SIFIs will be subject to a 1 percent to 3.5 percent capital

surcharge above the minimum capital level, capital conservation, and counter-cyclical buffer requirements.

Key Takeaways

* Basel III contains various measures aimed at improving both the quantity and quality of capital, with the ultimate aim to improve loss-absorption capacity in both the going-concern and the liquidation (gone-concern) scenarios.
* Under Basel III, capital is mostly made up of ordinary shares termed "**common equity tier 1 capital**" (CET1), non-common equity tier 1 capital, also known as "**additional tier 1 capital**," and **tier 2 capital**. Another important part of CET1 is retained earnings.
* Capital ratio requirements increase significantly. The CET1 ratio increased from 2.0 percent under Basel II to 4.5 percent in 2015 under Basel III, before buffers. The tier 1 ratio increased from 4.0 percent under Basel II to 6.0 percent in 2015 under Basel III, before buffers.
* Basel III also introduces additional buffers, which are introduced in later chapters.

Contingent Convertible Capital Instruments (CoCos)

Contingent convertible capital instruments (CoCos) are hybrid capital securities that absorb losses when the capital of the issuing bank falls below a certain level. CoCo issuance is primarily driven by the instruments' potential to satisfy regulatory capital requirements. According to the Bank for International Settlements (BIS), the bulk of the demand for CoCos has come from small investors, while institutional investors have been relatively restrained so far. Spreads of CoCos over other subordinated debt greatly depend on their two main design characteristics—the trigger level and the loss-absorption mechanism. Typically, CoCo spreads are more correlated with the spreads of other subordinated debt than with CDS spreads and equity prices.

Of course, private investors are usually reluctant to provide additional external capital to banks in times of financial distress. As we observed in numerous examples during the financial crisis, the government can end up injecting capital to prevent the disruptive insolvency of a large financial institution simply because nobody else is willing to do so. Such public sector support costs taxpayers, fractures the relationship between banks and society, and distorts the incentives of bankers. CoCos offer a way to address this problem.

CoCos are hybrid capital securities that absorb losses in accordance with their contractual terms when the capital of the issuing bank falls below a certain level, typically the common equity tier 1 (CET1) capital ratio. Then debt is reduced and bank capitalization gets a boost. Owing to their capacity to absorb losses, CoCos have the potential to satisfy regulatory capital requirements.

In response to changes in the regulatory environment, there is a steadily growing market for CoCos. As the BIS notes in a survey, the market is still small: some $70 billion of CoCos have been issued since 2009, as against $550 billion of non-CoCo subordinated debt and $4 trillion of senior debt.[19]

Structure and Design of CoCos

The structure of CoCos is shaped by their primary purpose as a readily available source of bank capital in times of crisis. In order to achieve that objective, they need to possess several characteristics:

---

[19]"CoCos: a Primer," Basel Committee on Banking Supervision, Bank for International Settlements, BIS Quarterly Review, September 2013.

1. CoCos need to automatically absorb losses prior to or at the point of insolvency.
2. The activation of the loss-absorption mechanism must be a function of the capitalization levels of the issuing bank.
3. Their design has to be robust to price manipulation and speculative attacks.

As Figure 4.1 illustrates, CoCos have two main defining characteristics: the loss-absorption mechanism and the trigger that activates that mechanism. CoCos can absorb losses either by converting into common equity or by suffering a principal write-down. The trigger can be either mechanical (i.e., defined numerically in terms of a specific capital ratio) or discretionary (i.e., subject to supervisory judgment).

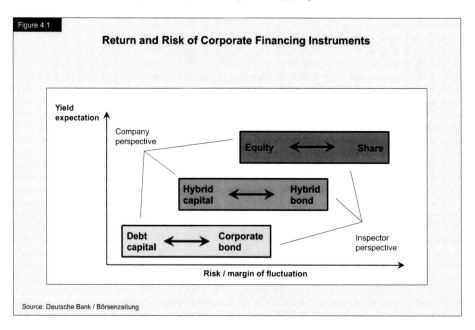

Figure 4.1

Return and Risk of Corporate Financing Instruments

Source: Deutsche Bank / Börsenzeitung

Contingent Convertible Capital Instrument (CoCo):

The term CoCo is used to describe a type of convertible bond that is automatically converted into a predetermined amount of shares when a predefined trigger is breached. Since this type of bond is transformed into equity upon conversion, it would be available for further loss absorption and therefore satisfies the regulatory requirements of hybrid capital instruments under Basel III / Capital Requirements Directive IV (CRD IV).

CoCo Triggers

One of the most important features in the design of a CoCo is the definition of the trigger, i.e., the point at which the loss-absorption mechanism is activated. A CoCo can have one or more triggers. In cases of multiple triggers, the loss-absorption mechanism is activated when any trigger is breached. Triggers can be based on a mechanical rule or supervisors' discretion. The loss-absorption mechanism is activated when the capital of the CoCo-issuing bank falls below a pre-specified fraction of its risk-weighted assets. The capital measure, in turn, can be based on book values or market values.

- Book-value triggers, also known as accounting-value triggers, are typically set contractually in terms of the book value of CET1 capital as a ratio of risk-weighted assets (RWA).
- Market-value triggers are set at a minimum ratio of the bank's stock market capitalization to its assets. However, market-value triggers may be difficult to price and could create incentives for stock price manipulation.
- Discretionary triggers, or point of non-viability (PONV) triggers, are activated based on supervisors' judgment about the issuing bank's solvency prospects. In particular, supervisors can activate the loss-absorption mechanism if they believe that such action is necessary to prevent the issuing bank's insolvency. PONV triggers allow regulators to trump any lack of timeliness or unreliability of book-value triggers. However, unless the conditions under which regulators will exercise their power to activate the loss-absorption mechanism are made clear, such power could create uncertainty about the timing of the activation.

Under Basel III, the minimum trigger level—in terms of CET1 to risk-weighted assets (RWAs)—required for a CoCo to qualify as additional tier 1 (AT1) capital is 5.125 percent. As a result, over the past couple of years, there has been a trend towards issuing CoCos with a trigger set exactly at that level. CoCos with such triggers are attractive for issuing banks due to the fact that they qualify as AT1 capital, while simultaneously being cheaper to issue than CoCos with higher trigger levels.

Basically, a distinction can be made between high and low conversion triggers. A high trigger (such as falling below a core capital ratio of 7 percent) means that the bonds can be converted relatively quickly when a bank suffers losses. Already, contingent capital with a high trigger—and hence CoCos too—have a positive impact with rating agencies and on International Capital Adequacy Assessment Process (ICAAP) stress tests. On the other hand, a low trigger (e.g., falling below a 5 percent core capital ratio) would result in conversion taking place only in an emergency. In that case CoCos would act as insurance against hard times. This kind of instrument would appeal more to institutional investors as it clearly targets exceptional crisis situations and is thus easier to assess.

The trigger level can therefore also be used to help fine-tune the purpose of CoCos: Are these convertibles intended more as catastrophe bonds providing capital insurance in systemic crises (low trigger) or as a continuous pre-emptive buffer in hard times (high trigger)? There is another factor, too: the higher the trigger, the more expensive the CoCo because from the investor's point of view a higher trigger implies a greater conversion risk. Market interest rates rise with the conversion risk. A low trigger, by contrast, would have the merit of making conversion less likely, and the risk premium for CoCos would therefore presumably be lower.

Loss-Absorption Mechanism

The loss-absorption mechanism is the second key characteristic of each CoCo. A CoCo can boost the issuing bank's equity in one of two ways. A conversion-to-equity (CE)

CoCo increases CET1 by converting into equity at a pre-defined conversion rate. By contrast, a principal write-down (PWD) CoCo raises equity by incurring a write-down.

For CoCos with a CE loss-absorption mechanism, the conversion rate can be based on:

(i) The market price of the stock at the time the trigger is breached;
(ii) A pre-specified price (often the stock price at the time of issuance); or
(iii) A combination of (i) and (ii).

The first option could lead to substantial dilution of existing equity holders as the stock price is likely to be very low at the time the loss-absorption mechanism is activated. But this potential for dilution would also increase the incentives for existing equity holders to avoid a breach of the trigger. By contrast, basing the conversion rate on a pre-specified price would limit the dilution of existing shareholders, but also probably decrease their incentives to avoid the trigger being breached. Finally, setting the conversion rate equal to the stock price at the time of conversion, subject to a pre-specified price floor, preserves the incentives for existing equity holders to avoid a breach of the trigger, while preventing unlimited dilution.

The principal write-down of a PWD CoCo could be either full or partial; most PWD CoCos have a full write-down feature.

Investors in CoCos

The bulk of the demand for CoCos has come from retail investors and small private banks. According to the Bank for International Settlements, large institutional investors have been relatively timid in the past. The main factors suppressing the growth of the investor base at the moment are the absence of complete and consistent credit ratings for most CoCos and the inherent tension between the objectives of issuers' regulators and prospective buyers' regulators. However, the market has been growing significantly.

Ultimately, though, participation by traditional bond investors, most importantly investors in fixed income, will be vital to create a sufficiently large potential market for CoCos to tap. Another decisive factor will be whether traditional bond investors with a low-to-medium appetite for risk, such as pension funds, will be prepared to venture into riskier territory with CoCos. Alongside traditional bond investors, some of whom may not be in a position to hold CoCos, new target groups with a higher risk/return profile than investors in previous hybrids are also likely to emerge as potential buyers of CoCos. These include hedge funds or high-net-worth individuals utilizing CoCos to diversify their portfolios, and similarly the expanding market for responsible investments.

Figure 4.2 illustrates CoCos' (hybrids) place between equity and debt in terms of its risk and return profile.

CoCos Issuance by Deutsche Bank in 2014

In its May 2014 CoCo issuance, Deutsche Bank raised €3.5 billion ($4.8 billion) that will recapitalize the bank if it hits trouble. Just a few weeks prior to a jumbo rights issue of new stock, the bank attracted over €25 billion of demand for the CoCos. The bank sold more than it had planned of the hybrid bonds in three denominations—euros, dollars,

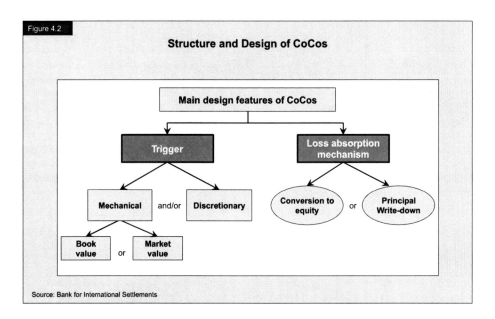

Figure 4.2

Structure and Design of CoCos

Source: Bank for International Settlements

and pounds—paying interest of between 6 percent and 7.125 percent just two days after saying it would raise €8 billion in a separate fundraising to address concerns about its capital strength.

CoCos – Key Takeaways

- CoCos are convertible bonds that convert automatically into common stock at a predetermined ratio during their maturity when a pre-arranged trigger is met. Therefore, they qualify—subject to meeting all regulatory requirements—as "going-concern" capital.
- Triggers are typically based on book values, e.g., CET1 capital as a ratio of risk-weighted assets or market values / a minimum ratio of the bank's stock market capitalization to its assets.
- Under Basel III, the minimum trigger level (in terms of CET1/RWA) required for a CoCo to qualify as additional tier 1 (AT1) capital is 5.125 percent.

Prudential Filters and Deductions

The Basel III standard harmonizes regulatory adjustments, i.e., deductions from capital and prudential filters, that will generally be applied at the level of common equity tier 1 (CET1) capital or its equivalent.

Goodwill and Other Intangibles (except Mortgage-Servicing Rights)

Goodwill and all other intangibles must be deducted in the calculation of CET1, including any goodwill included in the valuation of significant investments in the capital of banking, financial, and insurance entities that are outside the scope of regulatory consolidation. With the exception of mortgage-servicing rights, the full amount is to be deducted net of any associated deferred tax liability that would be extinguished if the intangible assets become impaired or derecognized under the relevant accounting standards.

Subject to prior supervisory approval, banks that report under local GAAP may use the International Financial Reporting Standards (IFRS) definition of intangible assets to determine which assets are classified as intangible and are thus required to be deducted.

Goodwill in Bank Balance Sheets

Goodwill, a type of intangible asset, is created in an acquisition and reflects the value—from an accounting standpoint—of a company that is not attributed to its other assets and liabilities. Goodwill is calculated by subtracting the target's book value, written up to fair market value, from the equity purchase price paid for the company. This equation is sometimes referred to as the "excess purchase price." Accounting rules state that goodwill no longer should be amortized each period, but must be tested once per year for impairment. Absent impairment, goodwill can remain on a company's balance sheet indefinitely.

Of course, goodwill and intangibles are not the biggest items on bank's balance sheets. However, Figure 5.1 illustrates that a deduction of goodwill and other intangibles significantly impacts major institutions: JPMorgan Chase lists goodwill and intangibles in the consolidated balance sheet of the institution in the amount of nearly $50 billion.

Figure 5.1

**Goodwill and Other Intangibles
Example: JPMorgan Chase & Co.**

	2013		2012	
	In $million	In Percent of Total Assets	In $million	In Percent of Total Assets
Total Assets	2,415,689		2,359,141	
thereof Goodwill and other Intangibles	49,699	2.06	50,410	2.14

Source: Annual Report 2013 JPMorgan Chase & Co., Consolidated Balance Sheet, page 186

Deferred Tax Assets (DTAs)

Deferred tax assets (DTAs) that rely on future profitability of the bank to be realized are to be deducted in the calculation of CET1. DTAs may be netted with associated deferred tax liabilities (DTLs) only if the DTAs and DTLs relate to taxes levied by the same taxation authority and offsetting is permitted by the relevant taxation authority.

An over installment of tax or, in some jurisdictions, current year tax losses carried back to prior years may give rise to a claim or receivable from the government or local tax authority. Such amounts are typically classified as current tax assets for accounting purposes. The recovery of such a claim or receivable would not rely on the future profitability of the bank and would be assigned the relevant sovereign risk weighting.

Deferred Tax Assets

Deferred tax assets are assets on a company's balance sheet that may be used to reduce any subsequent period's income tax expense. They can arise due to net-loss carryovers, which are only recorded as assets if it is deemed more likely than not that the asset will be used in future fiscal periods.

Cash Flow Hedge Reserve

The amount of the cash flow hedge reserve that relates to the hedging of items that are not fair valued on the balance sheet (including projected cash flows) should be derecognized in the calculation of common equity tier 1 capital. This means that positive amounts should be deducted and negative amounts should be added back.

This treatment specifically identifies the element of the cash flow hedge reserve that is to be derecognized for prudential purposes. It removes the element that gives rise to artificial volatility in common equity, as in this case the reserve only reflects one half of the picture (the fair value of the derivative, but not the changes in fair value of the hedged future cash flow).

Hedge Accounting

Firms are typically exposed to some form of market risk. For example, gold mines are exposed to the price of gold, airlines to the price of oil, borrowers to interest rates, and importers and exporters to exchange rate risks. Many financial institutions and non-bank institutions, i.e., large corporations, energy companies, and trading companies, use derivative financial instruments to hedge their exposure to different risks (for example interest rate risk, foreign exchange risk, commodity risk, etc.). Further, entities active in the credit markets hedge their credit risk from bonds or corporate loans by using credit default swaps. Accounting for derivative financial instruments under international accounting standards (IAS) is covered by IAS39 (Financial Instruments: Recognition and Measurement). IAS39 requires that all derivatives are marked-to-market with changes in the mark-to-market being taken to the profit and loss account. For many entities this can result in a significant amount of profit and loss volatility arising from the use of derivatives. An entity can mitigate the profit and loss effect arising from derivatives used for hedging through an optional part of IAS39 relating to hedge accounting.

Shortfall of the Stock of Provisions to Expected Losses

The deduction from capital in respect to a shortfall of the stock of provisions to expected losses under the internal ratings-based (IRB) approach should be made in the calculation of common equity tier 1. The full amount is to be deducted and should not be reduced by any tax effects that could be expected to occur if provisions were to rise to the level of expected losses.

Expected Loss

In statistical terms, the expected loss is the average credit loss that we would expect from an exposure or a portfolio over a given period of time.

$$Expected\ Loss = EaD \times PD \times LGD$$

The total expected loss of a portfolio will simply be the summation of expected losses of individual assets. This is because the mean of the sum is the same as the sum of the mean. Since the expected loss is what a business expects to lose in a year, the business will generally have budgeted for it and the losses can be borne as a part of the normal operating cash flows.

Naturally, allowance for loan and lease losses (ALLL) is a major item in the financial statements of any bank. Figure 5.2 illustrates ALLL in four selected large U.S. bank holding companies as of December 31, 2013. Of course, major deviations between ALLL and expected loss will result in a major impact on capital, i.e., loss-absorption potential.

Figure 5.2

Allowance for Loan Losses
Major U.S. Bank Holding Companies
As of 31-Dec-2013

	Total Assets	Loans	Allowance for Loan Losses	
	in $millions	in $millions	in $millions	in Percent of Loans
Bank of America Corporation	2,102,273	928,233	17,428	1.88
Citigroup Inc.	1,880,382	665,472	19,648	2.95
JPMorgan Chase & Co.	2,415,689	738,418	16,264	2.20
Wells Fargo	1,527,015	825,799	14,502	1.76

Source: Annuals Report 2013, Consolidated Balance Sheets

Gain on Sale Related to Securitization Transactions

Any increase in equity capital resulting from a securitization transaction, such as that associated with expected future margin income (FMI) resulting in a gain on sale, should be derecognized in the calculation of common equity tier 1 capital.

Cumulative Gains and Losses Due to Changes in Own Credit Risk on Fair Valued Financial Liabilities

All unrealized gains and losses that have resulted from changes in the fair value of liabilities that are due to changes in the bank's own credit risk should be derecognized in the calculation of common equity tier 1 capital.

Defined Benefit Pension Fund Assets and Liabilities

Defined benefit pension fund liabilities, as included on the balance sheet, must be fully recognized in the calculation of common equity tier 1 (i.e., CET1 cannot be increased through derecognizing these liabilities). For each defined benefit pension fund that is an asset on the balance sheet, the asset should be deducted in the calculation of common equity tier 1 net of any associated deferred tax liability that would be extinguished if the asset should become impaired or derecognized under the relevant accounting standards. Assets in the fund to which the bank has unrestricted and unfettered access can, with supervisory approval, offset the deduction. Such offsetting assets should be given the risk weight they would receive if they were owned directly by the bank.

This treatment addresses the concern that assets arising from pension funds may not be capable of being withdrawn and used for the protection of depositors and other creditors of a bank. The concern is that their only value stems from a reduction in future payments into the fund. The treatment allows for banks to reduce the deduction of the asset if they can address these concerns and show that the assets can be easily and promptly withdrawn from the fund.

Investments in Own Shares (Treasury Stock)

All of a bank's investments in its own common shares, whether held directly or indirectly, will be deducted in the calculation of common equity tier 1 (unless already derecognized under the relevant accounting standards). In addition, any own stock which the bank could be contractually obliged to purchase should be deducted in the calculation of common equity tier 1. The treatment described will apply irrespective of the location of the exposure in the banking book or the trading book.

In addition:

- Gross long positions may be deducted net of short positions in the same underlying exposure only if the short positions involve no counterparty risk.
- Banks should look through holdings of index securities to deduct exposures to own shares. However, gross long positions in own shares resulting from holdings of index securities may be netted against short positions in own shares resulting from short positions in the same underlying index. In such cases the short positions may involve counterparty risk (which will be subject to the relevant counterparty credit risk charge).

This deduction is necessary to avoid the double counting of a bank's own capital. Certain accounting regimes do not permit the recognition of treasury stock and so this deduction is only relevant where recognition on the balance sheet is permitted. The treatment seeks to remove the double counting that arises from direct holdings, indirect holdings via index funds, and potential future holdings as a result of contractual obligations to purchase own shares.

Reciprocal Cross Holdings in the Capital of Banking, Financial, and Insurance Entities

Reciprocal cross holdings of capital that are designed to artificially inflate the capital position of banks will be deducted in full. Banks must apply a "corresponding deduction approach" to such investments in the capital of other banks, other financial institutions, and insurance entities. This means the deduction should be applied to the same component of capital for which the capital would qualify if it was issued by the bank itself.

Investments in the Capital of Banking, Financial, and Insurance Entities that Are outside the Scope of Regulatory Consolidation and Where the Bank Does Not Own More Than 10 Percent of the Issued Common Share Capital of the Entity

As stated in the heading, the regulatory adjustment described in this section applies to investments in the capital of banking, financial, and insurance entities that are outside the scope of regulatory consolidation and where the bank does not own more than 10 percent of the issued common share capital of the entity.

But in addition:

- Investments include direct, indirect, and synthetic holdings of capital instruments.
- Holdings in both the banking book and trading book are to be included. Capital includes common stock and all other types of cash and synthetic capital instruments (e.g., subordinated debt). It is the net long position that is to be included (i.e., the gross long position net of short positions in the same underlying exposure where the maturity of the short position either matches the maturity of the long position or has a residual maturity of at least one year).
- Underwriting positions held for five working days or less can be excluded. Underwriting positions held for longer than five working days must be included.
- If the capital instrument of the entity in which the bank has invested does not meet the criteria for common equity tier 1, additional tier 1, or tier 2 capital of the bank, the capital is to be considered common shares for the purposes of this regulatory adjustment.
- National discretion applies to allow banks, with prior supervisory approval, to exclude temporarily certain investments where these have been made in the context of resolving or providing financial assistance to reorganize a distressed institution.

If the total of all holdings listed above in aggregate exceed 10 percent of the bank's common equity (after applying all other regulatory adjustments in full listed prior to this one) then the amount above 10 percent is required to be deducted, applying a corresponding deduction approach. This means the deduction should be applied to the same component of capital for which the capital would qualify if it were issued by the bank itself. Accordingly, the amount to be deducted from common equity should be calculated as the total of all holdings which in aggregate exceed 10 percent of the bank's common equity (as per above) multiplied by the common equity holdings as a percentage of the total capital holdings. This would result in a common equity deduction which corresponds to the proportion of total capital holdings held in common equity. Similarly, the amount to be deducted from additional tier 1 capital should be calculated as the total of all holdings which in aggregate exceed 10 percent of the bank's common equity (as per above) multiplied by the additional tier 1 capital holdings as a percentage of the total capital holdings. The amount to be deducted from tier 2 capital should be calculated as the total of all holdings which in aggregate exceed 10 percent of the bank's common equity (as per above) multiplied by the tier 2 capital holdings as a percentage of the total capital holdings.

If, under the corresponding deduction approach, a bank is required to make a deduction from a particular tier of capital and it does not have enough of that tier of capital to satisfy that deduction, the shortfall will be deducted from the next higher tier of capital (e.g., if a bank does not have enough additional tier 1 capital to satisfy the deduction, the shortfall will be deducted from common equity tier 1).

Amounts below the threshold, which are not deducted, will continue to be risk weighted. Thus, instruments in the trading book will be treated as per the market risk rules, and instruments in the banking book should be treated as per the internal ratings-based approach or the standardized approach (as applicable). For the application of risk weighting the amount of the holdings must be allocated on a pro-rata basis between those below and those above the threshold (see below).

Significant Investments in the Capital of Banking, Financial, and Insurance Entities that Are outside the Scope of Regulatory Consolidation

All investments included above that are not common shares must be fully deducted following a corresponding deduction approach. This means the deduction should be applied to the same tier of capital for which the capital would qualify if it was issued by the bank itself. If the bank is required to make a deduction from a particular tier of capital and it does not have enough of that tier of capital to satisfy that deduction, the shortfall will be deducted from the next-higher tier of capital (e.g., if a bank does not have enough additional tier 1 capital to satisfy the deduction, the shortfall will be deducted from common equity tier 1).

Investments included above that are common shares will be subject to the threshold treatment described in the next section.

Threshold Deductions

Instead of a full deduction, the following items may each receive limited recognition when calculating common equity tier 1, with recognition capped at 10 percent of the bank's common equity (after the application of all regulatory adjustments as described above):

- Significant investments in the common shares of unconsolidated financial institutions (bank, insurance, and other financial entities);
- Mortgage-servicing rights (MSRs); and
- DTAs that arise from temporary differences.

A bank must deduct the amount by which the aggregate of the three items above exceeds 15 percent of its common equity component of tier 1 (calculated prior to the deduction of these items but after application of all other regulatory adjustments applied in the calculation of common equity tier 1). The items included in the 15 percent aggregate limit are subject to full disclosure. As of January 1, 2018, the calculation of the 15 percent limit will be subject to the following treatment: the amount of the three items that remains recognized after the application of all regulatory adjustments must not exceed 15 percent of common equity tier 1 capital, calculated after all regulatory adjustments; and the amount of the three items that are not deducted in the calculation of common equity tier 1 will be risk weighted at 250 percent.

Transitional Arrangements under Basel III

Just like the increase in the capital ratios as described in Chapter 3, there will be a transition for prudential filters and deductions. The Basel Committee has defined these transitional arrangements for implementing the new standards to help ensure that the banking sector can meet the higher capital standards through reasonable earnings retention and capital raising, while still supporting lending to the economy.

The regulatory adjustments (i.e., deductions and prudential filters)—including amounts above the aggregate 15 percent limit for significant investments in financial institutions, mortgage-servicing rights, and deferred tax assets from temporary differences—would be fully deducted from common equity tier 1 by January 1, 2018.

In particular and as illustrated by Figure 5.3, the regulatory adjustments began at 20 percent of the required adjustments to common equity tier 1 on January 1, 2014, hit 40 percent on January 1, 2015, and will increase to 60 percent on January 1, 2016, 80 percent on January 1, 2017, and 100 percent on January 1, 2018.

During this transition, the remainder not deducted from common equity tier 1 will continue to be subject to existing national treatments. The same transition approach applies to deductions from additional tier 1 and tier 2 capital: 20 percent of the required deductions on January 1, 2014, 40 percent on January 1, 2015, 60 percent on January 1, 2016, 80 percent on January 1, 2017, and 100 percent on January 1, 2018. During this transition period, the remainder not deducted from capital will continue to be subject to existing national treatments.

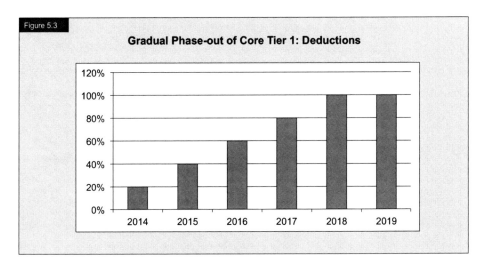

Figure 5.3

Gradual Phase-out of Core Tier 1: Deductions

Key Takeaways

- The Basel III standard harmonizes regulatory adjustments, i.e., deductions from capital and prudential filters, which will generally be applied at the level of common equity tier 1 (CET1) capital or its equivalent.
- Regulatory adjustments/deductions apply in a number of areas, e.g., goodwill and intangibles, deferred tax assets, cash flow hedge reserving, the calculation of the shortfall of the stock of provisions to expected losses, and others.
- Under Basel III, deductions became effective at a level of 20 percent on January 1, 2014. The required adjustments to common equity tier 1 stepped up to 40 percent on January 1, 2015, and will hit 60 percent on January 1, 2016, 80 percent on January 1, 2017, and the full 100 percent on January 1, 2018.

Capital Conservation Buffer

One of the most destabilizing elements of the crisis was the procyclical amplification of financial shocks throughout the banking system, financial markets, and the broader economy. The tendency of market participants to behave in a procyclical manner was amplified through a variety of channels, including through accounting standards for both mark-to-market assets and held-to-maturity loans, margining practices, and through the build-up and release of leverage among financial institutions, firms, and consumers. The Basel Committee is introducing a number of measures to make banks more resilient to such procyclical dynamics; these measures will help ensure that the banking sector serves as a shock absorber, instead of a transmitter of risk to the financial system and broader economy.

Basel III is introducing a series of measures to address procyclicality and raise the resilience of the banking sector in good times. These measures have the following key objectives:

- Dampen any excess cyclicality of the minimum capital requirement;
- Promote more forward-looking provisions;
- Conserve capital to build buffers at individual banks and the banking sector that can be used in stress; and
- Achieve the broader macro-prudential goal of protecting the banking sector from periods of excess credit growth.

As a result, the Basel Committee on Banking Supervision (BCBS) is introducing a framework to promote the conservation of capital and the build-up of adequate buffers above the minimum that can be drawn down in periods of financial and economic stress, lasting for a number of years.

In order to prevent large distributions in the form of dividends, share buybacks, and compensation payments, Basel III is introducing a framework that will give supervisors stronger tools to promote capital conservation in the banking sector.

Implementation of the framework through internationally agreed capital conservation standards will help increase sector resilience going into a downturn and will provide the mechanism for rebuilding capital during the economic recovery.

The capital conservation buffer, expressed as a percentage of risk-weighted assets, (RWA) will be introduced in January 2016 and be gradually increased until 2019.

Capital Conservation Buffer, Gradual Phase-in

Date	In percent of RWA
1-Jan-2016	0.625
1-Jan-2017	1.250
1-Jan-2018	1.875
1-Jan-2019	2.500

The new buffer of eventually 2.5 percent of RWA must be met with common equity tier 1 (CET1) capital (tangible common equity capital). Considering the 4.5 percent CET1 capital ratio base, institutions must hold 7.0 percent CET1 capital on an individual and consolidated basis at all times. Institutions are expected to build up the capital in good economic times, as Figure 6.1 illustrates.

Under the framework, as a bank's capital ratio declines and it uses the conservation buffer to absorb losses, it will be required to retain an increasingly higher percentage of earnings and impose restrictions on distributable items such as dividends, share buybacks, and discretionary bonuses. It is not acceptable for banks that have depleted their capital buffers to use future predictions of recovery as justification for maintaining generous distributions to shareholders, other capital providers, and employees.

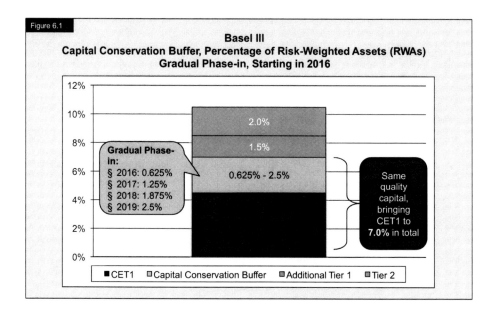

Figure 6.2 illustrates the minimum capital conservation ratios a bank must meet at various levels of CET1 capital ratios. For example, a bank with a CET1 capital ratio in the range of 5.125 percent to 5.75 percent is required to conserve 80 percent of its earnings in the subsequent fiscal year.

The Simple Idea behind the Capital Conservation Buffer:
Save for rainy days!

Figure 6.2

Basel III
Capital Conservation Buffer
Individual Bank Minimum Capital Conservation Standards

Common Equity Tier 1 Ratio	Minimum Capital Conservation Ratio (as percentage of earnings)
4.5% – 5.125%	100%
> 5.125% - 5.75%	80%
> 5.75% - 6.375%	60%
> 6.375% - 7.0%	40%
> 7.0%	0%

Capital Conservation Buffer – Key Takeaways

- The capital conservation buffer promotes the conservation of capital and the build-up of adequate buffers above the minimum that can be drawn down in periods of financial and economic stress.
- As of January 2019, banks will be required to hold a capital conservation buffer of 2.5 percent to withstand future periods of stress, bringing the total common equity requirement to 7 percent (4.5 percent common equity requirement plus the 2.5 percent capital conservation buffer).
- The conservation buffer will be introduced in January 2016 at level of 0.625 percent; it gradually increases until 2019 to a level of 2.5 percent.
- Banks that do not maintain the capital conservation buffer will face restrictions on payouts of dividends, share buybacks, and bonuses.
- The simple idea behind the buffer: Save for rainy days.

Countercyclical Buffer

In addition to the capital conservation buffer, Basel III is introducing a second cushion, the countercyclical buffer. This new buffer extends the capital conservation range during periods of extensive credit excess growth.

As witnessed during the financial crisis, losses incurred in the banking sector during a downturn preceded by a period of excess credit growth can be extremely large. Such losses can destabilize the banking sector, which can bring about or exacerbate a downturn in the real economy. This in turn can further destabilize the banking sector. These interlinkages highlight the particular importance of the banking sector building up its capital defenses in periods when credit has grown to excessive levels. The building up of these defenses should have the additional benefit of helping to moderate excess credit growth.

Therefore, Basel III is introducing a regime that will adjust the capital buffer range, established through the capital conservation mechanism outlined in Chapter 6, when there are signs credit has grown to excessive levels. The purpose of the countercyclical buffer is to achieve the broader macro-prudential goal of protecting the banking sector in periods of excess aggregate credit growth.

The buffer is to be imposed within a range of 0 percent and 2.5 percent comprising common equity when authorities judge credit growth is resulting in an unacceptable build-up of systemic risk. The buffer is released in an economic downturn.

National authorities will monitor credit growth and other indicators that may signal a build-up of system-wide risk. The countercyclical buffer will become effective in January 2016.

Countercyclical Buffer, in Percentage of Risk-Weighted Assets (RWAs):

- As of Jan. 1, 2016: Between 0 and 2.5 percent
- National discretion of the member countries via their respective national authorities, i.e., the European Central Bank in the European Union or the Federal Reserve in the United States

Just like the capital conservation buffer, the countercyclical buffer must be met by common equity tier 1 (CET1) capital, and therefore, further increases the burden for financial institutions, as Figure 7.1 illustrates.

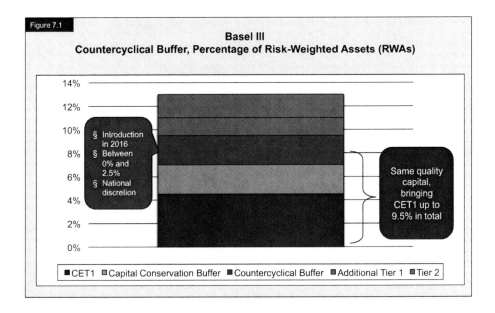

The following figure labels appear within Figure 7.1:

Figure 7.1

Basel III
Countercyclical Buffer, Percentage of Risk-Weighted Assets (RWAs)

§ Introduction in 2016
§ Between 0% and 2.5%
§ National discretion

Same quality capital, bringing CET1 up to 9.5% in total

■CET1 ▨Capital Conservation Buffer ■Countercyclical Buffer ■Additional Tier 1 ▨Tier 2

The Idea behind the Countercyclical Buffer:
Prevent excessive credit growth.

Most likely, it will be a difficult exercise to fix the exact buffer in a respective member country. The authorities that are responsible for setting will closely track key economic indicators, such as GDP, unemployment, and inflation. In addition, banking regulators will liaise closely with banking institutions, i.e., through periodic interviews to better and more quickly understand banks' current lending practices, policies, pricing, and behavior as well as customer trends in the market.

Obviously, there is an interrelationship with monetary policy by the central banks, which can be expansionary or contractionary. Monetary policy rests on the relationship between the rates of interest in an economy—that is, the price at which money can be borrowed—and the total supply of money.

Under what circumstances should policy be geared towards moderating high credit growth, or the contrary? This is not a straightforward question given uncertainty about what defines excessive credit growth under different circumstances.

How should authorities actually derive the buffer? One possibility could be based on a deviation of the ratio of credit to GDP from its long-term trend, e.g., on a quarterly basis.

In any case, an increase of the countercyclical capital buffer should generally be communicated well in advance, e.g., one year. A decrease of the buffer could be applicable immediately. The designated authority should give an indicative (not binding) period during which no increase in the buffer is expected.

Financial institutions that are not able to fulfill this regulatory requirement will face restrictions regarding distributions such as dividends, share buybacks, and compensation payments to staff. This guideline is in line with the regulations for the capital conservation buffer.

Key Takeaways

- The countercyclical buffer is an additional new buffer that extends the capital cushion of financial institutions—including the capital conservation buffer—during periods of extensive credit growth. The main purpose of the buffer is to prevent excessive credit growth.
- A buffer within a range of 0 to 2.5 percent of common equity or other fully loss-absorbing capital will be implemented within national discretion.
- The effective date will be January 1, 2016.
- Banks that do not maintain the countercyclical buffer will face restrictions on payouts of dividends, share buybacks, and bonuses.

Minimum Capital Standards / Phase-in Arrangements under Basel III Capital Requirements

Basel III establishes stricter capital standards through more-restrictive capital definitions, additional capital buffers, and higher requirements for minimum capital ratios for all banks that are governed under the new reform. These changes are fully described in Chapters 3 to 7. This chapter integrates the former issues and describes the new minimum capital standards in a comprehensive way. Further, it points out two unique distinctions: one for systemically important financial institutions (SIFIs) and one for community / regional banks, for example in the United States.

Minimum Total Capital – Pre Buffers

Figure 8.1 describes the minimum total capital requirements and their gradual phase-in arrangements until 2015, on a pre-buffer basis. The requirements are outlined in Chapter 3; the same information is described in graphical form in Figure 3.3.

Figure 8.1

Basel III Minimum Total Capital, Percentage of Risk-Weighted Assets (RWAs)
Gradual Phase-in Arrangements
(before Buffers)

	Going-Concern Capital			Gone-Concern Capital	Minimum Total Capital
	Common Equity Tier 1 (CET1)	Additional Tier 1	Total Tier 1 Capital	Tier 2	
Before 2013	2.0%	2.0%	4.0%	4.0%	8.0%
1-Jan-2013	3.5%	1.0%	4.5%	3.5%	8.0%
1-Jan-2014	4.0%	1.5%	5.5%	2.5%	8.0%
1-Jan-2015	4.5%	1.5%	6.0%	2.0%	8.0%

Minimum Total Capital – Including Capital Conservation and Countercyclical Buffers

Figure 8.2 describes the minimum total capital requirements and the gradual phase-in arrangements until 2019, including the main buffers that are relevant for any bank, independent of size: the capital conservation and the countercyclical buffers. Buffer requirements are outlined in Chapters 6 and 7.

As of 2019, minimum total capital will be in a range between 10.5 percent and 13 percent of RWAs, depending on how authorities will set the countercyclical buffer.

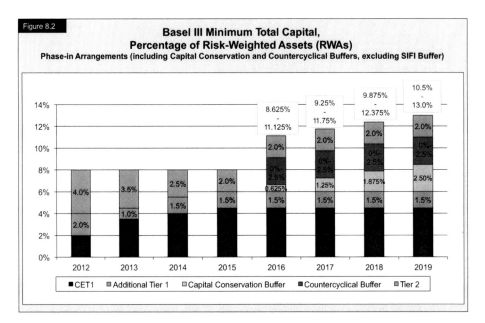

Figure 8.2

Basel III Minimum Total Capital, Percentage of Risk-Weighted Assets (RWAs)
Phase-in Arrangements (including Capital Conservation and Countercyclical Buffers, excluding SIFI Buffer)

Minimum Total Capital / Basel II versus Basel III – Including Capital Conservation Buffer and Countercyclical Buffer

Figure 8.3 compares Basel II and Basel III tier 1 capital—including capital conservation buffer and countercyclical buffer but excluding the buffer for systemically important institutions—broken down into the main capital elements: common equity tier 1 (CET1), capital conservation buffer, countercyclical buffer, and additional tier 1 capital:

- Minimum total capital increases from 8.0 percent to 13.0 percent of RWAs.
- Until 2019, common equity tier 1 capital increases from 2.0 percent to 9.5 percent of RWAs, a factor of 4.75.
- Level of going-concern capital (CET1 capital plus additional tier 1 capital): 11.0 percent of RWAs.
- Level of gone-concern capital (tier 2 capital): 2.0 percent of RWAs.

The comparison assumes inclusion of the capital conservation buffer (in 2019: 2.5 percent) and the countercyclical buffer at its maximum potential of 2.5 percent.

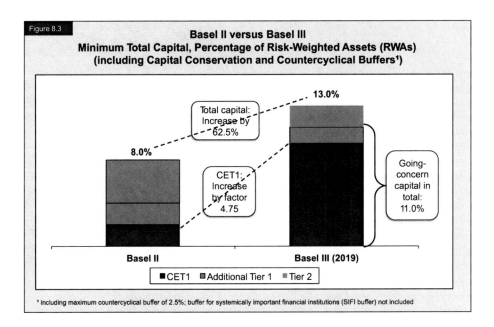

Figure 8.3

Basel II versus Basel III
Minimum Total Capital, Percentage of Risk-Weighted Assets (RWAs)
(including Capital Conservation and Countercyclical Buffers[1])

[1] including maximum countercyclical buffer of 2.5%; buffer for systemically important financial institutions (SIFI buffer) not included

Two Important Distinctions

Systemically Important Financial Institutions – All Member Countries

Large systemically important financial institutions will have a more onerous regulatory burden, including an additional capital buffer for SIFIs. Due to their importance, systemic risk in general, and special requirements, SIFIs in particular are covered in detail in Chapters 11 and 12.

Community Banks in the United States

The authorities in the United States have committed to implement Basel III; however, the Federal Reserve makes a strong distinction between large internationally active banks with a consolidated balance sheet of $50 billion and above on one side and the thousands of smaller institutions across the nation on the other side.

After careful analysis, including seeking input from community bankers and holding outreach sessions, the United States decided to maintain the objective of strengthening capital requirements for community banks, but without the more-onerous regulatory burden.

In order to reduce the burden for community banks, the United States is considering three issues in particular. In the Open Board Meeting of the Federal Reserve on July 2, 2013, the following remarks were made by the Federal Reserve governors:[21]

- *"First, in light of concerns about the burden of calculating the proposed risk weights for banking organizations' existing residential mortgage portfolios and the potential reduction in credit availability due to the interaction of the proposal with other mortgage-related rulemakings, the [U.S.] final rule would retain the current risk weights for residential mortgage loans.*
- *Second, the final rule would allow non-advanced approaches banking organizations to make a one-time election to opt out of the requirement to include most elements of AOCI [accumulated other comprehensive income] in regulatory capital. While these banks would not be required to recognize unrealized gains and losses in their regulatory capital, they would not be permitted to switch back and forth to take advantage of unrealized gains and ignore unrealized losses.*
- *Third, community banks [would be] subjected to the phase-out of trust-preferred securities as part of their tier 1 capital. In recognition of community banking organizations' limited access to capital markets, the final rule would effectively grandfather certain existing trust-preferred securities, as permitted by the Dodd-Frank Act. Ultimately, the relevant measure of the final rule is not to compare it to the proposal, but to evaluate it against existing regulatory capital requirements."*

Daniel K. Tarullo, Member of the Federal Reserve Board:

"In characterizing this rule [Basel III] as a milestone in financial regulatory reform, I should note that this marker has quite different meanings for banking organizations of systemic importance on the one hand and the thousands of smaller banks on the other."

Governor Elizabeth A. Duke, Member of the Federal Reserve Board

"I want to begin by emphasizing that having adequate levels of high quality capital is just as crucial for smaller banks as it is for the largest institutions. The recent financial crisis demonstrated that community banks can still be devastated by economic turbulence, even when they did nothing to cause the problem. Banks that were able to withstand the adverse economic conditions and continue to serve their communities were those that started with solid capital positions."

There is, of course, another side to the coin. As American community banks are facing a less-onerous regulatory burden, large U.S. bank holding companies are facing a more onerous one. This opens interesting future questions about one of the main Basel III objectives, which is to achieve level playing fields in the industry.

Most recently, the Federal Reserve hinted that the regulatory threshold in the United States may be raised from a $50 billion consolidated balance sheet to $75 billion or even $100 billion.

---

[21]Remarks by Federal Reserve Governors Daniel K. Tarullo and Elizabeth A. Duke, Federal Reserve Open Board Meeting, July 2, 2013. http://www.federalreserve.gov/mediacenter/files/open-board-meeting-transcript-20130702.pdf

Key Takeaways

- Minimum total capital increases from 8.0 percent to 13.0 percent of RWAs.
- Common equity tier 1 capital increases from 2.0 percent to 9.5 percent of RWAs.
- Level of going-concern capital (CET1 capital plus additional tier 1 capital): 11.0 percent of RWAs.
- Level of gone-concern capital (tier 2 capital): 2.0 percent of RWAs.
- Additional capital requirements for systemically important financial institutions (SIFIs): See Chapters 11 and 12.
- United States implementation of Basel III: less-onerous regulatory burden (capital requirements) for thousands of community banks on one side and more-onerous regulatory burden for large, internationally active U.S. banking organizations on the other.

Macroeconomic and Systemic Issues

Ending Too Big to Fail

One of the main objectives of Basel III and other major banking reforms, such as Dodd-Frank, is to mitigate or even control systemic risk. For governments and regulators—and, of course, for other market participants—the worst-possible scenario is another banking crisis, starting at one major bank with a knock-on effect on a second bank, and a domino effect from thereon. Therefore, a key focus of the banking reforms relates to large internationally active banks. Let's explore the issue of ending "too big to fail."

The financial crisis proved that certain financial institutions were so large and so interconnected that their failure would be disastrous to the financial system and the real economy. The term "too big to fail" became a part of the mainstream consciousness. In capitalism, it is "normal business" that some companies succeed while others fail. A failure of any given institution has, of course, negative effects on its main stakeholders such as shareholders, bond investors, management, and staff. However, such a failure should not have a major negative effect on another company or start a domino effect that could threaten any number of institutions and eventually the whole system and the prosperity of a nation.

A too-big-to-fail bank is one deemed too important to be allowed to fail because that may have significant knock-on effects for other financial institutions. The results could become catastrophic.

Such a company or bank has the implicit support of the federal government. In order to prevent even bigger costs and threats to the real economy as a result of the financial crisis, many governments stepped in to support major banks. In 2008-9 the U.S. Treasury and the Federal Reserve, and governments of EU countries and European central banks, bailed out numerous very large institutions.

Definition[22]

In 2010, the Federal Reserve chair at that time, Ben Bernanke, said, "A too-big-to-fail firm is one whose size, complexity, interconnectedness, and critical functions are such that, should the firm go unexpectedly into liquidation, the rest of the financial system and the economy

---

[22]Ben Bernanke, "Causes of the Recent Financial and Economic Crisis," federalreserve.gov, September 2, 2010.

would face severe adverse consequences." He continued, "Governments provide support to too-big-to-fail firms in a crisis not out of favoritism or particular concern for the management, owners, or creditors of the firm, but because they recognize that the consequences for the broader economy of allowing a disorderly failure greatly outweigh the costs of avoiding the failure in some way. Common means of avoiding failure include facilitating a merger, providing credit, or injecting government capital, all of which protect at least some creditors who otherwise would have suffered losses....If the crisis has a single lesson, it is that the too-big-to-fail problem must be solved."

Bernanke cited several risks with too-big-to-fail institutions:

1. These firms generate severe moral hazard. "If creditors believe that an institution will not be allowed to fail, they will not demand as much compensation for risks as they otherwise would, thus weakening market discipline; nor will they invest as many resources in monitoring the firm's risk-taking. As a result, too-big-to-fail firms will tend to take more risk than desirable, in the expectation that they will receive assistance if their bets go bad."

2. They create an uneven playing field between big and small firms. "This unfair competition, together with the incentive to grow that too big to fail provides, increases risk and artificially raises the market share of too-big-to-fail firms, to the detriment of economic efficiency as well as financial stability."

3. The firms themselves become major risks to overall financial stability, particularly in the absence of adequate resolution tools. Bernanke wrote, "The failure of Lehman Brothers and the near-failure of several other large, complex firms significantly worsened the crisis and the recession by disrupting financial markets, impeding credit flows, inducing sharp declines in asset prices, and hurting confidence. The failures of smaller, less-interconnected firms, though certainly of significant concern, have not had substantial effects on the stability of the financial system as a whole."

Moral Hazard

A moral hazard is a situation where a party may have a tendency to take risks because the costs that could result will not be felt by the party taking the risk. In other words, there may be a tendency to be more willing to take a risk knowing that the potential costs or burdens will be borne, in whole or in part, by others.

Some critics of the financial system and the new regulatory reforms argue that moral hazard continues to be a real concern. One could argue that "too big to fail" is actually "too big to allow."

Large Banking Groups – a Continuous Concern

Table 9.1 presents a selection of prominent mergers and takeovers in the United States that the market has observed as a result of the financial crisis.

Banks have grown significantly in terms of balance sheet volume, and even more importantly, risk. Today, the largest U.S. banks are bigger than ever, as Figure 9.1 illustrates. The balance sheet volume (total assets) of JPMorgan Chase, America's largest bank, is nearing the $2.5 trillion mark.

Table 9.1	List of Large U.S. Financial Institutions Acquired by Other Banks During the Financial Crisis
Acquired Institution	**Acquirer**
Bear Stearns	JPMorgan Chase
Washington Mutual	JPMorgan Chase
Countrywide Financial	Bank of America
Merrill Lynch	Bank of America
Lehman Brothers	Barclays / Nomura
Wachovia	Wells Fargo

Banks in the EU have also grown since the financial crisis, mainly because of takeovers; prominent examples include Deutsche Bank and its takeover of German retail institute Deutsche Postbank and Barclays' acquisition of the U.S.portfolio of the former "bulge bracket" investment bank Lehman Brothers.

European and American banks have grown by asset size, indeed. However, the largest banks in the world today are not headquartered in New York, London, Frankfurt, or Paris; in fact, they are domiciled in China. The People's Republic's largest banks reported total assets as follows:

- Industrial and Commercial Bank of China: $3.2 trillion (CNY19.7 trillion), as of 1Q2014.
- Bank of China: $2.3 trillion (CNY13.9 trillion) as of FY2013.[23]

Today, at least 20 international banking groups report total assets larger than $1.5 trillion. Examples besides the banks listed above include HSBC and Royal Bank of Scotland of the United Kingdom, Deutsche Bank of Germany, Crédit Agricole and BNP Paribas of France, and Santander Group of Spain, just to name a few.

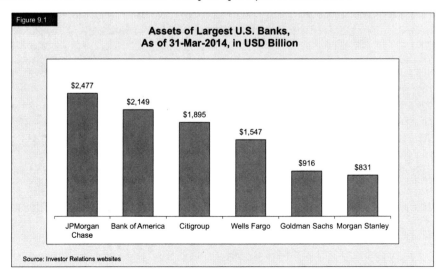

Figure 9.1

Assets of Largest U.S. Banks, As of 31-Mar-2014, in USD Billion

Source: Investor Relations websites

---

[23]Bank of China, Industrial and Commercial Bank of China.

For both governments and credit analysts, the too-big-to-fail issue remains an element of concern, and in fact, observation. A special framework for systemically important banks has been developed under Basel III and also plays a key role in other major banking reforms throughout the world, i.e., Dodd-Frank, Banking Reform in the United Kingdom, and the enhanced regulations of the Swiss Financial Market Supervisory Authority (FINMA).

The aforementioned regulatory developments may differ in detail but they all share the same overall key objectives:

- Reduce the probability of failure of global systemically important banks (G-SIBs) by increasing their going-concern loss absorbency; and
- Reduce the extent or impact of failure of G-SIBs by improving global recovery and resolution frameworks.

Financial Stability Board (FSB)

The Financial Stability Board (FSB) is an international body that monitors and makes recommendations about the global financial system. It was established after the G-20 London summit in April 2009 as a successor to the Financial Stability Forum (FSF). The board includes all G-20 economies, FSF members, and the European Commission.

The FSB has been established to coordinate at the international level the work of national financial authorities and international standard-setting bodies and to develop and promote the implementation of effective regulatory, supervisory, and other financial sector policies. It brings together national authorities responsible for financial stability in significant international financial centers, international financial institutions, sector-specific international groupings of regulators and supervisors, and committees of central bank experts.

The FSB is chaired by Mark Carney, governor of the Bank of England. Its secretariat is located in Basel, Switzerland, and hosted by the Bank for International Settlements (BIS).

The FSB is governments' main "early warning tool" to control systemic risk.

"Strengthening the Resilience of International Banking" – Excerpt of Speech by Mark Carney, Governor of the Bank of England and Chairman of the Financial Stability Board, at an Event to Celebrate the 125th Anniversary of the Financial Times, London, October 24, 2013.

"Making international banks safer is fundamental to a renewed globalization. To this end, new global standards for capital and liquidity have been agreed. The major global banks have raised $500 billion of new equity over the past few years and are on course as a group to meet the Basel III standards more than four years in advance of the deadline. In the UK, all major banks and building societies now have in place credible plans to achieve the Bank of England's thresholds for capital and leverage.

"To finish the job, international regulators need to agree over the next year [on] new rules for capital to be held in banks' trading books, a simple leverage ratio, and a guideline which governs the stability of banks' funding.

"Alongside these efforts to increase resilience, our focus is on solving the problem of banks that are too big to fail. Systemic resilience depends on being able to resolve failing banks in a way that does not threaten the entire system. Fairness demands the end of a system that privatizes gains but socializes losses. And simple economics dictates that the UK state cannot stand behind a banking system that is already many times the size of the economy.

"Moreover, without a credible means to resolve failing banks, regulatory Balkanization will continue as national regulators seek to protect their own interests, threatening the efficient operation of the international financial system and accordingly London's competitiveness.

"To avoid these risks, we need to make the resolution of global banks a real option.

"Successful cross-border resolution requires coordination and cooperation between authorities across multiple jurisdictions. This will only work if all authorities are confident that global resolutions will deliver domestic financial stability and protect local services. Cross-border cooperative agreements will help, but fine words must also be backed up by harsh economic incentives. Operating structures of banks must be made consistent with resolvability and, above all, banks must have substantial loss-absorbing capacity that cascades through their group structures."

Buffer for Systemically Important Financial Institutions (SIFIs)

One of the key measures of the Basel Committee is, of course, an additional buffer for SIFIs. Naturally, due to their importance for the overall system, SIFIs must expect higher regulatory scrutiny, especially in risk management. The SIFI buffer is described in Chapter 10.

Key Takeaways

- One of the main objectives of Basel III and other major banking reforms, such as Dodd-Frank in the United States, is to mitigate or even control systemic risk. For governments and regulators, and of course also for other market participants, the worst possible scenario is another banking crisis, starting at one major bank with a knock-on effect on a second bank, and a domino effect from thereon.
- A too-big-to-fail firm is one whose size, complexity, interconnectedness, and critical functions are such that, should the firm go unexpectedly into liquidation, the rest of the financial system and the economy would face severe adverse consequences.

- Contrary to the idea of "too big to fail," large banking organizations have increased their balance sheets since the financial crisis. Balance sheets of large European and U.S. banks have well passed the $2 trillion mark, e.g., Deutsche Bank (€1.6 trillion or $2.3 trillion) and JPMorgan Chase (nearly $2.5 trillion), as of the first quarter of 2014.
- One of the key measures of the Basel Committee is, of course, an additional buffer for SIFIs. Naturally, due to their importance for the overall system, SIFIs must expect higher regulatory scrutiny, especially in risk management.
- The Financial Stability Board (FSB) is an international body that monitors and makes recommendations about the global financial system.

Requirements for Systemically Important Financial Institutions under Basel III

The Basel Committee on Banking Supervision (BCBS) issued rules and requirements for systemically important financial institutions (SIFIs), in particular global systemically important banks (G-SIBs).

The G-SIB rules text was endorsed by the G-20 leaders at their November 2011 summit meeting in Cannes, France. The G-20 leaders also asked the BCBS and the Financial Stability Board to work on modalities to extend the global systemically important financial institution (G-SIFI) framework to domestic systemically important banks (D-SIBs).

The committee has developed a set of principles that constitutes the systemically important bank framework, which can be broken down in two broad categories:

- Assessment methodology; and
- Higher going-concern loss-absorbency capacity.

Characteristics of Systemically Important Financial Institutions

The impact of a SIFI's failure on the economy should, in principle, be assessed having regard to bank-specific factors:

Bernanke cited several risks with too-big-to-fail institutions:

- Size;
- Interconnectedness;
- Substitutability;
- Complexity; and
- Global (cross-jurisdictional) activity.

The committee has developed a methodology for assessing the systemic importance of G-SIBs. The methodology is based on an indicator-based measurement approach. The selected indicators are chosen to reflect the different aspects of what generates negative externalities and makes a bank critical for the stability of the financial system. The advantage of the multiple indicator-based measurement approach is that it encompasses many dimensions of systemic importance, is relatively simple, and is more robust than currently available model-based measurement approaches and methodologies that rely on only a small set of indicators or market variables.

Indicator-Based Measurement Approach under Basel III

Basel III has defined an indicator-based measurement approach that looks at global systemic importance in terms of the impact that a bank's failure can have on the global financial system and the wider economy, rather than the risk that a failure could occur. This can be thought of as a global, system-wide, loss-given-default (LGD) concept rather than a probability-of-default (PD) concept.

The selected indicators reflect the size of banks, their interconnectedness, the lack of readily available substitutes or financial institution infrastructure for the services they provide, and their global (cross-jurisdictional) activity. A measure of complexity is also added, since G-SIBs with greater complexity are likely to be more difficult to resolve and therefore cause significantly greater disruption to the wider financial system and economic activity.

The methodology gives an equal weight of 20 percent to each of the five categories of systemic importance. The categories, the individual indicators, and their weighting are illustrated in Figure 10.1.

Figure 10.1

Indicator-Based Measurement Approach under Basel III for Systemically Important Financial Institutions

Category and Weighting	Individual Indicator	Indicator Weighting
Size (20%)	• Total exposures as defined for use in the Basel III leverage ratio	20%
Interconnectedness (20%)	• Intra-financial system assets • Intra-financial system liabilities • Securities outstanding	6.67% 6.67% 6.67%
Substitutability / Financial Institution Infrastructure (20%)	• Assets under custody • Payments activity • Underwritten securities (debt/equities)	6.67% 6.67% 6.67%
Complexity (20%)	• OTC derivatives notional value • Level 3 assets • Trading and available for sale securities	6.67% 6.67% 6.67%
Cross-jurisdictional activity (20%)	• Cross-jurisdictional claims • Cross-jurisdictional liabilities	10% 10%

Under Basel III, for each bank the score for a particular indicator is calculated by dividing the individual bank amount (expressed in currency) by the aggregate amount for the indicator summed across all banks in the respective sample. This amount is then multiplied by 10,000 to express the indicator score in terms of basis points. For example, if a bank's size divided by the total size of all banks in the sample is 0.03 (i.e., the bank makes up 3 percent of the sample total) its score will be expressed as 300 basis points. Each category score for each bank is determined by taking a simple average of the indicator scores in that category. The overall score for each bank is then calculated by taking a simple average of its five category scores. The maximum total score, i.e., the score that a bank would have if it were the only bank in the sample, is 10,000 basis points (i.e., 100 percent).

1. Size

A bank's distress or failure is more likely to damage the global economy or financial markets if its activities comprise a large share of global activity. The larger the bank, the more difficult it is for its activities to be quickly replaced by other banks and therefore the greater the chance that its distress or failure would cause disruption to the financial markets in which it operates. The distress or failure of a large bank is also more likely to damage confidence in the financial system as a whole. Size is therefore a key measure of systemic importance. One indicator is used to measure size: the measure of total exposures used in the Basel III leverage ratio.

2. Interconnectedness

Financial distress at one institution can materially increase the likelihood of distress at other institutions given the network of contractual obligations in which these firms operate. A bank's systemic impact is likely to be positively related to its interconnectedness vis-à-vis other financial institutions. Three indicators are used to measure interconnectedness:

(i)   Intra-financial system assets;
(ii) Intra-financial system liabilities; and
(iii) Securities outstanding.

The interconnectedness between is mainly a result of

a) Interbank wholesale lending between banks (money markets); and
b) The over-the-counter (OTC) derivatives markets.

The OTC derivatives market is huge. As Figure 10.2 illustrates, the latest BIS statistics on OTC derivatives markets show that notional amounts outstanding totaled $710 trillion at end of June 2013.[24]

That is a multiple of the size of the entire world economy. Incredibly, there is a significant lack of transparency about these derivatives and their implications for the strengths and sustainability of any large market participant. Of course, the bulk of this derivatives trading is conducted by the strong capital market players, in other words the G-SIBs.

---

[24]Derivatives statistics as of end of December 2013, Bank for International Settlements, May 8, 2014.

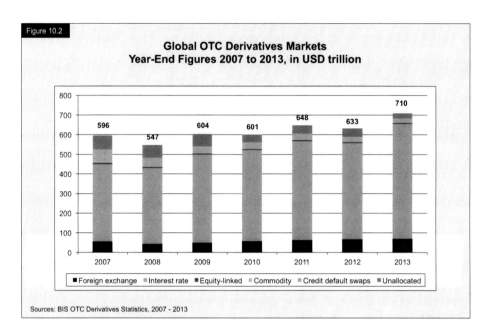

Figure 10.2

Global OTC Derivatives Markets
Year-End Figures 2007 to 2013, in USD trillion

Sources: BIS OTC Derivatives Statistics, 2007 - 2013

> *How many zeros in a trillion?*
> *1 trillion = 1,000,000,000,000*

3. Substitutability / Financial Institution Infrastructure

The systemic impact of a bank's distress or failure is expected to be negatively related to its degree of substitutability as both a market participant and client service provider, i.e., it is expected to be positively related to the extent to which the bank provides financial institution infrastructure. For example, the greater a bank's role in a particular business line, or as a service provider in underlying market infrastructure (e.g., payment systems), the larger the disruption will likely be following its failure, in terms of both service gaps and reduced flow of market and infrastructure liquidity. At the same time, the cost to the failed bank's customers in having to seek the same service from another institution is likely to be higher for a failed bank with relatively greater market share in providing the service.

Three indicators are used to measure substitutability / financial institution infrastructure:

(i) Assets under custody;
(ii) Payments activity; and
(iii) Underwritten transactions in debt and equity markets.

4. Complexity

The systemic impact of a bank's distress or failure is expected to be positively related to its overall complexity—that is, its business, structural, and operational complexity. The more complex a bank is, the greater are the costs and time needed to resolve the bank. Three indicators are used to measure complexity:

(i) Notional amount of over-the-counter derivatives;
(ii) Level 3 assets; and[25]
(iii) Trading and available-for-sale securities.

5. Cross-Jurisdictional Activity

Given the focus on G-SIBs, the objective of this indicator is to capture banks' global footprint. Two indicators in this category measure the importance of the bank's activities outside its home (headquarters) jurisdiction relative to overall activity of other banks in the sample:

(i) Cross-jurisdictional claims; and
(ii) Cross-jurisdictional liabilities. The idea is that the international impact of a bank's distress or failure would vary in line with its share of cross-jurisdictional assets and liabilities.

The greater a bank's global reach, the more difficult it is to coordinate its resolution and the more widespread the spillover effects from its failure.

Sample of Banks

The indicator-based measurement approach under Basel III uses a large sample of banks as its proxy for the global banking sector. Data supplied by this sample of banks is then used to calculate banks' scores. Banks fulfilling any of the following criteria will be included in the sample:

- The 75 largest global banks, based on the financial year-end Basel III leverage ratio exposure measure.
- Banks that were designated as G-SIBs by the BCBS in the previous year (unless supervisors agree that there is compelling reason to exclude them).
- Banks that have been added to the sample by national supervisors using supervisory judgment (subject to certain criteria).

These banks will be required to submit the full set of data used in the assessment methodology to their supervisors.

Bucketing Approach under Basel III

Banks that have a score produced by the indicator-based measurement approach that exceeds a cutoff level set by the BCBS will be classified as G-SIBs. Supervisory judgment may also be used to add banks with scores below the cutoff to the list of G-SIBs.

---

[25]For definition see chapter on Liquidity Coverage Ratio in part 6.

Most likely, the number of G-SIBs, and their bucket allocations, will evolve over time as banks change their behavior in response to the incentives of the G-SIB framework as well as other aspects of Basel III and country-specific regulations. Moreover, after the bucket thresholds have been fixed, if a bank's score increases such that it exceeds the top threshold of the fourth bucket, new buckets will be added to accommodate the bank. New buckets will be equal in size in terms of scores to each of the initial four populated buckets, and will have incrementally higher loss-absorbency requirements, as illustrated in Figure 10.3. This is to provide incentives for banks to avoid becoming more systemically important.

Figure 10.3

Basel III, the Magnitude of the Higher Loss Absorbency Requirement Bucketing Approach

Bucket	Score Range	Higher Loss Absorbency Requirement (Common Equity As a Percentage of Risk-Weighted Assets)
5	D-E	3.5%
4	C-D	2.5%
3	B-C	2.0%
2	A-B	1.5%
1	Cutoff point-A	1.0%

Capital Quality of the Higher Loss-Absorbency Requirements for Systemically Important Financial Institutions (SIFI Buffer)

The higher loss-absorbency requirement for systemically important financial institutions must be comprised of common equity tier 1 capital.

Under Basel III, the SIFI buffer will become effective in 2019. Figure 10.4 illustrates the total capital levels for SIFIs, which can be as high as 16.5 percent (14.5 percent tier 1 capital).

Additional Disclosure Requirements under Basel III for SIFIs

In addition to meeting the Basel III requirements, G-SIFIs must disclose the 12 indicators (middle column in Figure 10.1) used in the assessment methodology.

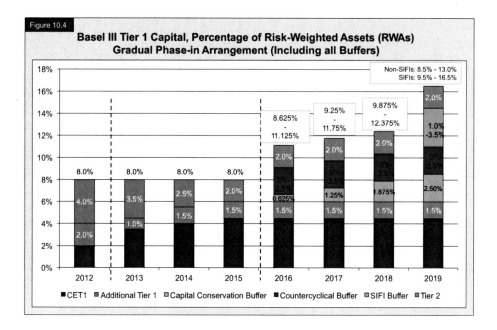

Figure 10.4

Basel III Tier 1 Capital, Percentage of Risk-Weighted Assets (RWAs) Gradual Phase-in Arrangement (Including all Buffers)

Basel III has set a €200 billion threshold with the objective of ensuring that the 75 largest banks in the world are subject to the public disclosure requirements, as these are the banks that are automatically included in the sample used to calculate banks' scores.

Banks below this threshold that have been added to the sample by supervisory judgment or as a result of being classified as a G-SIB in the previous year would also be required to comply with the disclosure requirements.

Although publication of the 12 indicators is the minimum requirement, national authorities may also wish to require that banks disclose the full breakdown of the indicators as set out in the template that sample banks use to report their data to the committee's data hub.

Disclosures must either be included in banks' published financial statements or, at a minimum, these statements must provide a direct link to the completed disclosures on their websites or on publicly available regulatory reports.

Stress Testing / Comprehensive Capital Analysis and Review (CCAR)

The financial and sovereign debt crises have highlighted how important it is for banks to have solid capital buffers that enable them to withstand extreme and unexpected shocks to their balance sheets and thus ensure that they can act as effective financial intermediaries even in periods of turbulence.

A macro stress-testing framework is often used by central banks to assess in a forward-looking manner the resilience of the banking sector to (adverse) macroeconomic and financial developments. In line with their responsibility for safeguarding financial stability in their economies, central banks employ macro stress-testing tools in their regular macro-prudential assessments:

- The European Central Bank has developed a "top down" stress-testing framework that currently covers the largest 80-90 banking groups in the European Union.
- In the United States, the Comprehensive Capital Analysis and Review (CCAR) and Dodd-Frank Act (DFA) stress tests are regulatory tools the Federal Reserve uses to ensure that financial institutions have robust capital planning processes and adequate capital. CCAR is an annual exercise by the Federal Reserve and applies to large bank holding companies with total consolidated assets of $50 billion or more. DFA stress test requirements apply to a broader range of companies and include bank holding companies, savings and loan companies, and state member banks with total assets greater than $10 billion and nonbank financial firms that are designated by the Financial Stability Oversight Council for supervision by the Federal Reserve.

Stress testing and CCAR are among the most important subjects in banking regulations and modern bank risk management; central elements apply to financial institutions of any size. Due to their importance, stress testing and CCAR are covered in Part 7 of this book.

Key Takeaways

- In addition to meeting the Basel III requirements, global systemically important financial institutions (G-SIFIs) must have higher loss-absorbency capacity to reflect the greater risks that they pose to the financial system.
- The Basel Committee has developed a methodology under Basel III that includes both quantitative indicators and qualitative elements to identify global systemically important banks (SIBs).
- Category and weighting quantitative indicators include size, interconnectedness, substitutability, complexity, and global (cross-jurisdictional) activity, each with a 20 percent weighting; the five categories can be broken down into 12 individual indicators, which must be disclosed by SIFI banks in their published financial statements (or openly on their websites).
- The additional loss-absorbency requirements are to be met with a progressive common equity tier 1 (CET1) capital requirement ranging from 1 percent to 3.5 percent, depending on a bank's systemic importance.
- Special stress testing requirements apply to systemically important financial institutions. In addition, central banks perform an annual assessment on institutions' loss-absorbency capacity and ability to withstand extreme and unexpected shocks.

Global Implementation of Basel III

As described in Chapter 2, Basel III is a global, voluntary regulatory standard endorsed by the G-20 governments. As more than 90 percent of the world's economy is represented by the G-20 endorsement, it should be expected that Basel III will be, eventually, signed into national law in all of the Basel Committee's member countries.

The members of the Basel Committee on Banking Supervision (BCBS) have actively developed the new capital, liquidity, and leverage standards, while making sure that specificities and issues related to their banking industries are appropriately addressed.

The new rules therefore respect the balance and level of ambition of Basel III. However, there are the following three reasons why Basel III cannot simply be copied/pasted into national legislation and, therefore, a faithful implementation of the Basel III framework must be assessed in all member countries and beyond having regard to the substance of the rules.

1. Basel III is not a law; it is the latest configuration of an evolving set of internationally agreed standards developed by supervisors and central banks, which has to go through a process of democratic control in the member countries as it is transposed into national laws. It needs to fit with existing national laws or arrangements.

2. The Basel capital adequacy agreements apply primarily, but not exclusively, to "internationally active banks" rather than small and midsize institutions, i.e., the thousands of regional and community banks in both the European Union and the United States.

3. The maturity of economic development, key economic indicators such as unemployment and inflation, and the central government's macroeconomic policy flexibility are very different in the individual member countries. In July 2014 benchmark interest rates in the BCBS member countries ranged from 0 percent in Japan and Switzerland to more than 17 percent; and were 0.15 percent in the European Union, as fixed by the European Central Bank (ECB); and a quarter percent in the United States, as fixed by the Federal Reserve.

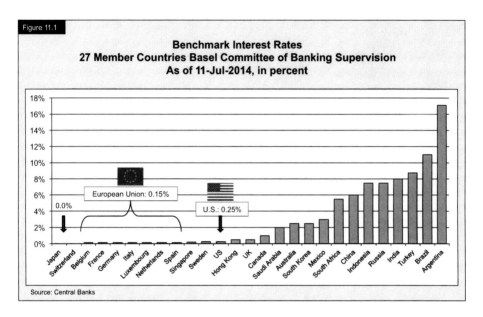

Source: Central Banks

Global Perspective

In August 2013, the BCBS reported the following progress of Basel III implementation to G-20 leaders:[26]

Capital

"Of the 27 Basel Committee member jurisdictions, only 24 have implemented Basel II fully. The United States, which is one of the three jurisdictions yet to fully implement Basel II, has issued final regulations on Basel II; however, its largest banks are still in parallel run for implementing the advanced approaches. The remaining two jurisdictions, Argentina and Russia, have also initiated the process to complete the implementation of Basel II.

"Of the 27 member jurisdictions, 11 have now issued final Basel III capital rules that are legally in force. The number of members that have issued final rules but not yet brought them into force has increased to 14 (this includes Argentina, Brazil, Russia, South Korea, the United States, and the nine EU member states that are members of the Basel Committee). The two remaining member jurisdictions (Indonesia and Turkey) have issued draft rules."

Liquidity

"Regarding the adoption of regulations relating to the liquidity coverage ratio (LCR), 11 member jurisdictions have issued final rules (South Africa, Switzerland, and EU member states), while four member jurisdictions have started the implementation process by issuing draft rules (Australia, Hong Kong SAR, India, and Turkey)."

---

[26]Report to G-20 Leaders on Monitoring Implementation of Basel III Regulatory Rreforms," Basel Committee on Banking Supervision, Bank for International Settlements, August 2013

Basel III Implementation in the European Union

The European Union (Figure 11.2) has actively contributed to developing the new capital, liquidity, and leverage standards in the Basel Committee on Banking Supervision, while making sure that major European banking specificities and issues are appropriately addressed.

Within the European Union, the European Commission has decided to implement Basel III through the use of a Regulation and a Directive. The European Commission published its original formal proposals for the Capital Requirements Regulation (CRR) and amended Capital Requirements Directive (CRD) in July 2011. This collective package of legislation is commonly referred to simply as 'CRD IV'. The EU implements Basel III nearly completely.

Under CRD IV, the most fundamental change is that, in implementing the Basel III agreement within the EU, the reform moves—as suggested by Basel III—from a uni-dimensional reform with only capital as a prudential reference to a multi-dimensional regulation and supervision with a wider scope, in particular capital, liquidity, and leverage, in order to cover the whole balance sheet of banks.

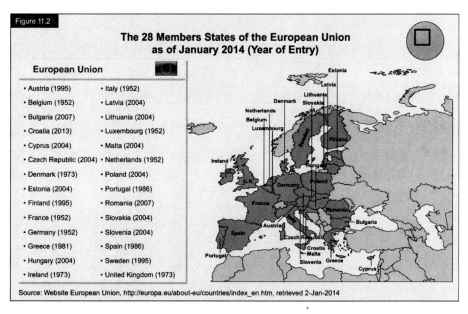

Figure 11.2

The 28 Members States of the European Union as of January 2014 (Year of Entry)

European Union

• Austria (1995)	• Italy (1952)
• Belgium (1952)	• Latvia (2004)
• Bulgaria (2007)	• Lithuania (2004)
• Croatia (2013)	• Luxembourg (1952)
• Cyprus (2004)	• Malta (2004)
• Czech Republic (2004)	• Netherlands (1952)
• Denmark (1973)	• Poland (2004)
• Estonia (2004)	• Portugal (1986)
• Finland (1995)	• Romania (2007)
• France (1952)	• Slovakia (2004)
• Germany (1952)	• Slovenia (2004)
• Greece (1981)	• Spain (1986)
• Hungary (2004)	• Sweden (1995)
• Ireland (1973)	• United Kingdom (1973)

Source: Website European Union, http://europa.eu/about-eu/countries/index_en.htm, retrieved 2-Jan-2014

CRD IV applies to all banks in the EU (more than 8,300) as well as investment firms. Further, it fully implements the Basel III suggestions for capital, liquidity, and the leverage ratio (as explained in other chapters in detail):

- Minimum common equity tier 1 (CET1) ratio of 4.5 percent (excluding buffers).
- Minimum tier 1 ratio of 6 percent (excluding buffers).
- Minimum total capital 8 percent (excluding buffers).
- Introduction of a capital conservation buffer (all banks): 2.5 percent.
- Introduction of a countercyclical capital buffer (national discretion): 0 – 2.5 percent.

- Introduction of a systemic buffer (systemically important institutions only): 1.0 percent – 3.5 percent.
- Liquidity coverage ratio ≥ 100 percent.
- Net stable funding ratio > 100 percent.
- Leverage ratio of 3.0 percent.

CRD IV applies to all banks in the European Union (more than 8,300), independent of size, as well as investment firms.

In addition to Basel III implementation, CRD IV introduces a number of important changes to the banking regulatory framework:

- Remuneration.
- Enhanced governance.
- Diversity.
- Enhanced transparency.

Figure 10.4 in Chapter 10 describes the individual Basel III / CRD IV elements, including their gradual phase-ins until 2019. In 2019, banks governed by Basel III / CRD IV will face the following going-concern capital requirements (tier 1):

Going-Concern Capital (Tier 1, incl. buffers)	Non-SIFIs	SIFIs
Minimum Capital Ratio	8.5%	9.5%
Maximum Capital Ratio	11.0%	14.5%

In addition, all banks are required to hold an additional 2.0 percent gone-concern capital (tier 2):

Total Capital (Tier 1 and Tier 2, incl. buffers)	Non-SIFIs	SIFIs
Minimum Capital Ratio	10.5%	11.5%
Maximum Capital Ratio	13.0%	16.5%

Timeline CRD IV

The original European Commission proposal followed the timeline as agreed in the Basel Committee and in the framework of the G-20: application of the new legislation from January 1, 2013, and full implementation on January 1, 2019, in line with the international commitments. Given the detailed discussions and their impact on the length of the legislative process, the new legislation was published in June 2013 and fully entered into force in July 2013. Institutions were required to apply the new rules starting from January 1, 2014, with full implementation on January 1, 2019.

Will EU States Have the Potential to Require Higher Capital Levels?

The EU in general and the euro area in particular have a very high degree of financial and monetary integration. Decisions on the level of capital requirements therefore need to be taken for the single market as a whole, as the impact of such requirements is felt by all member states. Financial stability can only be achieved by the EU acting together; not by each member state on its own.

Capital Requirements under the UK Banking Reform

In the United Kingdom, the government has introduced the Financial Services Bill (UK Banking Reform) in order to deliver stability and to support a sustainable UK economy. In its June 2012 white paper,[27] the UK government continues to support a PLAC (primary loss-absorbing capacity) requirement of up to 17 percent for UK-headquartered global, systemically important banks (G-SIBs) and ring-fenced banks, and takes the view that it is appropriate to calibrate this requirement against RWAs in line with the principle that the primary determinant of a bank's loss-absorbency requirement should take account of the riskiness of its assets. This is illustrated in Figure 11.3.

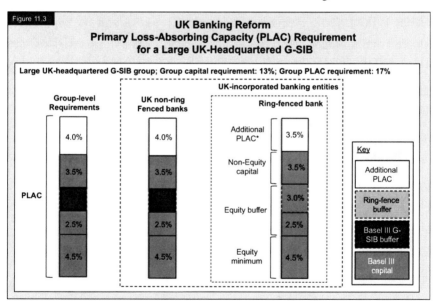

Figure 11.3

UK Banking Reform Primary Loss-Absorbing Capacity (PLAC) Requirement for a Large UK-Headquartered G-SIB

Basel III Implementation in the United States

In the United States, the Dodd-Frank Act (DFA) was signed into federal law by President Barack Obama in July 2010 in order to promote the financial stability of the United States by improving accountability and transparency in the financial system, to end "too

---

[27]"Banking Reform: Delivering Stability and Supporting a Sustainable Economy." Gov.UK. June 2012.

big to fail," to protect the American taxpayer by ending bailouts, to protect consumers from abusive financial services practices, and for other purposes.

The aforementioned reforms have very similar objectives and have comparable general architectures. Naturally, all reforms endeavor to establish a "level playing field" for market participants, even though Dodd-Frank in the U.S. has a wider reach. Surprisingly, the reforms have different requirements regarding loss-absorbency capacity, i.e., the capital ratio and the leverage ratio.

Capital Requirements under the Dodd-Frank Act in the United States

The following capital ratios apply:

Dodd-Frank-Act Minimum Risk-Based Capital Ratios		
	Tier 1 Capital	**Total Capital**
Well Capitalized	6.0%	10.0%
Adequately Capitalized	4.0%	8.0%

What is the Difference between a Bank's Liquidity and its Capital?[28]

Capital and liquidity are distinct but related concepts. Each plays an essential role in understanding a bank's viability and solvency.

Liquidity is a measure of the ability and ease with which assets can be converted to cash. Liquid assets are those that can be converted to cash quickly if needed to meet financial obligations; examples of liquid assets generally include cash, central bank reserves, and government debt. To remain viable, a financial institution must have enough liquid assets to meet its near-term obligations, such as withdrawals by depositors.

Capital acts as a financial cushion to absorb unexpected losses and is the difference between all of a firm's assets and its liabilities. To remain solvent, the value of a firm's assets must exceed its liabilities.

A typical family's household finances help to illustrate the differences between these two concepts. On the liquidity side, money in a family's checking account can be used to quickly and easily pay its bills, so a gauge of the family's liquidity position would include how much money is in the checking account as well as how much cash the family has on hand.

On the capital side, the family's assets include not just the money in the checking account, but also its home, savings accounts, and other investments. The family debt, or money it owes, such as a mortgage, constitutes its liabilities. So the difference between the family's debt and its assets would provide a measure of the family's capital position.

Over time, banks have failed or required government assistance because they had inadequate capital, a lack of liquidity, or a combination of the two.

---

[28]"Current FAQs: What Is the Difference Between a Bank's Liquidity and its Capital?" Federal Reserve Website. http://www.federalreserve.gov/faqs/cat_21427.htm

The Final Rule of July 2, 2013[29]

In July 2013, the U.S. bank regulatory agencies approved a Final Rule to help ensure that banks maintain strong capital positions. The rule brings the United States substantially into compliance with the Basel III international capital framework and implements various capital-related provisions of the Dodd-Frank Act. It includes higher minimum capital requirements, additional capital buffers above the minimum requirements, a more restrictive definition of capital, and higher risk weights for various assets, which together result in substantially more demanding capital standards for all U.S. banking organizations.

The Final Rule applies to all banking organizations subject to minimum capital requirements, including national banks, state member banks, state nonmember banks, state and federal savings associations, top-tier U.S. bank holding companies (BHCs) with more than $500 million in total consolidated assets, and most top-tier savings and loan holding companies (SLHCs). In a change from the proposed rules, SLHCs with significant commercial or insurance underwriting activities are not subject to the Final Rule. This is, of course, a major difference from the implementation of Basel III in Europe.

Therefore, the final rule minimizes the burden on smaller, less complex financial institutions. It establishes an integrated regulatory capital framework that addresses shortcomings in capital requirements, particularly for larger, internationally active banking organizations.

Ben Bernanke, Then-Chair of the Federal Reserve Board, on the Final Rule, July 2013

"This framework requires banking organizations to hold more and higher quality capital, which acts as a financial cushion to absorb losses, while reducing the incentive for firms to take excessive risks. With these revisions to our capital rules, banking organizations will be better able to withstand periods of financial stress, thus contributing to the overall health of the U.S. economy."

Under the Final Rule, minimum requirements will increase for both the quantity and quality of capital held by banking organizations. Consistent with the international Basel framework, the rule includes a new minimum ratio of common equity tier 1 capital to risk-weighted assets of 4.5 percent and a common equity tier 1 capital conservation buffer of 2.5 percent of risk-weighted assets that will apply to all supervised financial institutions. The rule also raises the minimum ratio of tier 1 capital to risk-weighted assets from 4 percent to 6 percent and includes a minimum leverage ratio of 4 percent for all banking organizations. In addition, for the largest, most internationally active banking organizations, the Final Rule includes a new minimum supplementary leverage ratio that takes into account off-balance sheet exposures.

Daniel K. Tarullo, Member of the Federal Reserve Board, on the Final Rule, July 2013

"Adoption of the capital rules today is a milestone in our post-crisis efforts to make the financial system safer. Along with the stress testing and capital re-

---

[29]Press Release: "Federal Reserve Proposes to Revise Market Risk Capital Rule," Federal Reserve Website, July 2, 2014.

view measures we have already implemented, and the additional rules for large institutions that are on the way, these new rules are an essential component of a set of mutually reinforcing capital requirements."

Basel III Implementation in China

The implementation framework for Basel III is stricter than the international standard, requiring a higher core tier 1 capital adequacy ratio (5 percent versus 4.5 percent) and a higher leverage ratio requirement (4 percent versus 3 percent).[30]

Special Challenge for Financial Institutions in Argentina and Russia

Financial institutions in both Argentina and Russia face the challenge of implementing three developments of the Basel Accord—Basel II, Basel 2.5, and Basel III—simultaneously, whereas other member countries of the BCBS have been working continuously on implementation of these regulatory standards for more than 10 years.

Basel III Implementation in Non-Basel Committee Jurisdictions

Central banks and regulatory authorities in a large number of countries—both member countries of the BCBS and others—are in the process of implementing, or have already implemented, the Basel standards, as Figure 11.4 illustrates.

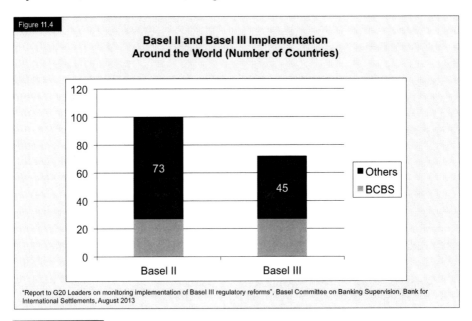

Figure 11.4

Basel II and Basel III Implementation Around the World (Number of Countries)

"Report to G20 Leaders on monitoring implementation of Basel III regulatory reforms", Basel Committee on Banking Supervision, Bank for International Settlements, August 2013

[30]"Basel III Implementation – Is the Industry Running out of Time?" JP Morgan Website. Retrieved July 14, 2014.

How have SIFIs Responded to the Additional Capital Requirements?

In recent years, many systemically important financial institutions (SIFIs) have raised capital by issuing new shares. Usually, these new shares were placed with institutional investors, and, of course, existing shareholders, who have to accept significant dilutions in their investments. For all banks, the purpose of the capital increases was to strengthen the equity capitalization and, therefore, loss-absorbency capacity.

Figures 11.5 and 11.6 illustrate the massive efforts by G-SIBs to increase their total equity and capital ratios.

In the time period FY2008 (the year of the Wachovia-Wells Fargo merger) to FY2013, Wells Fargo increased its total equity from $130 billion to $176 billion, an increase of 35.2 percent, as Figure 11.5 illustrates.

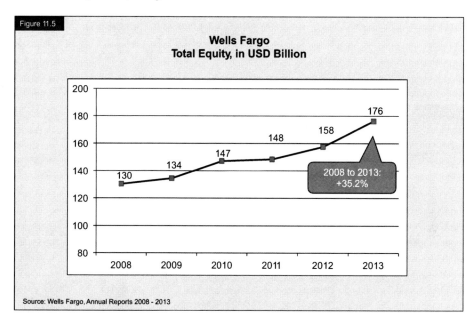

Figure 11.5

Wells Fargo
Total Equity, in USD Billion

Source: Wells Fargo, Annual Reports 2008 - 2013

In the time period 1Q2012 to 1Q2014, Citigroup increased its tier 1 common ratio under Basel III from 7.2 percent to 10.4 percent, an increase of 44.4 percent, as Figure 11.6 illustrates.

Citigroup is not unique in strengthening its capital base; other banks have gone through similar exercises. Gross proceeds of recent share issuances were of significant sizes; for example, Deutsche Bank raised €3 billion in 2Q2013 and an astonishing additional €8 billion in 2Q2014. This latest issuance improved Deutsche Bank's CET1 ratio from 9.5 percent to a rather comfortable level of 11.8 percent.[31]

Figure 11.7 illustrates the 1Q2014 levels of Basel III CET1 ratios at some of the largest banks in the world; these ranged from 9 percent to 13.2 percent. It must be noted

---

[31]Deutsche Bank Interim Report 2Q2014 and Update on Capital and Strategy 2015+. Deutsche Bank Web site.

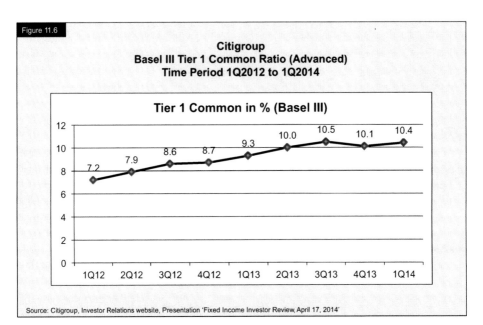

Figure 11.6

Citigroup
Basel III Tier 1 Common Ratio (Advanced)
Time Period 1Q2012 to 1Q2014

Source: Citigroup, Investor Relations website, Presentation 'Fixed Income Investor Review, April 17, 2014'

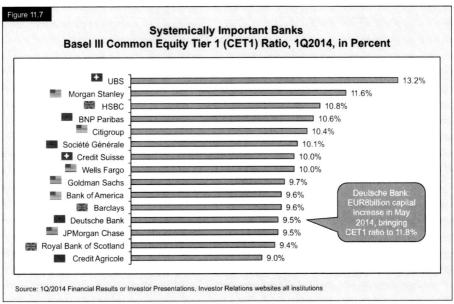

Figure 11.7

Systemically Important Banks
Basel III Common Equity Tier 1 (CET1) Ratio, 1Q2014, in Percent

Source: 1Q/2014 Financial Results or Investor Presentations, Investor Relations websites all institutions

that the comparison is still somewhat fragile. This is due to the fact that the Basel rule has not been fully finalized and that reported data is still calculated by institutions according to their own (best effort) interpretations of the (difficult) rules. Nevertheless, the figure illustrates clearly the actual trend of building up capital ratios, and therefore, loss-absorbency capacity.

Following the requirements by Basel III and the integration into CRD IV, the UK Banking Reform, and Dodd-Frank, it becomes clear that SIFIs need to continue their efforts in strengthening their capital ratios, either by raising additional capital or by reducing risk-weighted assets. This particular issue has been discussed in detail in Part 3.

A number of institutions have made announcements about their target capital structure, an issue which depends significantly on the exact regulatory requirement and whether the institution is primarily governed under CRD IV, the UK Banking Reform, or Dodd-Frank.

Figure 11.8 illustrates Barclays' target capital structure, which was disclosed in its Q12013 results. As a UK-headquartered bank, Barclays targets a total capital ratio of 17 percent, broken down as follows:

- Common equity tier 1: 10.5 percent (compared to 9.6 percent as of 1Q2014).
- Additional tier 1: 1.5 percent.
- Tier 2 capital: 5.0 percent.

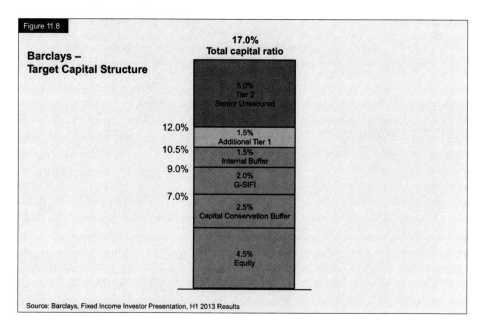

Figure 11.8

Barclays – Target Capital Structure

Source: Barclays, Fixed Income Investor Presentation, H1 2013 Results

Key Takeaways

- Within the European Union, the European Commission has decided to implement Basel III through the use of a Regulation and a Directive; the Commission published its original formal proposals for the Capital Requirements Regulation (CRR) and amended Capital Requirements Directive (CRD) in July 2011. This collective package of legislation is commonly referred to simply as "CRD IV."
- The EU implements Basel III nearly completely; CRD IV applies to all banks in the European Union (more than 8,300), independent of size, as well as investment firms.

- In the United Kingdom, the government has introduced the Financial Services Bill (UK Banking Reform) in order to deliver stability and to support a sustainable UK economy.
- The U.S. bank regulatory agencies approved a Final Rule to help ensure banks maintain strong capital positions. The Final Rule brings the United States substantially into compliance with the Basel III international capital framework and implements various capital-related provisions of the Dodd-Frank Act.
- Many non-Basel Committee countries are also in the process of implementing, or have implemented already, the Basel standards.
- Basel III requires going-concern capital levels (tier 1) of up to 11 percent for non-SIFIs and 14.5 percent for SIFIs. In addition, banks of any size need to hold gone-concern capital of 2 percent, bringing total capital ratios (tier 1 and tier 2) to up to 13 percent for non-SIFIs and 16.5 percent for SIFIs. These requirements are binding for financial institutions in the European Union.
- Large systemic banks have significantly increased their levels of capital and reduced assets, hence strengthening their capital ratios; these institutions will continue the process throughout 2014 and probably beyond.
- Different capital requirements in different jurisdictions and higher capital requirements endanger one of Basel III's main goals: achieving fairness and level playing fields.

Risk-Weighted Assets

Risk-Weighted Assets – Counterparty Credit Risk

The defaults or near-defaults of large, renowned banking organizations during the financial crisis have dramatically refocused risk managers onto trading-related credit risks.

As a result of the losses, the interconnectedness of large, systemically important financial institutions (SIFIs), and the complexity of their portfolios and products, the center of attention of both regulators and financial institutions today is credit risk from trading, in particular the derivatives business. Trading-related credit risk can be split into issuer risk and counterparty risk.

Issuer Risk

Issuer risk is the risk that the borrower, e.g., the issuer of a bond, defaults and is not able to fulfill the obligation, i.e., the issuer is unable to make full repayments. Issuer risk is similar to institutions' credit risk from commercial bank loans, where the lender is at risk that the borrower is unable to make payments on debt.

Counterparty Credit Risk

Counterparty credit risk (CCR) is the risk that the counterparty to a transaction could default before the final settlement of the transaction's cash flows. An economic loss would occur if the transaction, or portfolio of transactions with the counterparty, has a positive economic value at the time of default. Different than issuer risk, counterparty risk is often a risk to both parties and should be considered by both institutions when evaluating a contract or a portfolio of contracts. Counterparty risk occurs specifically in the over-the-counter (OTC) derivatives markets as transactions are done directly between two parties, without any supervision or role of an exchange.

Counterparty credit risk can be further broken down into three sub-categories:

- *Default risk,* the risk that a counterparty defaults and transactions fail to pay. Double-default risk occurs when collateral is also impaired.
- *Replacement risk,* the risk that, after a default, replacing the transaction under the same conditions (price) is not possible.
- *Settlement risk,* the risk that a party involved in the settlement fails before a transaction has completely settled.

Table 12.1 illustrates the main risk categories, their definitions, and how they apply to commercial loans and to capital markets products, i.e., exchange-traded products and OTC transactions. Trading partners—in particular, derivatives players—are the source for counterparty risk, not borrowers.

Table 12.1		**Definition of Counterparty Risk**			
				Capital markets	
Main Risk Categories		Description	Loan	Exchange-traded	OTC
Credit risk	Issuer risk		λ	λ	λ^1
	Counterparty risk	**Default risk:** the risk that a counterparty defaults and transactions fail to pay; double-default risk occurs when collateral is also impaired			λ
		Replacement risk: the risk that, after a default, replacing the transaction under the same conditions (price) is not possible			λ
		Settlement risk: the risk that a party involved in the settlement fails before a transaction has completely settled			λ
Market risk		Risk that the value of assets decreases and/or liabilities increase because of changes in market prices and/or volatility		λ	λ
Operational risk		Risk of loss resulting from inadequate or failed internal processes, people, and systems, or from external events (includes legal risk)	λ	λ	λ
Liquidity risk		The risk of being unable to meet payments due to a situation where the institution (1) has a lack of cash or cash equivalents to meet the needs of depositors/creditors, (2) cannot solve that shortage through the sale of liquid assets due to assets yielding less than the fair value, (3) cannot sell illiquid assets at the desired time due to a lack of buyers	λ	λ	λ

[1] Issuer risk for some products, e.g., credit default swaps

Basel III Requirements for Counterparty Credit Risk (CCR)

In its efforts to raise the level of institutions' capital bases, the Bank for International Settlements (BIS) has increased its capture of material risks into risk-weighted assets (RWA), i.e., the denominator of the capital ratio. Failure to capture major on- and off-balance-sheet risks, mainly counterparty risk, was a key factor that amplified the financial crisis.

In response to these shortcomings, the BIS in July 2009 completed a number of critical reforms to the Basel II framework. These reforms raise capital requirements for the trading book and complex securitization exposures, a major source of losses for many internationally active banks. The reforms became law in the European Union on April 16, 2013.

The framework established under Basel II has broadened and banks seeking to use their internal models for calculating their CCR regulatory capital must now deal with new rules and constraints, while the stakes for using the internal model method (IMM) approach in terms of capital have become more important and sometimes strategic for banks, in particularly large derivatives payers.

Review of Basel II for CCR

Basel II introduced major amendments under Pillar I (capital adequacy) and provided two approaches for the calculation of CCR:

1. The current exposure method (CEM), a fixed price version—based on a market price valuation—offering a hybrid measure between exposure and volume.
2. An "internal models" version that was created in line with the previous developments for market risk to enable banks to simulate mark-to-market future variations, with the objective of using such simulations both for their internal risk monitoring and for calculating regulatory capital.

Figure 12.1 describes the current exposure at default (EAD) method, which is based on the market value of a transaction (or its replacement value), an add-on for potential future risk, and an adjustment for collateral.

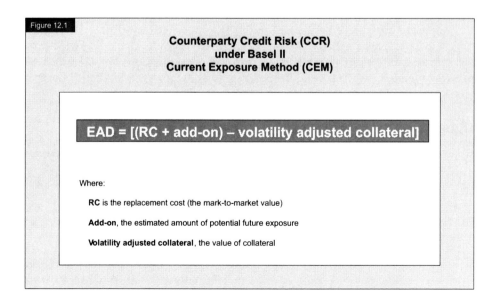

Figure 12.1

Counterparty Credit Risk (CCR)
under Basel II
Current Exposure Method (CEM)

EAD = [(RC + add-on) – volatility adjusted collateral]

Where:

RC is the replacement cost (the mark-to-market value)

Add-on, the estimated amount of potential future exposure

Volatility adjusted collateral, the value of collateral

Regarding the internal model for CCR, the Basel Committee adopted in 2005 changes to Basel II capital requirements for counterparty credit risk that allowed firms to use expected positive exposure (EPE) as the basis for regulatory capital requirements. EPE is the average over time of the forecast of the mean exposure to a counterparty at various horizons over the next year.

Expected positive exposure is the basis for calculating EAD in Basel II and involves the following steps:

1. **Find the Distribution of Market Values for Trades with a Counterparty.** For future dates find the probability distribution of net market values of transactions within a netting set for some future date given the realized market value of those transactions up to the present time.
2. **Find the Distribution of Exposures.** Adjust the probability distribution of market values for each of those future dates by setting cases of negative net market values equal to zero within the distribution (this takes account of the fact that, when the bank owes the counterparty money, the bank does not have an exposure to the counterparty).
3. **Find the Expected Exposure (EE).** For each date find the mean (average) of the distribution of exposures at any particular future date before the longest-maturity transaction in the netting set matures. An expected exposure value is typically generated for many future dates up until the longest maturity date of transactions in the netting set.
4. **Find Expected Positive Exposure (EPE).** Take the weighted average over time of expected exposures where the weights are the proportion that an individual expected exposure represents of the entire time interval. When calculating the minimum capital requirement, the average is taken over the first year or over the time period of the longest-maturity contract in the netting set.

Exposure at default (EAD), of course, must be linked with probability of default (PD) and loss given default (LGD) to generate risk-weighted assets.

Despite the analytical advantages of the internal model method (IMM), most banks subject to Basel II regulation decided to use the current exposure method (CEM) assessment method for their CCR calculations— mainly because it is quite simple and less expensive to implement—and avoid the heavy application process to have their internal model tested and finally approved by the regulatory authorities.

Glossary Basel / Counterparty Credit Risk

- **Internal Model Method (IMM):** The IMM is the most risk sensitive (and favored) method for calculating a bank's trade exposure and is based on the bank's own internal calculations of its risk exposure. In line with the internal models for market risk, the IMM must obtain regulatory approval.
- **Standardized Model (SM):** The SM is designed for banks that do not qualify to use the IMM, but wish to run a more risk sensitive method for calculating their trade exposures than the CEM allows for.
- **Current Exposure Method (CEM):** The CEM is the simplest and least risk-sensitive method for calculating a bank's trade exposure. Under the CEM, a bank's

trade exposure is calculated by taking the current replacement cost of all marked-to-market contracts currently "in the money" and then adding a factor (the "add on") to reflect the potential future exposure over the remaining life of the contract.

- **Standardized Approach (SA):** The SA enables banks to calculate the risk weightings to be applied to their exposures in a standardized manner, based on external credit ratings supplied by external assessment institutions (rating agencies).
- **Internal Ratings-Based (IRB) Approach:** The IRB approach enables banks to use their own internal rating systems to calculate the risk weightings to be applied to their exposures. Banks wishing to use the IRB approach must obtain regulatory approval.

Basel III Requirements for Counterparty Credit Risk

The Basel III standards include a series of proposals for new measures and adjustments to existing Basel II requirements related to counterparty credit risk.

Stressed Effective Expected Positive Exposure (EEPE) Calculation

For banks using an internal model method to calculate counterparty credit exposure regulatory capital, Basel III requires determining the default risk capital charge by using the greater of the portfolio-level capital charge based on effective expected positive exposure (EEPE) using current and stressed market data. EEPE is calculated as an average of effective expected exposure throughout the one-year horizon. Under Basel III, the EEPE measure is completed by a "stressed" EEPE calculation based on the calibration of diffusion model parameters over a period of three years, including a period of rapid increases in credit spreads. The greater of the EEPEs should not be applied on a counterparty-by-counterparty basis, but on a total portfolio level.

Credit Value Adjustments (CVA)

Basel III introduces an additional capital charge to cover the risk of change in credit valuation adjustments of a trading portfolio. The adjustment of credit valuation (credit valuation adjustment) materializes the market value of counterparty credit risk on the market transactions of the trading portfolio. The CVA charge represents a new capital add-on for potential mark-to-market losses associated with a deterioration in the creditworthiness of a counterparty. Effectively, CVA measures the difference between the present value of a derivative without counterparty default risk and the value when risk is taken into account.

Banks with IMM approval for CCR risk and approval to use the market risk internal-models approach for the specific interest rate risk of bonds must calculate the additional capital charge by modeling the impact of changes in the counterparty's credit spread on the CVAs of all OTC derivatives using the internal value-at-risk (VaR) model for bonds, as illustrated in Figure 12.2.

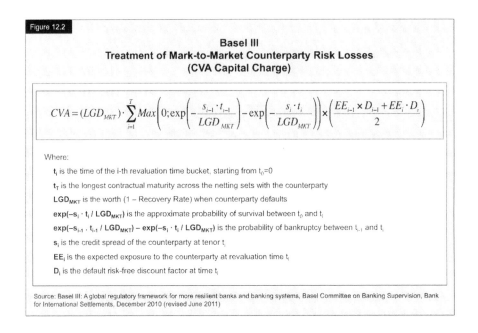

Figure 12.2

**Basel III
Treatment of Mark-to-Market Counterparty Risk Losses
(CVA Capital Charge)**

$$CVA = (LGD_{MKT}) \cdot \sum_{i=1}^{T} Max\left(0; \exp\left(-\frac{s_{i-1} \cdot t_{i-1}}{LGD_{MKT}}\right) - \exp\left(-\frac{s_i \cdot t_i}{LGD_{MKT}}\right)\right) \times \left(\frac{EE_{i-1} \times D_{i-1} + EE_i \cdot D_i}{2}\right)$$

Where:

t_i is the time of the i-th revaluation time bucket, starting from $t_0 = 0$

t_T is the longest contractual maturity across the netting sets with the counterparty

LGD_{MKT} is the worth (1 − Recovery Rate) when counterparty defaults

$\exp(-s_i \cdot t_i / LGD_{MKT})$ is the approximate probability of survival between t_0 and t_i

$\exp(-s_{i-1} \cdot t_{i-1} / LGD_{MKT}) - \exp(-s_i \cdot t_i / LGD_{MKT})$ is the probability of bankruptcy between t_{i-1} and t_i

s_i is the credit spread of the counterparty at tenor t_i

EE_i is the expected exposure to the counterparty at revaluation time t_i

D_i is the default risk-free discount factor at time t_i

Source: Basel III: A global regulatory framework for more resilient banks and banking systems, Basel Committee on Banking Supervision, Bank for International Settlements, December 2010 (revised June 2011)

Specific Wrong-Way Risk (WWR)

Specific WWR for unfavorable correlation quantifies the negative correlation between the risk exposure to a counterparty and its credit quality, for instance a put option purchase on a counterparty legally bound to the counterparty issuing the underlying instrument. When the Basel III capital requirements regulation (CRR) takes effect, transactions carrying specific wrong-way risk unfavorable correlation will have to be identified, isolated from the overall compensation node of origin, and assigned to a particular computational processing to calculate their exposure at default.

General Wrong-Way Risk

The overall risk of unfavorable correlation quantifies a systemic risk coming from the positive correlation between risk factors and counterparty creditworthiness.

Examples of general wrong-way risk:

- Higher oil prices can directly lead to an increase in the probability of default of airline companies, as the value of some of their exposures increase.
- Fluctuations in interest rates cause changes in the value of the derivative transactions but could also impact the creditworthiness of the counterparty.

Increase of the Margin Period of Risk (MPR)

The margin period of risk is the time period covering the last exchange of collateral used to cover netting transactions with a defaulting counterpart and when the closing out of the counterparty and the resulting market risk is re-hedged. With this indicator it is possible to model the change in market value of the collateral exchanged during a theoretical date of collateral exchange and the calculation date of subsequent exposure. In some situations, notably for all "illiquid" netting sets, banks will have to move from 10 days (the Basel II requirement) to 20 days of the regulatory threshold (with the possible doubling of this threshold coming into play if at least two disputes on the same set of compensation have been observed over the last six months).

Collateral Management

Basel III requires the implementation of a strengthened operational management of collateral, through the creation of a "collateral management" unit responsible for monitoring, reporting, and analyzing received and paid collateral, including categories of collateralized assets, the amount of margin calls exchanged, concentration, disputes, rehypothecations, and other elements.

Collateral management is vastly important for institutions active in the derivatives markets. The concept is described in detail in Chapter 13.

Application of a Coefficient of Correlation between Asset Values for Large Financial Institutions

Basel III requires the use of a correlation factor greater than 1.25 times the one used in calculating the Basel II regulatory capital for institutions of significant size, i.e., setting a threshold for those institutions with a trading book exposure over $100 billion.

Central Counterparty Clearing Houses (CCPs)

Banks are required to use a minimum risk weighting of 2 percent of the exposure value of all their trade exposures with the CCP. Even if this results in a new capital charge, when compared to Basel II, Basel III intends to enhance the role and the importance of central counterparties in the OTC market. These counterparties are to serve as intermediaries between buyers and sellers of products and thus help reduce counterparty risk, and therefore, systemic risk. The Basel Committee has therefore designed the new CCP requirements to act as an incentive to this end by ensuring OTC transactions will be more demanding in terms of capital requirements, whereas cleared derivatives contracts will tend to increase liquidity needs through initial and variation margins callable by clearing houses.

Clearing transactions via CCPs is tremendously important for institutions active in the derivatives markets. The concept is described in detail in Chapter 13. .

Validation and Backtesting Credit Counterparty Risk Models

Banks must conduct a regular program of backtesting, i.e., an ex-post comparison of the risk measures generated by the model against realized risk measures, as well as comparing hypothetical changes based on static positions with realized measures. Banks must carry out an initial validation and an ongoing periodic review of their IMM model and the risk measures generated by it.

The new requirements are in line with the requirements for the internal model for market risk. Validation and backtesting are key elements in assessing the quality of risk models and are therefore an important tool for risk control.

Impact on Banking Organizations

Large Banks

For those banks with significant derivatives portfolios, the impact on capital is potentially huge. However, large banking organizations will focus on credit risk mitigation tools and on clearing transactions via central counterparties, as described in Chapter 13. Implementation effort and costs depend on the state of sophistication in various institutions.

Impact on Small Banks

The Basel III requirements for counterparty credit risk have only minor impacts on small banks, provided that they are not active in the derivatives market in great volumes.

Securitization under Basel III

In December 2013, the Basel Committee on Banking Supervision issued a consultative paper on revisions to the Basel securitization framework. The committee proposed a simple framework akin to that used for credit risk:

- Where banks have the capacity and supervisory approval to do so, they may use an internal ratings-based approach to determine the capital requirement based on the risk of the underlying pool of exposures, including expected losses.
- If this internal ratings-based approach cannot be used for a particular securitization exposure, an external ratings-based approach may be used (assuming that the use of ratings is permitted within the relevant jurisdiction).
- Finally, if neither of these approaches can be used, a standardized approach would be applied. This is based on the underlying capital requirement that would apply under the standardized approach for credit risk, and other risk drivers.

Figure 12.3 illustrates the Basel III risk weights for securitization.

Figure 12.3

Basel III
Securitization / Risk Weights

	Securitization	Re-securitization
AAA	20%	40%
A+ to A-	50%	100%
BBB+ to BBB-	100%	225%
BB+ to BB-	350%	650%
B+ to unrated	Deduction	Deduction

Credit Risk – The Loan Book

The Basel III requirements under risk coverage or risk-weighted assets focus primarily on counterparty credit risk, derivatives, securitization, and off-balance-sheet commercial banking activities such as trade finance. The commercial loan book, i.e., risk coverage in capital adequacy, was completely overhauled with the introduction of Basel II.

For most banks in the world, the loan book is still the largest single asset. Under Basel II, the credit risk component can be calculated in three different ways, each with a varying degree of sophistication, namely:

- Standardized approach;
- Foundation internal ratings-based approach;
- Advanced internal ratings-based approach.

Further, Basel II allowed banks to choose between using internal and external ratings, and emphasized a common set of credit terminology:

- Exposure at default (EAD), an estimation of the extent to which a bank may be exposed to a counterparty in the event of, and at the time of, that counterparty's default;
- Probability of default (PD), an estimate of the likelihood that a borrower will be unable to meet its debt obligations;
- Loss given default (LGD), the share of an asset that is lost when a borrower defaults;
- Default (a loan is placed on non-accrual, a charge-off has already occurred, the obligor is more than 90 days past due, or the obligor has filled bankruptcy);
- Expected loss and unexpected loss.

Definition of PD:

"PD is the risk that the borrower will be unable or unwilling to repay its debt in full or on time. The risk of default is derived by analyzing the obligor's capacity to repay the debt in accordance with contractual terms. PD is generally associated with financial characteristics such as inadequate cash flow to service debt, declining revenues or operating margins, high leverage, declining or marginal liquidity, and the inability to successfully implement a business plan. In addition to these quantifiable factors, the borrower's willingness to repay also must be evaluated."

Office of the Comptroller of the Currency

Key Takeaways

- Risk coverage under Basel III (risk-weighted assets) focuses mainly on trading-related credit risks, i.e., counterparty credit risk (CCR) and securitization.
- CCR is seen as a major risk type and regulatory scrutiny has increased significantly; banking organizations have responded accordingly.

▪ CCR can be broken down into three sub-categories: (a) default risk—the risk that a counterparty defaults and transactions fail to pay; (b) replacement risk—the risk that, after a default, replacing the transaction under the same conditions (price) is not possible; and (c) settlement risk—the risk that a party involved in the settlement fails before a transaction has completely settled. Trading partners, in particular derivatives players, are the source for counterparty risk, not borrowers.

▪ Banks should implement adequate risk assessment tools and focus on risk mitigation, e.g., collateralization and clearing via central counterparties.

Key Requirements for OTC Derivatives

The Pittsburgh G-20 Summit in September 2009 marked a crucial step in the critical transition from crisis to recovery. The G-20 responded forcefully by committing to a co-ordinated set of policy actions that were unprecedented in scale and effect. Those actions pulled the world economy back from the brink of a depression.

Besides agreeing to strong international standards for bank capital—calling on banks to hold more and higher quality capital—the G-20 agreed on vital reforms in order to reduce systemic risk from the over-the-counter (OTC) derivatives markets, i.e., making the business more transparent.

G20 Statement, Pittsburgh, September 2009:

"All standardized OTC derivative contracts should be traded on exchanges or electronic trading platforms, where appropriate, and cleared through central counterparties by end-2012 at the latest. OTC derivative contracts should be reported to trade repositories. Non-centrally cleared contracts should be subject to higher capital requirements."

Figure 13.1 describes the multiples between outstanding derivatives (notional amounts) and total assets in two systemically important financial institutions (SIFIs) as

Figure 13.1 Total Assets and Notional Amounts of Derivatives Transactions Deutsche Bank / Bank of America Corporation / JPMorgan Chase & Co. Annual Reports 2013						
Assets and Derivatives in EUR(€) and USD($) **million** Equivalents using ECB exchange rate as per 31-Dec-2013: EUR/USD = 1.3791	Deutsche Bank†	Multiple of Total Assets	Bank of America Corporation	Multiple of Total Assets	JPMorgan Chase & Co.	Multiple of Total Assets
Total Assets	1,611,400€ equals $2,222,282		$2,102,273		$2,415,689	
Exchange-trades Derivatives	5,125,006€ equals $7,067,896	3.2				
OTC Derivatives	49,527,077€ equals $68,302,792	30.7				
thereof maturities > 5 years	11,290,048€ equals $15,570,105	7.0				
All Derivatives	54,652,083€ equals $75,370,688	33.9	$55,932,200	26.6	$70,430,000	29.2

Sources: Deutsche Bank, Annual Report 2013 page 72 and Annual Report / Management Report 2013 page 101 / Bank of America Corporation, Annual Report 2013 pages 16 and 165, JPMorgan Chase & Co., Annual Report 2013, pages 2 and 223

per 2013FY. While the size of the balance sheets alone is noteworthy—at Deutsche Bank, Bank of America, and JPMorgan Chase the balance sheets have well passed the $2 trillion mark—the derivative multiple to total assets is 33.9 times at Deutsche Bank, 26.6 times at Bank of America, and 29.2 at JP Morgan Chase. These multiples and the outstanding volumes in derivatives are simply amazing and speak for themselves.

Figure 10.2 in Chapter 10 illustrated that outstanding OTC volumes have remained high, even after the financial crisis. The latest Bank of International Settlements (BIS) statistics on over-the-counter derivatives markets show that notional amounts outstanding totaled $710 trillion at the end of June 2013.[32]

Volumes in derivatives remain significant. Large capital markets conglomerates such as the aforementioned Deutsche Bank, Bank of America, and JP Morgan act as counterparties in OTC contracts for a fee called spreads.. For example, swap dealers are the market makers for the swap market. The spread represents the difference between the wholesale price for trades and the "retail" price. As banks need to hedge their market risks—interest rates, foreign exchange, commodities, equities, etc.—on a macro (portfolio) or micro (individual transaction) basis, they enter into offsetting transactions with other market players. Effectively, these other market players act as a sort of reinsurance. Since the business is fee based, volumes have grown to the levels BIS has reported. Just to compare: according to the World Bank, the GDP of the entire United States stands at $16.2 trillion.

Amounts outstanding of OTC derivatives as of 31-Dec-2013:
$710.2 trillion
in full number: 710,182,000,000,000

For comparison, GDP 2012 of major economies, in $:[33]
United States: 16,244,600,000,000
United Kingdom: 2,208,002,878,868
Australia: 926,710,311,519

Figure 13.2 represents the interconnectedness between the institutions. In simple terms, every institution does business with other market participants in one or more products, in small, medium or large volumes—hence the total global OTC derivatives volume of $710 trillion.

Regulations have been designed to increase the stability of the over-the-counter (OTC) derivative markets throughout the European Union and the United States, including:

- Clearing obligations for eligible OTC derivatives.
- Reporting obligations for OTC derivatives.
- Measures to reduce counterparty credit risk and operational risk for bilaterally cleared OTC derivatives.
- Common rules for central counterparties (CCPs).
- Common rules for trade repositories (TRs).

In the U.S., the bulk of these reform initiatives was embedded in the Dodd-Frank Act and implemented primarily by the Commodity Futures Trading Commission

---

[32]Derivatives statistics as at end of December 2013, Bank for International Settlements, May 8, 2014.
[33]http://data.worldbank.org/indicator/NY.GDP.MKTP.CD, World Bank

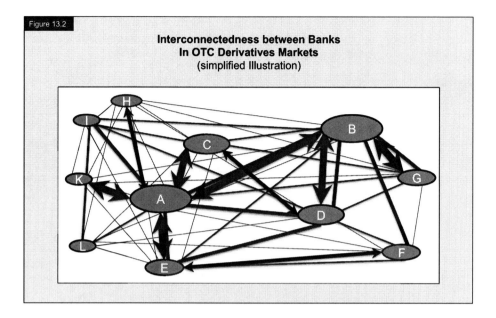

Figure 13.2

**Interconnectedness between Banks
In OTC Derivatives Markets**
(simplified Illustration)

(CFTC), working in conjunction with the Securities and Exchange Commission (SEC). In the European Union, the regulatory landscape is a bit more fragmented, as the majority of derivatives reforms are addressed in the Markets in Financial Instruments Directive (MiFID) and European Market Infrastructure Regulation (EMIR).

A key regulator in the European Union is the European Securities and Markets Authority (ESMA), the independent EU authority that contributes to safeguarding the stability of the European Union's financial system by ensuring the integrity, transparency, efficiency, and orderly functioning of securities markets, as well as enhancing investor protection. In particular, ESMA fosters supervisory convergence both amongst securities regulators and across financial sectors by working closely with the other European Supervisory Authorities competent in the field of banking (the European Banking Authories, or EBA), and insurance and occupational pensions (the European Insurance and Occupational Pensions Authority, or EIOPA).

Clearing Obligations for Eligible OTC Derivatives

All standardized OTC derivative contracts should be traded on exchanges or electronic trading platforms, where appropriate, and cleared through central counterparties. Clearing is the process of establishing positions, including the calculation of net obligations, and ensuring that financial instruments, cash, or both, are available to secure the exposures arising from those positions.

Financial institutions must arrange for all derivative contracts deemed "clearing eligible" by the responsible regulatory authorities (CFTC/ESMA) to be centrally cleared by a central counterparty. Central clearing imposes a central counterparty between each side of a trade, thus reducing credit risk between market participants. The CFTC and EMIR also set out margin and collateral standards for trades cleared through CCPs.

Non-financial counterparties will be subject to clearing requirements only if their derivatives positions exceed a clearing threshold set out under the regulations. Figure 13.3 illustrates the EMIR clearing thresholds for non-financial entities.

Figure 13.3

EMIR
Clearing Thresholds for Non-Financial Entities

Class of Derivatives	Threshold (Gross Notional Value, in Euro Billion)
Credit derivatives	1
Equity derivatives	1
Interest Rate derivatives	3
Foreign exchange derivatives	3
Commodity or other derivatives	3

Sources: ESMA

What is a Derivative:

A derivative is a financial instrument whose price is dependent upon or de-rived from one or more underlying assets. The derivative itself is merely a contract between two or more parties. Its value is determined by fluctuations in the underlying asset. The most common underlying assets include stocks, bonds, commodities, currencies, interest rates, and market indexes.

A derivative is generally used as an instrument to hedge risk, but can also be used for speculative purposes. For example, a European investor purchas-ing shares of an American company on a U.S. exchange (using U.S. dollars to do so) would be exposed to exchange-rate risk while holding that stock. To hedge this risk, the investor could purchase a put to hedge the equity compo-nent of the transaction and/or enter in an FX forward contract to lock in a specified exchange rate for the future stock sale and currency conversion back into euros.

Central Clearing / Central Counterparties

Central clearing is the process in which financial transactions are cleared by a single (central) counterparty to reduce individual risk. Each party in the transaction enters into a contract with the central counterparty, so each party does not take on the risk of the other defaulting. In this way, the counterparty is essentially involved in two mutually opposing contracts.

Central clearing of derivatives reduces counterparty risk and strengthens overall market integrity. It also helps with position segregation and portability in the event of a default, improves transparency for regulatory requirements, and benefits the central management of trade lifecycle events, such as cash settlement with central counterparties and credit events in the credit default swap (CDS) market.

CCPs provide a means for centralization, mutualization, and reduction of counterparty risk, as illustrated in Figure 13.4, and have two main objectives:

▪ Reduce counterparty risk; and
▪ Increase transparency,

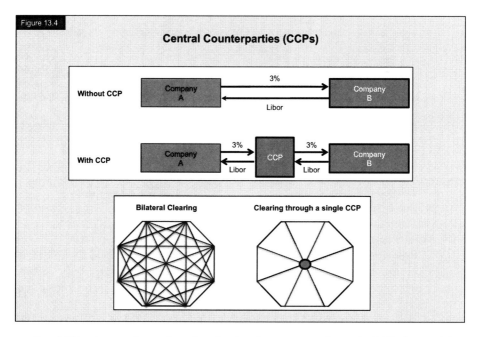

Basel III enhances incentives for clearing instruments through CCPs by applying lower own-funds requirements relative to OTC transactions. Also, the additional credit valuation adjustment (CVA) charge does not apply to exposures towards eligible CCPs.

CCPs are viewed as having strong creditworthiness but exposures to them were not given zero capitalization—a zero capital charge would create moral hazard and lead to the assumption that the CCP would never fail. Trade-related exposures arise from the current mark-to-market exposure and both initial and variation margin contributions only in the case of CCP failure. CCPs have a low risk weight of 2 percent.

The new provisions are designed to provide the industry with the following benefits:

▪ Central clearing lowers the counterparty credit risk. Once a trade is accepted by a clearinghouse, the clearinghouse becomes the counterparty. The regulatory agencies require clearinghouses to have rigorous risk management practices and governance.

- Central clearing will lead to greater standardization of derivative products and trading practices.
- Public trading venues will provide increased market and price transparency for participants.
- Regular trade reporting to central data repositories will improve transparency and operational efficiencies.
- Standardized collateral and default management practices will lead to better counterparty risk management.
- Standardization of trading venues and collateral mechanisms will provide greater protection to less sophisticated investors.

Regulatory requirements for clearinghouses are enormous and include the following:

- Organizational requirements, for example:
  - Roles and responsibilities, including senior management and the board.
  - Experience.
  - Independence / conflict of interest.
  - Establishment of a risk committee, which must be composed of representatives of the CCP'S clearing members, independent members of the board, and representatives of its clients.
  - Record-keeping (at least 10 years).
  - Outsourcing.
  - Business continuity.
- Conduct of business rules, for example:
  - General provisions.
  - Participation requirements.
  - Transparency.
- Prudential requirements, mainly:
  - **Exposure management:** A CCP shall measure and assess its liquidity and credit exposures to each clearing member and, where relevant, to another CCP with which it has concluded an interoperability arrangement, on a near to real-time basis.
  - **Margin requirements:** The prudential requirements shall be sufficient to cover losses that result from at least 99 percent of the exposures' movements over an appropriate time horizon. They shall also ensure that a CCP fully collateralizes its exposures with all its clearing members, and, where relevant, with CCPs with which it has interoperability arrangements, at least on a daily basis.
  - **Establishment of a default fund:** Of course, CCPs shall establish a minimum amount below which the size of the default fund is not to fall under any circumstances.
  - **Liquidity risk controls:** A clearing member, parent undertaking, or subsidiary of that clearing member together shall not provide more than 25 percent of the credit lines needed by the CCP.
  - **Collateral requirements:** A CCP shall accept highly liquid collateral with minimal credit and market risk to cover its initial and ongoing exposure to its clearing members and apply market-accepted haircuts when and where necessary.

▪ **Investment policy:** A CCP shall invest its financial resources only in cash or in highly liquid financial instruments with minimal market and credit risk.

▪ Rigorous **risk management practices and governance**, including policies and procedures, risk measurement tools / models, stress testing, and back testing.

Figure 13.5 lists the central counterparties that have been authorized to offer services and activities under EMIR in the European Union, as of April 2014.

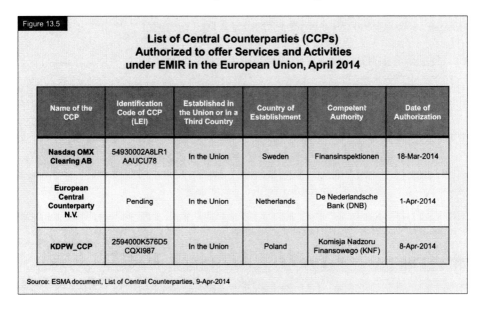

Figure 13.5

List of Central Counterparties (CCPs) Authorized to offer Services and Activities under EMIR in the European Union, April 2014

Name of the CCP	Identification Code of CCP (LEI)	Established in the Union or in a Third Country	Country of Establishment	Competent Authority	Date of Authorization
Nasdaq OMX Clearing AB	54930002A8LR1 AAUCU78	In the Union	Sweden	Finansinspektionen	18-Mar-2014
European Central Counterparty N.V.	Pending	In the Union	Netherlands	De Nederlandsche Bank (DNB)	1-Apr-2014
KDPW_CCP	2594000K576D5 CQXI987	In the Union	Poland	Komisja Nadzoru Finansowego (KNF)	8-Apr-2014

Source: ESMA document, List of Central Counterparties, 9-Apr-2014

Reporting Obligations

Firms must report exchange-traded and OTC-traded derivative contracts to trade repositories (TRs); the reporting requirements will allow regulators to monitor the build-up of systemic risk through excessive risk concentrations.

Firms must assess the data-reporting requirements against their system capabilities and strategies; they may delegate reporting to third parties and should assess reporting services as part of a suite of clearing related services.

Naturally, the information that needs to be provided to the TR must include both counterparty data, such as name of counterparty, corporate sector, etc., and common data, type of contract, currency, maturity, and notional value.

Few exemptions from the reporting obligations exist. Brokers and dealers do not have a reporting obligation when they act purely in an agency capacity.

a) Unique Trade Identifier (UTI)

Unique global trade IDs are required in order to ensure accurate identification of reported trades. This will improve the ability to reconcile trades both with and between counterparties, CCPs, and trade repositories, and reduce the likelihood of duplicate reporting. Regulators, for example ESMA, have placed the responsibility of creating UTIs on the counterparties to the contract. However, it is possible to delegate the generation of the UTI.

b) Legal Entity Identifier (LEI)

Identification of counterparties, CCPs, beneficiaries, and brokers will be achieved by using a global legal entity identifier. Third-party entities, i.e., trade repositories, have developed a global solution to the identification of legal entities.

c) Universal/Unique Product Identifier (UPI)

There has been an industry request for adoption of the ISDA UPI taxonomy; however, concerns were raised that it may not capture exotic/bespoke/hybrid products.

In the event that a globally agreed product identifier is not available, a number of alternatives have been identified:

- International Securities Identification Number (ISIN).
- Alternative Instruments Identifier (AII).
- Classification of Financial Instruments code (CFI).

Hybrid trades may also be reported, on the basis that both counterparties agree to use the asset class the hybrid closely resembles.

d) Valuation

Data reported to repositories should include fields that provide an indication of the exposure between counterparties and allow regulators to see a comprehensive picture of the positions of firms with each other, including collateral exchanged. Based on this, daily valuation is required in order to obtain the mark-to-market valuation of the outstanding contracts. Mark-to-market or mark-to-model valuation will assist in ensuring a more accurate quantification of the counterparty's exposure. CCPs are required to provide valuation data on cleared OTC contracts.

e) Collateral

Collateral information must complement the information on exposures. Counterparties can report collateral exchanged for an individual contract to trade repositories and may report collateral exchanged on a portfolio basis (using a unique code applicable to the portfolio) if individual contract information is unavailable. Portfolio information should include collateral value and currency.

Trade Repositories

A trade repository (TR), sometimes also called swap data repository, is an entity that centrally collects and maintains the records of OTC derivatives. These electronic platforms, acting as authoritative registries of key information regarding open OTC derivatives trades, provide an effective tool for mitigating the inherent opacity of OTC deriva-tives markets. This market infrastructure is defined and supervised in Europe by the European Securities and Markets Authority under the European Markets Infrastructure Regulation. Similar regulatory initiatives are conducted in the United States where the Commodity Futures Trading Commission (CFTC) has developed the Dodd-Frank Act regulation, under which swap data repositories are regulated.

A trade repository must register with ESMA or CFTC, or other similar regulatory authorities in its jurisdiction. To be eligible to be registered, a trade repository shall be a legal person established in the European Union (under EMIR) or United States (under Dodd-Frank) and meet stringent requirements:

a) General Requirements

TRs must have robust governance arrangements that include a clear organizational structure with well defined, transparent, and consistent lines of responsibility and ade-quate internal control mechanisms—including sound administrative and accounting procedures—that prevent any disclosure of confidential information. Further, they must maintain and operate effective written organizational and administrative arrange-ments to identify and manage any potential conflicts of interest concerning their man-agers, employees, or any person directly or indirectly linked to them by close links. As it is good practice in risk management, TRs must also establish policies and procedures sufficient to ensure compliance.

b) Operational Reliability

A trade repository shall identify sources of operational risk and minimize them through the development of appropriate systems, controls, and procedures. Such systems shall be reliable and secure and have adequate capacity to handle the information received. TRs must establish, implement, and maintain an adequate business continuity policy and disaster recovery plan.

c) Safeguarding and Reporting

Privacy concerns exist wherever personally identifiable information or other sensitive information is collected and stored—in digital form or otherwise. Improper or nonex-istent disclosure control can be the root cause for privacy issues. Data privacy issues can arise in response to information from a wide range of sources such as financial institu-tions and transactions. Therefore, it is of the utmost importance that TRs ensure the confidentiality, integrity, and protection of the information received. A trade repository may only use the data it receives for commercial purposes if the relevant counterparties have provided their consent.

d) Transparency and Data Availability

A trade repository must regularly, and in an easily accessible way, publish aggregate po-sitions by class of derivatives on the contracts reported to it. A trade repository shall collect and maintain data and shall ensure that entities have direct and immediate access to the details of derivatives contracts they need to fulfill their respective responsibilities and mandates. A trade repository shall make the necessary information available to the entities listed in Figure 13.6 to enable them to fulfill their respective responsibilities and mandates.

The figure lists the registered trade repositories that have been authorized to offer services and activities under EMIR in the European Union as of April 2014.

Figure 13.6

List of Registered Trade Repositories (TRs) Authorized to Offer Services and Activities under EMIR in the European Union, April 2014

Trade Repository	Derivatives Asset Classes	Effective Date
DTCC Derivatives Repository Ltd. (DDRL)	All asset classes	14-Nov-2013
Krajowy Depozyt Papierów Wartosciowych S.A. (KDPW)	All asset classes	14-Nov-2013
Regis-TR S.A.	All asset classes	14-Nov-2013
UnaVista Limited	All asset classes	14-Nov-2013
CME Trade Repository Ltd. (CME TR)	All asset classes	5-Dec-2013
ICE Trade Vault Europe Ltd. (ICE TVEL)	Commodities, credit, equities, interest rates	5-Dec-2013

Source: ESMA, http://www.esma.europa.eu/page/Trade-repositories, retrieved 21-Apr-2014

Key Takeaways

- Regulations have been designed to increase the stability of the over-the-counter (OTC) derivative markets throughout the European Union and the United States, including clearing obligations for eligible OTC derivatives, reporting obligations for all OTC derivatives, and measures to reduce counterparty credit risk and operational risk for bilaterally cleared OTC derivatives.
- This market infrastructure is defined and supervised in the European Union by the European Securities and Markets Authority (ESMA) under the European Markets Infrastructure Regulation (EMIR). In the United States, related regulatory initiatives are conducted by the Commodity Futures Trading Commission (CFTC) under the Dodd-Frank Act.
- All standardized OTC derivative contracts should be traded on exchanges or electronic trading platforms, where appropriate, and cleared through central counterparties (CCPs).
- Regulatory requirements for clearinghouses/CCPs are enormous and include organizational requirements, conduct of business rules, and prudential requirements.

- CCPs must register with the ESMA or CFTC, or other similar regulatory authorities in their respective jurisdiction.
- Financial institutions and non-financial firms above a defined threshold must report exchange-traded and OTC-traded derivative contracts to trade repositories (TRs); the reporting requirements will allow regulators to monitor the build-up of systemic risk through excessive risk concentrations.
- Trade repositories are entities that centrally collect and maintain the records of OTC derivatives. These electronic platforms, acting as authoritative registries of key information regarding open OTC derivatives trades, provide an effective tool for mitigating the inherent opacity of OTC derivatives markets.
- A trade repository must register with the ESMA or CFTC, or other similar regulatory authorities in their respective jurisdiction; prudent risk management requirements apply.

Risk-Weighted Assets – Market Risk and Other Risks

Market risk is the risk of losses in positions arising from movements in market prices. Typically, market risks for banking institutions include:

- *Interest rate risk,* the risk that interest rates, e.g., Libor, Euribor, etc., and/or their implied volatility will change. Naturally, interest rates affect both the banking book and the trading book of institutions.
- *Currency (foreign exchange) risk,* the risk that foreign exchange rates, e.g., EUR/USD, EUR/GBP, etc., and/or their implied volatility will change.
- *Equity risk,* the risk that stocks or stock indices, e.g., S&P500, DAX, etc., and/or their implied volatility will change.
- *Commodity risk,* the risk that commodity prices, e.g., crude oil, copper, wheat, etc., and/or their implied volatility will change.

Banking Book versus Trading Book

The trading book is an accounting term that refers to assets held by a bank that are regularly traded. The trading book is required under Basel II and III to be marked to market daily. The value-at-risk (VaR) for assets in the trading book is measured on a 10-day time horizon under Basel II.

The banking book is also an accounting term, and refers to assets on a bank's balance sheet that are expected to be held to maturity. Banks are not required to mark these to market. Unless there is reason to believe that the counterparty will default on its obligation, they are held at historical cost.

If a client wishes to sell debt securities to a bank instead of taking a loan, the asset will now be assigned to the trading book instead. The bank will then keep specific risk capital for the securities as well as market risk capital.

The main differences are:

1. Assets that are held for trading are put in the trading book; assets that are held to maturity are held in the banking book.
2. Assets in the trading book are marked-to-market daily; assets in the banking book are held at historic cost.

3. The value-at-risk for assets in the trading book is calculated at a 99 percent confidence level based on a 10-day time horizon. The value-at-risk for assets in the banking book is calculated at a 99.9 percent confidence level on a one-year horizon. This issue has been significantly enhanced under Basel III; see under "Basel III Requirements for Market Risk" below.

Trading Market Risk Deutsche Bank[34]

"The vast majority of our businesses are subject to market risk, defined as the potential for change in the market value of our trading and investing positions. Risk can arise from adverse changes in interest rates, credit spreads, foreign exchange rates, equity prices, commodity prices, and other relevant parameters, such as market volatility and market implied default probabilities. The primary objective of Market Risk Management, a part of our independent Risk function, is to ensure that our business units optimize the risk-reward relationship and do not expose us to unacceptable losses outside of our risk appetite. To achieve this objective, Market Risk Management works closely together with risk takers ('the business units') and other control and support groups. We distinguish between three substantially different types of market risk:

- *Trading market risk arises primarily through the market-making activities of the CB&S [Corporate Banking & Securities] Division. This involves taking positions in debt, equity, foreign exchange, other securities and commodities as well as in equivalent derivatives.*
- *Traded default risk arising from defaults and rating migrations relating to trading instruments.*
- *Nontrading market risk arises from market movements, primarily outside the activities of our trading units, in our banking book and from off-balance sheet items. This includes interest rate risk, credit spread risk, investment risk and foreign exchange risk as well as market risk arising from our pension schemes, guaranteed funds and equity compensation. Nontrading market risk also includes risk from the modeling of client deposits as well as savings and loan products."*

Market Risk in Large Banks – Regulatory Concerns

1. High Levels of Market Risk in the Overall Portfolio

With the emergence of derivative products in the 1980s and 1990s, many banks have committed even more financial and human resources to their respective capital markets business. Markets had bullish phases in that period; i.e., stock markets increased significantly. Figure 14.1 illustrates that the U.S. blue chip equity market, the Dow Jones Industrial Average (DJIA / Dow 30), increased from 824.57 in 1980 to 11,497.12 in 1999. Consequently, banks continuously increased their willingness to take market risk positions, especially in the trading book.

---

[34]Deutsche Bank Annual Report 2013, Risk Report, Trading Market Risk, Page 154.

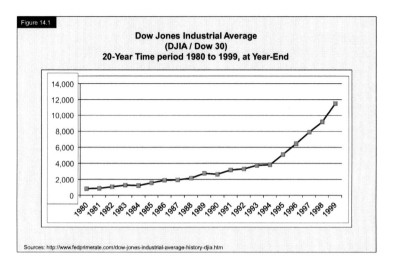

Back in 1980, banks of course had market risk, in particular interest rate and foreign exchange-related exposures; however, annual reports did not disclose much about those particular risks. While banks back then informed their shareholders and other stakeholders about general interest rate levels and outlook, the trends in the FX markets regarding increasing international and capital market risks and value-at-risk were only at the brink of development.

Definition of Market Risk at HSBC:[35]

"The risk that movements in market factors, including foreign exchange rates and commodity prices, interest rates, credit spreads, and equity prices, will reduce our income or the value of our portfolios."

Today, market risk levels in major banks are significant. As Figure 14.2 illustrates, Deutsche Bank disclosed in its 2013 annual report an economic capital usage for market

Figure 14.2

Deutsche Bank
Risk Position As Measured by Economic Capital Usage
As of 31-Dec-2013

In EUR million, as of 31-Dec-2013	
Credit risk	12,013
Market risk	12,738
• Trading market risk	4,197
▪ Nontrading market risk	8,541
Operational risk	5,253
Diversification effects	(4,515)
Sub-total credit, market and operational risk	25,489
Business risk	1,682
Total economic capital usage	**27,171**

Before Diversification Effects

17.5%
28.5%
14.0%

■ Credit risk
▨ Trading market risk
☐ Nontrading market risk
▩ Operational risk

Source: Deutsche Bank, Annual Report 2013, Risk Report, Overall Risk Position, Page 223

---

[35]HSBC Annual Report / Risk Report / Page 137.

risk of 42.5 percent of the sum of economic capital usage for all major risk types (credit risk, market risk, operational risk), before diversification effects.

Market Risk at HSBC[36]

Exposure to Market Risk
"Exposure to market risk is separated into two portfolios:

- *Trading portfolios comprise positions arising from market making and warehousing of customer-derived positions.*
- *Non-trading portfolios comprise positions that primarily arise from the interest rate management of our retail and commercial banking assets and liabilities, financial investments designated as available for sale and held to maturity, and exposures arising from our insurance operations."*

Monitoring and Limiting Market Risk Exposures
"Our objective is to manage and control market risk exposures while maintaining a market profile consistent with our risk appetite. We use a range of tools to monitor and limit market risk exposures, including:

- *Sensitivity analysis measures the impact of individual market factor movements on specific instruments or portfolios including interest rates, foreign exchange rates, and equity prices, for example the impact of a one basis point change in yield;*
- *Value-at-risk is a technique that estimates the potential losses that could occur on risk positions as a result of movements in market rates and prices over a specified time horizon and to a given level of confidence; and*
- *In recognition of VaR's limitations we augment it with stress testing to evaluate the potential impact on portfolio values of more extreme, though plausible, events or movements in a set of financial variables. Examples of scenarios reflecting current market concerns are the slowdown of mainland China and the potential effects of a sovereign debt default, including its wider contagion effects."*

2. Value-at-Risk Models

The growing magnitude and complexity of trading accounts, coupled with increased volatility in the financial markets, have pushed both institutions and regulators to adopt large-scale risk measurement models—i.e., VaR. Today, VaR is widely used for internal risk measurement/management purposes by banks of various sizes, and by many regulators world-wide to define regulatory capital requirements for market risks. VaR is particularly popular because it is simple and fairly easy to implement.

Financial institutions utilize VaR to estimate the potential loss from adverse market moves in a normal market environment consistent with the day-to-day risk decisions

---

[36]HSBC Annual Report / Risk Report / Page 231.

made by the lines of business.

Firms typically have one overarching VaR model framework, used for risk management purposes across the institution. Most large banks have implemented a historical simulation approach, which is based on historical data, e.g., the previous 12 months. Other institutions use a Monte Carlo simulation, using computational algorithms that rely on repeated random sampling to obtain numerical results; typically one runs simulations many times over in order to obtain the distribution of an unknown probabilistic entity. Of course, the data sample is again built on historical data, i.e., market rates and prices.

For the daily assessment of market risk in the trading portfolio, VaR is calculated by institutions assuming a one-day holding period and an expected tail-loss methodology which approximates a 97.5 percent (alternatively 95.0 percent or other more conservative confidence level). This means that, assuming current changes in market values are consistent with the historical changes used in the simulation, one would expect to incur VaR "band breaks," defined as losses greater than that predicted by VaR estimates, not more than 2.5 times every 100 trading days. The number of VaR band breaks observed can differ from the statistically expected number of band breaks. That can occur if the current level of market volatility is materially different from the level of market volatility during the 12 months of historical data used in the historical simulation VaR calculation, or the sample data set used for Monte Carlo Simulation. Data sources used in VaR models must be the same as those used for financial statement valuations.

Institutions' models aggregate portfolio market risk exposure for capital adequacy purposes into one single number by using a 99 percent confidence level and by applying a 10-day holding period.

3. Weaknesses of Value-at-Risk Models

VaR, unfortunately, has a number of weaknesses. These have been known to risk experts, at both financial institutions and regulatory authorities, for years, and mainly include:

- The simplicity of VaR—aggregating positions and exposures into one figure—is actually its biggest weakness. Market risk is more than one figure.
- VaR is backward looking and analyzes historical data. This implicitly assumes that historical data is a good predictor of future outcomes. This assumption is lacking in financial market risk management, especially in periods of stressed markets.
- VaR assumes that positions are liquid; the 10-day holding period assumes that exposures can be closed in a period of 10 days. First of all, a significant number of positions in large banks' trading books are not liquid and, secondly, positions cannot be closed out and hedged in 10 days in stressed markets. VaR assumes that positions can be marked-to-market. In fact, a large number of positions can only be evaluated on a mark-to-model basis. Mark-to-model refers to the practice of pricing a position or portfolio at prices determined by financial models, in contrast to allowing the market to determine the price. Often the use of models is necessary where a market for the financial product is not available, such as with complex financial instruments. One shortcoming of mark-to-model is that it gives an artificial illusion of liquidity, and the actual price of the product depends on the accu-

racy of the financial models used to estimate the price. Further, pricing models are based on underlying assumptions, which can be questionable in certain markets, i.e., in periods of stress. Back in the mid-1990s, when models and their inclusion in regulator concepts were developed, a number of experts criticized the short holding period of 10 days.

- The confidence level to measure capital adequacy for market risk has always been, since its introduction as a regulatory tool for the measurement of capital adequacy for market risk, set at 99 percent. The level suggests that the forecasting by risk management is off on average 2.5 times a year, assuming a total of 250 trading days per annum. In previous times, regulators considered this gap to be covered assuming a qualitative scaling factor (m) of a minimum of 3.0 to be multiplied by VaR. The concept of VaR covers the unexpected part of the risk curve in still "normal" markets, where volatility goes bad. However, the concept has never tried to answer the question, "How much will we lose in extremely stressed markets?"

Bank Capital Requirements for Market Risk in the United States: The Internal Model Approach – Quotes from the Federal Reserve[37]

- "By substituting banks' internal risk measurement models for broad, uniform regulatory measures of risk exposure, [the new rule] should lead to capital charges that more accurately reflect individual banks' true risk exposures."
- "By itself, even a perfectly measured 10-day, 99th percentile value-at-risk figure may not provide a sufficient degree of risk coverage to serve as a prudent capital standard."
- "In addition to tightening the link between [market] risk exposures and capital requirements, a capital charge based on internal models may provide supervisors and the financial markets with a consistent framework for making comparisons across institutions."
- "Although the task of assessing value-at-risk models requires supervisors to maintain staff with a high degree of technical skill and experience in reviewing banks' trading operations, it is largely an extension of the activities routinely performed by U.S. bank supervisors in overseeing the trading operations of major banks."

4. Proprietary Trading

Many banks had, previous to the financial crisis—intentionally or possibly even unconsciously—redesigned their business models within their capital markets divisions towards higher income contribution from proprietary trading. As a result, institutions traded for direct gain instead of commission income. Essentially, those firms had decided to profit from the market rather than from commissions from processing trades. Banks that engaged in proprietary trading believed that they had a competitive advantage that would enable them to earn excess returns compared to their "bread and butter"

---

[37]"Bank Capital Requirements for Market Risk: The Internal Model Approach," Federal Reserve Bank of New York Economic Policy Review, December 1997.

businesses—i.e., net interest margins (NIM) from corporate lending or consumer financing, in particular residential mortgages.

Proprietary trading has been responsible for some large losses and has come under heavy scrutiny by regulators. Further, there is a risk of moral hazard (the trader is using the firm's capital and therefore may take more risks). However, it is also often a highly profitable part of a bank, i.e., the investment bank. Proprietary traders usually have access to extremely sophisticated software and information systems to enable them to gain a competitive edge. Under the Dodd-Frank legislation and Volcker Rule in the U.S., proprietary trading is being made more and more difficult to do and is under significant scrutiny. The Volcker Rule is described in Chapter 15 in more detail.

Basel III Requirements for Market Risk

Under Basel III, the trading functions of institutions come under the highest degree of regulatory scrutiny given the nature of the business they conduct and the perceived complexity surrounding certain financial transactions. The Bank for International Settlements (BIS) recognizes that the 1996 Amendment to the Capital Accord to incorporate market risks, a major milestone in the overall process of the Basel Accord, did not capture some key risks, especially in stressed markets.

In response, the BIS supplements the former current VaR-based trading book framework with an incremental risk capital charge, which includes default risk as well as migration risk, for unsecuritized credit products. For securitized products, the capital charges of the banking book will apply with a limited exception for certain so-called correlation trading activities, where banks may be allowed by their supervisor to calculate a comprehensive risk capital charge subject to strict qualitative minimum requirements as well as stress testing requirements. These measures will reduce the incentive for regulatory arbitrage between the banking and trading books.

An additional response by Basel to the crisis is the introduction of a stressed value-at-risk requirement. According to the Bank for International Settlements (BIS), losses in most banks' trading books during the financial crisis had been significantly higher than the minimum capital requirements under the former Pillar 1 market risk rules. Basel III therefore requires banks to calculate a stressed value-at-risk taking into account a one-year observation period relating to significant losses, which must be calculated in addition to the value-at-risk based on the most recent one-year observation period. The additional stressed VaR requirement will also help reduce the procyclicality of the minimum capital requirements for market risk.

Implementation of the Basel III Requirements for Market Risk in the United States – The Market Risk Final Rule

In July 2012, agencies in the United States approved the Market Risk Final Rule (Final Rule) to implement changes to the Market Risk Capital Rule that requires large banking organizations with significant trading activities to adjust their capital requirements to better account for the market risks of those activities.

The Final Rule:

- Represents the most complete overhaul of U.S. bank capital standards since the U.S. adoption of Basel I in 1989;
- Implements many aspects of the Basel III capital framework agreed upon by the Basel Committee, but also incorporates changes required by the Dodd-Frank Act;
- Applies to all U.S. banks and savings associations (national and state chartered), federal savings associations, and U.S.-domiciled bank holding companies with consolidated assets of $500 million and greater.

In line with Basel III, the Final Rule looks to refine the scope of covered positions, increase risk sensitivity, and increase transparency throughout enhanced disclosures. Not surprisingly, the Final Rule includes specific guidance around the quantitative aspects to calculate market risk capital and also addresses many of the qualitative aspects around governance, oversight, and disclosures.

Key elements of the Market Risk Final Rule include:

- Updated definitions for covered positions that place greater emphasis on trading products.
- Standards for use of internal models for VaR calculations and stressed VaR in market risk capital calculations, including treatment of credit spread risk, correlations within and across risk categories, and risks arising from non-linear price movements.
- Standards for specific risk capital requirements including use of internal models and application of specific risk add-on factors.
- An incremental risk capital requirement that addresses default risk and migration risk.
- A comprehensive risk capital requirement to measure comprehensive price risk for correlated trading activities.
- Disclosure requirements including information on an organization's market risk modeling methodologies and quantitative disclosures relating to a firm's risk measures for each material portfolio of covered positions.
- The Market Risk Final Rule became effective in the United States on Jan. 1, 2013.

Capital Requirement for Market Risk

The Market Risk Final Rule requires that a banking organization calculate its risk-based capital ratio denominator as the sum of its adjusted risk-weighted assets (RWA) and market risk equivalent assets. However, Advanced Approaches organizations will be required to calculate both a general risk-based requirement as well as an advanced risk-based capital requirement. Each measure of market risk (general or advanced) will need to be multiplied by 12.5 to determine its market risk equivalent assets. The Final Rule dictates that general and advanced measures for market risk total the sum of its components including:

(VaR-based capital requirement) + (Stressed VaR-based capital requirement) + (Specific risk capital charge) + (Incremental risk capital requirement) + (Comprehensive risk capital requirements) + (Capital charge for de minimis exposures)

Each component has to be calculated according to the specific guidance and methodologies provided in the Final Rule.

VaR and Stressed VaR Capital Requirements

The Final Rule requires a large banking organization to use an internal model to calculate its VaR-based risk capital requirement on a daily basis for all covered positions, including a multiplication factor based on backtesting results and qualitative factors. In addition, banks will be required to calculate the VaR-based capital requirement in a stressed market environment, at minimum on a weekly basis. The VaR-based risk measure will include risk factors such as credit spread risk, correlations within and across risk categories, and risks arising from the non-linear price movements inherent in positions with optionality. Of course, banking organizations must be able to justify to the regulator the omission of any risk factors from their VaR methodology and demonstrate the appropriateness of any proxies used and assumptions used.

VaR is calculated using a:

- One-tail, 99 percent confidence level;
- Ten-business-day holding period; and
- Historical observation period of at least one year.

Calculation of the stressed VaR measure requires that banks use that same VaR model, but with model inputs calibrated based upon historical data during a one-year period of significant financial stress appropriate to the banking institution's current portfolio.

Modeling Standards for Specific Risk

A banking organization has to have well-defined processes to identify covered positions that have specific risk. Institutions are permitted to use an internal model to measure specific risk for covered positions including debt and equity positions consistent with the requirements detailed in the rule. However, use of an internal model to measure specific risk for correlation positions is required, except for securitizations.

Model Risk: JPMorgan Chase & Co.[38]

"By substituting banks' internal risk measurement models for broad, uniform regulatory measures of risk exposure, [the new rule] should lead to capital charges that more accurately reflect individual banks' true risk exposures. The firm uses models, for many purposes, but primarily for the measurement, monitoring, and management of risk positions. Valuation models are employed by the firm to value certain financial instruments which cannot otherwise be valued using quoted prices. These valuation models may also be employed as inputs to risk management models, including VaR and economic stress models. The firm also makes use of models for a number of

---

[38]JPMorgan Chase & Co. Annual Report 2013, Risk Report, Model Risk, Page 153.

other purposes, including the calculation of regulatory capital requirements and estimating the allowance for credit losses.

"Models are owned by various functions within the firm based on the specific purposes of such models. For example, VaR models and certain regulatory capital models are owned by the line-of-business aligned risk management functions. Owners of models are responsible for the development, implementation, and testing of their models, as well as referral of models to the model risk function (within the model risk and development unit) for review and approval. Once models have been approved, model owners are responsible for the maintenance of a robust operating environment and must monitor and evaluate the performance of the models on an ongoing basis. Model owners may seek to enhance models in response to changes in the portfolios and for changes in product and market developments, as well as to capture improvements in available modeling techniques and systems capabilities.

"The model risk function is part of the firm's model risk and development unit, which in turn reports to the chief risk officer. The model risk function is independent of the model owners and reviews and approves a wide range of models, including risk management, valuation, and certain regulatory capital models used by the firm.

"Models are tiered based on an internal standard according to their complexity, the exposure associated with the model, and the firm's reliance on the model. This tiering is subject to the approval of the model risk function. A model review conducted by the model risk function considers the model's suitability for the specific uses to which it will be put. The factors considered in reviewing a model include whether the model accurately reflects the characteristics of the product and its significant risks, the selection and reliability of model inputs, consistency with models for similar products, the appropriateness of any model-related adjustments, and sensitivity to input parameters and assumptions that cannot be observed from the market. When reviewing a model, the model risk function analyzes and challenges the model methodology and the reasonableness of model assumptions and may perform or require additional testing, including back-testing of model outcomes. Model reviews are approved by the appropriate level of management within the model risk function based on the relevant tier of the model.

"Under the firm's model risk policy, new models, as well as material changes to existing models, are reviewed and approved by the model risk function prior to implementation in the operating environment.

"In the event that the model risk function does not approve a model, the model owner is required to remediate the model within a time period agreed upon with the model risk function. The model owner is also required to re-submit the model for review to the model risk function and to take appropriate actions to mitigate the model risk if it is to be used in the interim. These actions will depend on the model and may include, for example, limitation of trading activity. The firm may also implement other appropriate risk measurement tools to augment the model that is subject to remediation.

"Exceptions to the firm's model risk policy may be granted by the head of the model risk function to allow a model to be used prior to review or approval."

Incremental Risk Capital Requirement

A banking organization that calculated the specific risk for debt positions using an internal model must also calculate a measure of incremental risk, a measure of default risk, and credit migration risk of a position no less frequently than weekly. The model must calculate incremental risk over a one-year time horizon using a one-tail, 99.9 percent confidence level, and using an assumption of either a constant level of risk or of constant positions. In addition, the model must incorporate a liquidity horizon consistent with the time that would be required for a bank to reduce its exposure to, or hedge all of its material risk in, a stressed market. The liquidity horizon may not be less than the shorter of three months or the contractual maturity of the position. In line with general model requirements, optionality must be covered as well.

Comprehensive Risk Capital Requirement

Banking organizations must calculate a comprehensive risk measure to assess material price risk for portfolios of correlation trading positions. In addition, banking organizations will be required to apply a specific set of supervisory stress scenarios to their portfolios of correlation trading positions no less than weekly.

Basel III in the United States – Which Organizations Are Affected?

U.S. Basel III Applies to:	U.S. Basel III Does Not Apply to:
▪ National banks ▪ State member banks ▪ State nonmember banks ▪ U.S. bank holding companies (BHCs) other than small BHCs ▪ State savings associations ▪ Federal savings associations ▪ Covered savings and loan holding companies (SLHCs) ▪ Any of the above that are subsidiaries of foreign banks	▪ Small BHCs with <U.S.-$500 million in total consolidated assets that: 　▪ are not engaged in significant nonbank activities; 　▪ do not conduct significant off-balance sheet activities; and 　▪ do not have a material amount of SEC-registered debt or equity securities ▪ Non-covered SLHCs ▪ Holding companies of industrial loan companies (unless designated as systemically important)

Operational Risk

Operational risk means the risk of loss resulting from inadequate or failed internal processes, people, and systems or from external events, and includes legal risk.

Operational risk excludes business and reputational risk. Particular prominent examples of operational risks are the following:

- **Fraud Risk** is the risk of incurring losses as a result of an intentional act or omission by an employee or by a third party involving dishonesty that is for personal and/or business gain, or to avoid personal and/or business loss. Examples include falsification and/or alteration of records and/or reports; facilitation; breach of trust; intentional omission; misrepresentation; concealment; misleading; abuse of position in order to obtain personal gain, business advantage, and/or conceal improper/unauthorized activity.
- **Business Continuity Risk** is the risk of incurring losses resulting from the interruption of normal business activities. Interruptions to the firm's infrastructure as well as to the infrastructure that supports the businesses (including third-party vendors) and the communities in which firms are located (including public infrastructure like electrical, communications, and transportation) can be caused by (i) deliberate acts such as sabotage, terrorist activities, bomb threats, strikes, riots, and assaults on the bank's staff; (ii) natural calamities such as hurricanes, snow storms, floods, disease pandemic, and earthquakes; or (iii) other unforeseen incidents such as accidents, fires, explosions, utility outages, and political unrest.
- **Regulatory Compliance Risk** is the potential that institutions may incur regulatory sanctions (such as restrictions on business activities, fines, or enhanced reporting requirements) or financial and/or reputational damage arising from failure to comply with applicable laws, rules, and regulations.
- **Information Technology Risk** is the risk that a firm's information technology will lead to quantifiable losses. This comes from inadequate information technology and processing in terms of manageability, exclusivity, integrity, controllability, and continuity.
- **Vendor Risk** arises from adverse events and risk concentrations due to failures in vendor selection, insufficient controls and oversight over a vendor, and/or services provided by a vendor.

Legal risk may materialize in any of the above risk categories. This may be due to the fact that in each category banks may be the subject of a claim or proceedings alleging non-compliance with contractual or other legal or statutory responsibilities, or banks may otherwise be subject to losses allegedly deriving from other legal circumstances applicable to any of the above categories.

Operational Risk in the Basel Accord

Basel II and various supervisory bodies of the countries have prescribed various soundness standards for operational risk management for banks and similar financial institutions. To complement these standards, Basel II has given guidance regarding three broad methods of capital calculation for operational risk:

- Basic Indicator Approach (BIA): based on annual revenue of the financial institution.

- Standardized Approach (SA): based on annual revenue of each of the broad business lines of the financial institution.
- Advanced Measurement Approach (AMA): based on the internally developed risk measurement framework of the bank adhering to the qualitative and quantitative standards, i.e., an internal proprietary model including internal and external data collection and loss-distribution analysis.

Under Basel II, the operational risk management framework includes identification, measurement, monitoring, reporting, control, and mitigation frameworks for operational risk.

Since the regulatory standards and methodologies for operational risk, in particular RWA for operational risk, were developed under Basel II, regulators did not overhaul methodologies under Basel III.

Other Risks

Banks do have other risks but they are not included in RWA calculations; examples include strategic and reputational risk.

Definition of Reputational Risk at HSBC:[39]

"The risk that illegal, unethical or inappropriate behavior by the group itself, members of staff, or clients or representatives of the group will damage HSBC's reputation, leading potentially to a loss of business, fines, or penalties."

Key Takeaways

- The trading functions of banks in general and market risk in particular come under the highest degree of regulatory scrutiny given the nature of the business they conduct and the perceived complexity surrounding certain financial transactions.
- Trading risks, in particular market risk, remain major contributors to institutions' income. Percentages of market risk in banks' overall risk positions remain high, e.g., Deutsche Bank.
- Market risk under Basel III has been significantly enhanced; it supplements the value-at-risk (VaR)-based trading book framework with an incremental risk capital charge, which includes default risk and also focuses on unsecuritized and securitized credit products. Further, Basel III introduces a stressed value-at-risk requirement.
- The Volcker Rule under Dodd-Frank in the United States greatly restricts banks from proprietary trading.
- Since the regulatory standards and methodologies for operational risk, in particular RWA for operational risk, were developed under Basel II, regulators did not overhaul methodologies under Basel III.

---

[39]HSBC Annual Report / Risk Report / Page 138.

The Volcker Rule under the Dodd-Frank Act in the United States

The Volcker Rule refers to section 619 of the Dodd-Frank Wall Street Reform and Consumer Protection Act. It was proposed by American economist and former United States Federal Reserve Chairman Paul Volcker (see Figure 15.1) to restrict United States banks from making certain kinds of speculative investments that do not benefit their customers. Volcker argued that such speculative activity played a key role in the financial crisis. The rule is often referred to as a ban on proprietary trading by commercial banks, whereby deposits are used to trade on the bank's own accounts, although a number of exceptions to this ban were included in the Dodd-Frank law. The rule's provisions were scheduled to be implemented as a part of Dodd-Frank on July 21, 2012, with preceding ramifications, but were delayed. On December 10, 2013, the necessary agencies approved regulations implementing the rule, which were scheduled to go into effect April 1, 2014. On January 14, 2014, after a lawsuit by community banks over provisions concerning specialized securities, revised final regulations were adopted.

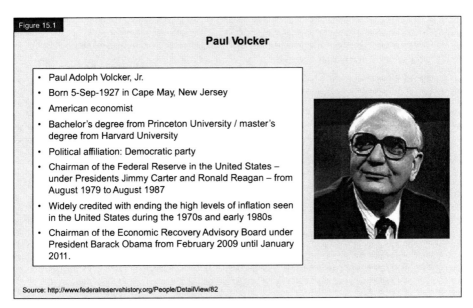

Figure 15.1

Paul Volcker

- Paul Adolph Volcker, Jr.
- Born 5-Sep-1927 in Cape May, New Jersey
- American economist
- Bachelor's degree from Princeton University / master's degree from Harvard University
- Political affiliation: Democratic party
- Chairman of the Federal Reserve in the United States – under Presidents Jimmy Carter and Ronald Reagan – from August 1979 to August 1987
- Widely credited with ending the high levels of inflation seen in the United States during the 1970s and early 1980s
- Chairman of the Economic Recovery Advisory Board under President Barack Obama from February 2009 until January 2011.

Source: http://www.federalreservehistory.org/People/DetailView/82

The Volcker Rule contains two broad prohibitions for banking entities:

- No proprietary trading.
- No ownership interest in or sponsorship of a private equity or hedge fund.

The statutory Volcker Rule contains other requirements:

- Prohibition of transactions that would result in material conflicts of interest or material exposure to high-risk assets or activities, threaten the safety or soundness of the banking entity, or pose a threat to U.S. financial stability.
- Certain financial relationships with covered funds are prohibited.
- Nonbank financial firms may be subject to capital charges / restriction of activities.
- Agencies must issue rules covering internal controls and recordkeeping to insure compliance with statute.

Testimony of Paul Volcker before the U.S. Senate Banking Committee, February 2, 2010:

"The basic point is that there has been, and remains, a strong public interest in providing a 'safety net'—in particular, deposit insurance and the provision of liquidity in emergencies—for commercial banks carrying out essential services. There is not, however, a similar rationale for public funds—taxpayer funds—protecting and supporting essentially proprietary and speculative activities. Hedge funds, private equity funds, and trading activities unrelated to customer needs and continuing banking relationships should stand on their own, without the subsidies implied by public support for depository institutions."

Permitted Activities under the Volcker Rule

- Underwriting: the process by which large financial institutions (banks, investment houses) raise investment capital from investors on behalf of corporations and governments that are issuing securities, i.e., equity and debt capital, typically in a public offering. This is a way of distributing newly issued securities, such as stocks or bonds, to investors. A syndicate of banks (the lead managers) underwrites the transaction, which means they have taken on the risk of distributing the securities. Should they not be able to find enough investors, they will have to hold some securities—and therefore, risk—themselves. Underwriters make their income from the price difference (the "underwriting spread") between the price they pay the issuer and what they collect from investors or from broker-dealers who buy portions of the offering; hence, institutions carry market risks.
- Market making: Financial institutions typically accept the risk of holding a certain number of shares of a particular security in order to facilitate trading in that security. Each market maker competes for customer order flow by displaying buy and sell quotations for a guaranteed number of shares. Once an order is received, the market maker immediately sells from its own inventory or seeks an offsetting order. This process takes place in mere seconds. Capital markets divisions of banks usually act as market makers in interest rate products, foreign exchange

transactions, equity markets, and commodities. In all of the aforementioned markets, large banks act as market makers in the derivatives markets. This particular activity is volume driven.

- Hedging: Banks, non-bank financial institutions, corporations, and other organizations are typically exposed to certain financial risks. For example, the treasurer of a non-U.S. airline such as Lufthansa faces various major financial risks: the price of fuel (crude oil), the level of the home currency against the U.S. dollar (as fuel is quoted in U.S. dollars), and interest rates (increased funding cost or lower yield on deposits or investments). Depending on its view on markets and risk appetite, Lufthansa may consider buying protection against its key risks. Therefore, the airline would make an investment to reduce the risk of adverse price movements in an asset or underlying position. Normally, a hedge consists of taking an offsetting position in a related security / position, such as a futures contract, a forward, a swap, or an option. Banks act as the "insurer" for such hedgers, taking the market risk onto their books. However, banks typically offset these market risks themselves by entering into offsetting micro- (individual position) or macro (portfolio) hedges with other large banks. This business is also volume driven, as banks earn a spread from their customers.
- Trading on behalf of customers for commission or fees.
- Trading in U.S. Treasuries, agencies, and municipals.

Statutory Definitions under the Volcker Rule

- "Proprietary trading" is defined as:
  - Engaging as principal for the trading account of the banking entity or non-bank financial company (NBFC).
  - Any transaction to purchase or sell, or otherwise acquire or dispose of, any security; any derivative; any contract of sale of a commodity for future delivery; any option on any such security, derivative, or contract; or "any other security or financial instrument" that the appropriate federal agencies may determine.
- "Trading account" is defined as:
  - Any account used for acquiring or taking positions principally for the purpose of selling in the near term (or otherwise with the intent to re-sell in order to profit from short-term price movements), or
  - Any such other accounts specified by rule.

Application of the Volcker Rule on Large Banks

The Volcker Rule applies to:

- Insured depository institutions.
- Any company that controls an insured depository institution.
- Foreign banks with a branch, agency, or subsidiary in the U.S.
- Any affiliate or subsidiary of those entities.

Impact of the Volcker Rule on Large Banks

The effect of the Volcker Rule is significant for large U.S. bank holding companies.. The loss of proprietary trading revenues puts pressure on profitability and may have negative consequences for the rating of the institutions, in particular the investment banks.

The Volcker Rule – the General Idea

Effectively, the general idea of the Volcker Rule is simply a new version of the U.S. Banking Act of 1933, commonly known as the Glass-Steagall Act, separating commercial and investment banking. Figure 15.2 illustrates the general idea, which is separating risky business such as capital markets from less-risky business such as commercial banking (i.e., lending money to corporations and retail customers at rates higher than the cost of deposits).

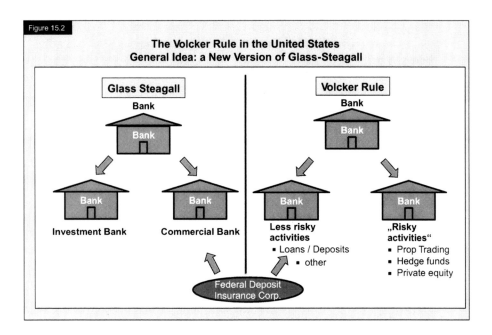

Glass-Steagall Act

The Glass–Steagall Act usually refers to four provisions of the U.S. Banking Act of 1933 that limited commercial bank securities activities and affiliations within commercial banks and securities firms. The term is also often used to refer to the entire Banking Act of 1933, which was named for its Congressional sponsors, Senator Carter Glass (Democrat) of Virginia, and Representative Henry B. Steagall (Democrat) of Alabama.

Impact on Banks

Large Banks

Besides implementing the technical requirements under Basel III, large banks will revisit their capital strategies. Banks have to clearly define/document what is banking book versus trading book and which businesses and activities are restricted under the Volcker Rule (proprietary trading).

Most likely, large banks will significantly reduce their market risks and shift focus, i.e., risk capital, towards their lending activities, both in corporate banking and consumer finance / retail banking. This, in effect, will lead to an increase in the quality of earnings—i.e., less volatility in banks' income statements—and therefore better bank ratings and, consequently, a safer banking system in general.

Small Banks

The Basel III requirements and the Volcker Rule have only minor impacts on small banks, if any. In case smaller banks carry positions that expose them to changes in market levels and/or volatility, institutions should have an appropriate market risk infrastructure in place, including a scenario-based methodology tool that calculates value-at-risk (VaR), stressed VaR, or equivalents. Parameters used such as confidence levels and holding period should be in line with the requirements for larger banking institutions as described above.

Key Takeaways

- The Volcker Rule under Dodd-Frank in the United States restricts banks from proprietary trading. The restriction has a significant impact on net income for all institutions with major capital markets divisions, not only those based in the United States.
- Most likely, banks will reduce their market risks and shift risk capital towards their lending activities, both in corporate banking and consumer finance / retail banking. This, in effect, will increase the quality of earnings—i.e., less volatility in banks' income statements and, therefore, better bank ratings and a safer banking system in general.

Leverage Ratio

Leverage Ratio

Leverage is an inherent part of banking activity; as soon as an entity's assets exceed its capital base it is levered.

An underlying feature of the financial crisis was the build-up of excessive on- and off-balance-sheet leverage in the banking system. In many cases, banks built up excessive leverage while maintaining strong risk-based capital ratios. At the height of the crisis, the market forced the banking sector to reduce its leverage in a manner that amplified downward pressure on asset prices. This deleveraging process exacerbated the feedback loop between losses, falling bank capital, and shrinking credit availability.

The Basel Commission has not proposed to eliminate leverage, but to rather reduce excessive leverage. As a consequence, Basel III introduced a transparent, non-risk-based leverage ratio to act as a credible supplementary measure to the risk-based capital requirements. This particular ratio is intended to:

- Restrict the build-up of leverage in the banking sector to avoid destabilizing deleveraging processes that can damage the broader financial system and the economy; and
- Reinforce the risk-based requirements with a simple, non-risk-based "backstop" measure.

Under Basel III, the leverage ratio is defined as the capital measure (the numerator) divided by the exposure measure (the denominator), with this ratio expressed as a percentage. The basis of calculation is the average of the three month-end leverage ratios over a quarter.

The new volume-based ratio:

- Puts a cap on a build-up of leverage.
- Provides an additional backstop against model risk and measurement errors.
- Is volume based, not risk based.
- Helps contain system-wide build up of leverage.

The Basel III leverage limit is set at 3 percent. In other words, the bank's total assets (volume-based, not risk-adjusted, including both on- and off-balance-sheet assets) should not be more than 33 times tier 1 capital.

Capital Measure

To reduce excessive leverage, Basel III introduced a transparent, non-risk-based leverage ratio to act as a credible supplementary measure to the risk-based capital requirements. This particular ratio is intended to:

- Restrict the build-up of leverage in the banking sector to avoid destabilizing deleveraging processes that can damage the broader financial system and the economy; and
- Reinforce the risk-based requirements with a simple, non-risk-based "back-stop" measure.

Exposure Measure

General Measurement Principles

The exposure measure for the leverage ratio should generally follow the accounting measure of exposure subject to the following principles:

- On-balance-sheet, non-derivative exposures are included in the exposure measure net of specific provisions and valuation adjustments, e.g., credit valuation adjustments;
- Netting of loans and deposits is not allowed.

Physical or financial collateral, guarantees, or credit risk mitigation purchased are not allowed to reduce on-balance-sheet exposures. A bank's total exposure measure is the sum of the following exposures:

- On-balance-sheet exposures;
- Derivative exposures;
- Securities-financing transaction exposures; and
- Other off-balance-sheet exposures.

On-Balance-Sheet Exposures

Banks must include all on-balance-sheet assets in their exposure measure including on-balance-sheet derivative collateral and collateral for securities-financing transactions (SFTs).

However, to ensure consistency, on-balance-sheet assets deducted from tier 1 capital must be deducted from the exposure measure.

Liability items must not be deducted from the measure of exposure. For example, gains/losses due to changes in own credit risk on fair valued liabilities should not be deducted from the measure of exposure.

Derivative Exposures

Derivatives create two types of exposure:

- An exposure arising from the underlying value of the contract; and
- A counterparty credit risk exposure.

Banks must calculate their derivatives exposures, including where a bank sells protection using a credit derivative, as the sum of the replacement cost for the current exposure plus an add-on for potential future exposure applying the regulatory bilateral netting rules and adjusting the exposure amount for the related collateral. Written credit derivatives are subject to additional treatment as described below.

For a single derivative exposure not covered by an eligible bilateral netting contract, the amount to be included in total exposures is determined as follows:

Total Exposure = Replacement Cost (RC) + Add-on

RC is the replacement cost of the contract (obtained by marking-to-market), where the contract has a positive value. Add-on is the amount of potential future credit exposure over the remaining life of the contract calculated by applying an add-on factor to the notional principal amount of the derivative.

When an eligible bilateral netting contract is in place, replacement cost (RC) for the set of derivative exposures covered by the contract will be the net replacement cost and the add-on.

Collateral received in connection with derivative contracts has two countervailing effects on leverage:

- It reduces counterparty exposure; but
- It can also increase the economic resources at the disposal of the bank, as the bank can use the collateral to leverage itself.

Collateral received in connection with derivative contracts does not reduce the economic leverage inherent in a bank's derivatives position. In particular, the exposure arising from the contract underlying is not reduced. As such, collateral received (cash or non-cash) may not be netted against derivatives exposures whether or not netting is permitted under the bank's operative accounting or risk-based framework. When calculating the exposure amount, a bank must not reduce the exposure amount by any collateral received from the counterparty. Furthermore, the replacement cost (RC) must be grossed up by any collateral amount used to reduce its value, including when collateral received by a bank has reduced the derivatives assets reported on-balance-sheet under its operative accounting framework.

Similarly, with regards to collateral provided, all banks must gross up their exposure measure by the amount of any derivatives collateral provided where the provision of that collateral reduced their on-balance-sheet assets under their operative accounting framework.

The above treatments apply whether the collateral is cash or non-cash; whether or not the collateral was received or provided as part of an eligible master netting agreement; or whether it was received or provided in relation to derivatives traded on an exchange, through a central counterparty, or otherwise.

Written credit derivatives create a notional credit exposure arising from the creditworthiness of the reference entity, in addition to the counterparty credit exposure arising from the fair value of contracts.

In order to capture the credit exposure to the reference entity, in addition to the above treatment for derivatives and related collateral, the full effective notional value referenced by a written credit derivative is to be incorporated into the exposure measure. The effective notional amount of a written credit derivative may be reduced by the effective notional amount of a purchased credit derivative on the same reference name and level of seniority if the remaining maturity of the purchased credit derivative is equal to or greater than the remaining maturity of the written credit derivative. The treatment recognizes a difference between cash instruments and credit derivatives; namely, that a bank closes a long cash position by selling the position, whereas with a credit derivative, a bank generally closes a long position by entering into an offsetting derivative transaction. Therefore, this treatment allows a bank that purchases credit protection using the same reference name under which it sold credit protection to net the bought and sold protection to reduce its exposure measure.

Since written credit derivatives are included in the exposure measure at their effective notional amounts and add-on amounts for written credit derivatives are also included in the exposure measure, exposure to written credit derivatives could be double counted. Banks may therefore choose to deduct the individual add-on amount relating to a written credit derivative from their gross add-on.

Securities-Financing Transaction (SFT) Exposures

Securities-financing transactions (SFTs) are included in the exposure measure according to a treatment that recognizes that secured lending and borrowing in the form of SFTs is an important source of leverage and ensures consistent international implementation by recognizing the main differences across accounting frameworks.

Other Off-Balance Sheet Exposures

Commercial banking off-balance sheet (OBS) items must also be included in the exposure measure. OBS items include commitments (including liquidity facilities), unconditionally cancellable commitments, direct credit substitutes, acceptances, standby letters of credit, trade letters of credit, failed transactions, and unsettled securities.

Naturally, these OBS items are a source of potentially significant leverage. Therefore, banks must include the above OBS items in the exposure measure by applying a uniform 100 percent credit conversion factor (CCF). For any commitments that are unconditionally cancellable at any time by the bank without prior notice, banks can apply a CCF of 10 percent to include such commitments in the exposure measure.

The committee will conduct further review to ensure that the 10 percent CCF is appropriately conservative based on historical experience.

The banking lobby has heavily criticized the 100 percent conversion factor and the potential impact on the trade finance business. Many large international banks such as

Deutsche Bank or JPMorgan have significant loan portfolios in this particular segment. Although the Basel Committee on Banking Supervision has responded favorably to industry concerns by waiving the one-year maturity floor and sovereign floor for certain trade finance transactions, the new Basel III rules are more than likely to increase the level of capital requirements required to undertake trade finance transactions. While Basel III's stringent requirements are necessary for strengthening the financial system in the aftermath of the global financial crisis, there is no doubt that market participants will continue to lobby in favor of less-demanding rules that are driving the cost of doing trade finance business higher.

This particular issue could also create problems for banks in emerging market countries, e.g., Indonesia. As the trade balance, i.e., import/export business, plays a key role in the growth of domestic GDP, high CCF for trade finance could jeopardize banks' ability to place liquidity, i.e. credit, into the economy.

Basel III Implementation Dates

The Basel Committee is testing a minimum requirement of 3 percent for the leverage ratio during a parallel run period from January 1, 2013, to January 1, 2017.

Based on the results of this parallel run period, any final adjustments to the definition and calibration of the Basel III leverage ratio will be carried out (expected in the first half of 2017) with the high likelihood of migrating the ratio into Pillar 1 on January 1, 2018, based on appropriate review and calibration.

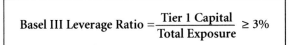

$$\text{Basel III Leverage Ratio} = \frac{\text{Tier 1 Capital}}{\text{Total Exposure}} \geq 3\%$$

Basel III Disclosure Requirements

Under Basel III, public disclosure by banks of their leverage ratio started on January 1, 2015.

To enable market participants to reconcile leverage ratio disclosures with banks' published financial statements from period to period, and to compare the capital adequacy of banks across jurisdictions with varying accounting frameworks, it is important that banks adopt a consistent and common disclosure of the main components of the leverage ratio while reconciling to their published financial statements.

To facilitate consistency and ease of use of disclosures relating to the composition of the leverage ratio, and to mitigate the risk of inconsistent formats undermining the objective of enhanced disclosure, the Basel Committee has agreed that internationally active banks across Basel-member jurisdictions will be required to publish their leverage ratio according to a common template.

Banks must disclose the leverage ratio on a quarterly basis in their published financial statements or, at a minimum, these statements must provide a direct link to the completed disclosures on their websites or on publicly available regulatory reports.

Leverage Ratio under CRD IV in the European Union

Under the Capital Requirements Directive IV (CRD IV), the European Union follows the new Basel III reforms. The ratio will be implemented as described above and is binding for banks of any size in the EU.

Leverage Ratio under the Dodd-Frank Act in the United States

The leverage ratio under Dodd-Frank has been defined in a more restrictive way than Basel III. For adequately capitalized banks, the ratio between assets and tier 1 capital has been set at 4 percent; well capitalized banks will have to hold 5 percent.

$$\text{Leverage Ratio DFA} = \frac{\text{Tier 1 Capital}}{\text{Total Exposure}} \geq 4\%$$

Responses by Banks and its Impact

Banks world-wide, in particular large, internationally active financial institutions, are managing their balance sheets in order to comply with the regulatory requirements, of course. Over recent quarters, banks have worked hard to improve their respective leverage ratios. Figure 16.1 describes—in a rather representative way for systemically important banks in general—how Royal Bank of Scotland, the second-largest British bank, and UBS, the largest Swiss bank, increased their respective leverage ratios in the time period FY2012 to 1Q2014.

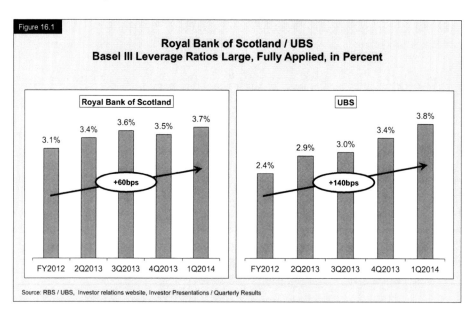

Figure 16.1

Royal Bank of Scotland / UBS
Basel III Leverage Ratios Large, Fully Applied, in Percent

Source: RBS / UBS, Investor relations website, Investor Presentations / Quarterly Results

The leverage ratio will make banks do one of two things: either raise more capital or reduce risk-weighted assets, either on- or off-balance sheet. However, both alternatives have their price.

First, raising capital leads to a reduction in the ownership percentage of a share of stock. As the number of shares outstanding increases, existing stockholders will own a smaller, or diluted, percentage of the company, making each share less valuable. Dilution also reduces the value of existing shares by reducing the stock's earnings per share.

Secondly, the reduction of risk-weighted assets reduces banks' risk levels on one side, but has a significant negative effect on net income. As the loan book decreases, net interest income decreases as well—or, a reduction in derivatives business leads to a reduction in market-sensitive income / operating revenues.

Key Takeaways

- Under Basel III, the leverage ratio is defined as the capital measure (the numerator) divided by the exposure measure (the denominator), with this ratio expressed as a percentage.
- The Basel III leverage limit is set at 3 percent. In other words, the bank's total assets—volume-based, not risk-adjusted, including both on- and off-balance- sheet assets—should not be more than 33 times tier 1 capital.
- The Basel Committee is testing a minimum requirement of 3 percent for the leverage ratio during a parallel run period from January 1, 2013, to January 1, 2017. It should be expected that the ratio will migrate to Pillar 1 in 2018.
- In the European Union, the leverage ratio will be implemented under CRD IV according to the Basel III definition, requirements, and timetable.
- The leverage ratio under the Dodd-Frank Act in the United States has been defined in a more-restrictive way than under Basel III. For adequately capitalized banks, the ratio between assets and tier 1 capital has been set at 4 percent; well capitalized banks will have to hold 5 percent.
- Banks, in particular internationally active institutions in the European Union and the United States, have worked hard in recent years to improve their respective leverage ratios. For example, UBS, the largest Swiss bank, has increased its leverage ratio by an impressive 140 basis points from 2.4 percent at FY2012 to 3.8 percent as of 1Q2014.

Liquidity Standards under Basel III

Principles for the Management and Supervision of Liquidity Risk[40]

Liquidity is the ability of a bank to fund increases in assets and meet obligations as they come due, without incurring unacceptable losses. The fundamental role of banks in the maturity transformation of short-term deposits into long-term loans makes banks inherently vulnerable to liquidity risk, both of an institution-specific nature and that which affects markets as a whole. Virtually every financial transaction or commitment has implications for a bank's liquidity. Effective liquidity risk management helps ensure a bank's ability to meet cash flow obligations, which are uncertain as they are affected by external events and other agents' behavior. Liquidity risk management is of paramount importance because a liquidity shortfall at a single institution can have system-wide repercussions. Financial market developments in the past decade have increased the complexity of liquidity risk and its management.

The market turmoil that began in mid-2007 re-emphasized the importance of liquidity to the functioning of financial markets and the banking sector. In advance of the turmoil, asset markets were buoyant and funding was readily available at low cost. The reversal in market conditions illustrated how quickly liquidity can evaporate and that illiquidity can last for an extended period of time. The banking system came under severe stress, which necessitated central bank action to support both the functioning of money markets and, in a few cases, individual institutions.

In February 2008 the Basel Committee on Banking Supervision published "Liquidity Risk Management and Supervisory Challenges." The difficulties outlined in that paper highlighted that many banks had failed to take account of a number of basic principles of liquidity risk management when liquidity was plentiful. Many of the most exposed banks did not have an adequate framework that satisfactorily accounted for the liquidity risks posed by individual products and business lines, and therefore incentives at the business level were misaligned with the overall risk tolerance of the bank. Many banks had not considered the amount of liquidity they might need to satisfy contingent obligations, either contractual or non-contractual, as they viewed funding of these obligations to be highly unlikely. Many firms viewed severe and prolonged liquidity disruptions as implausible and did not conduct stress tests that factored in the possibility of

---

[40]"Principles for Sound Liquidity Risk Management and Supervision," Basel Committee on Banking Supervision, Bank for International Settlements, September 2008.

139

market-wide strain or the severity or duration of the disruptions. Contingency funding plans (CFPs) were not always appropriately linked to stress test results and sometimes failed to take account of the potential closure of some funding sources.

In order to account for financial market developments as well as lessons learned from the turmoil, the Basel Committee has conducted a fundamental review of its 2000 "Sound Practices for Managing Liquidity in Banking Organizations." Guidance has been significantly expanded in a number of key areas. In particular, more detailed guidance is provided on:

- The importance of establishing a liquidity risk tolerance;
- The maintenance of an adequate level of liquidity, including through a cushion of liquid assets;
- The necessity of allocating liquidity costs, benefits, and risks to all significant business activities;
- The identification and measurement of the full range of liquidity risks, including contingent liquidity risks;
- The design and use of severe stress test scenarios;
- The need for a robust and operational contingency funding plan;
- The management of intraday liquidity risk and collateral; and
- Public disclosure in promoting market discipline.

Guidance for supervisors also has been augmented substantially. The guidance emphasizes the importance of supervisors assessing the adequacy of a bank's liquidity risk management framework and its level of liquidity, and suggests steps that supervisors should take if these are deemed inadequate. The principles also stress the importance of effective cooperation between supervisors and other key stakeholders, such as central banks, especially in times of stress.

This guidance focuses on liquidity risk management at medium and large complex banks, but the sound principles have broad applicability to all types of banks. The implementation of the sound principles by both banks and supervisors should be tailored to the size, nature of business, and complexity of a bank's activities. A bank and its supervisors also should consider the bank's role in the financial sectors of the jurisdictions in which it operates and the bank's systemic importance in those financial sectors. The Basel Committee fully expects banks and national supervisors to implement the revised principles promptly and thoroughly and will actively review progress in implementation.

This guidance is arranged around 17 principles for managing and supervising liquidity risk.

Fundamental Principles for the Management and Supervision of Liquidity Risk

Principle 1

A bank is responsible for the sound management of liquidity risk. A bank should establish a robust liquidity risk management framework that ensures it maintains sufficient liquidity, including a cushion of unencumbered, high quality liquid assets, to withstand a range of stress events, including those involving the loss or impairment of both unsecured and secured funding sources. Supervisors should assess the adequacy of both a bank's liquidity risk management framework and its liquidity position and should take prompt action if a bank is deficient in either area in order to protect depositors and to limit potential damage to the financial system.

Governance of Liquidity Risk Management

Principle 2

A bank should clearly articulate a liquidity risk tolerance that is appropriate for its business strategy and its role in the financial system.

Principle 3

Senior management should develop a strategy, policies, and practices to manage liquidity risk in accordance with the risk tolerance and to ensure that the bank maintains sufficient liquidity. Senior management should continuously review information on the bank's liquidity developments and report to the board of directors on a regular basis. A bank's board of directors should review and approve the strategy, policies, and practices related to the management of liquidity at least annually and ensure that senior management manages liquidity risk effectively.

Principle 4

A bank should incorporate liquidity costs, benefits, and risks in the internal pricing, performance measurement, and new-product approval process for all significant business activities (both on- and off-balance-sheet), thereby aligning the risk-taking incentives of individual business lines with the liquidity risk exposures their activities create for the bank as a whole.

Measurement and Management of Liquidity Risk

Principle 5

A bank should have a sound process for identifying, measuring, monitoring, and controlling liquidity risk. This process should include a robust framework for comprehensively projecting cash flows arising from assets, liabilities, and off-balance-sheet items over an appropriate set of time horizons.

Principle 6

A bank should actively monitor and control liquidity risk exposures and funding needs within and across legal entities, business lines, and currencies, taking into account legal, regulatory, and operational limitations to the transferability of liquidity.

Principle 7

A bank should establish a funding strategy that provides effective diversification in the sources and tenor of funding. It should maintain an ongoing presence in its chosen funding markets and strong relationships with funds providers to promote effective diversification of funding sources. A bank should regularly gauge its capacity to raise funds quickly from each source. It should identify the main factors that affect its ability to raise funds and monitor those factors closely to ensure that estimates of fund raising capacity remain valid.

Principle 8

A bank should actively manage its intraday liquidity positions and risks to meet payment and settlement obligations on a timely basis under both normal and stressed conditions and thus contribute to the smooth functioning of payment and settlement systems.

Principle 9

A bank should actively manage its collateral positions, differentiating between encumbered and unencumbered assets. A bank should monitor the legal entity and physical location where collateral is held and how it may be mobilized in a timely manner.

Principle 10

A bank should conduct stress tests on a regular basis for a variety of short-term and protracted institution-specific and market-wide stress scenarios (individually and in combination) to identify sources of potential liquidity strain and to ensure that current exposures remain in accordance with a bank's established liquidity risk tolerance. A bank should use stress test outcomes to adjust its liquidity risk management strategies, policies, and positions and to develop effective contingency plans.

Principle 11

A bank should have a formal contingency funding plan (CFP) that clearly sets out the strategies for addressing liquidity shortfalls in emergency situations. A CFP should outline policies to manage a range of stress environments, establish clear lines of responsibility, include clear invocation and escalation procedures, and be regularly tested and updated to ensure that it is operationally robust.

Principle 12

A bank should maintain a cushion of unencumbered, high-quality liquid assets to be held as insurance against a range of liquidity stress scenarios, including those that involve the loss or impairment of unsecured and typically available secured funding sources. There should be no legal, regulatory, or operational impediment to using these assets to obtain funding.

Public Disclosure

Principle 13

A bank should publicly disclose information on a regular basis that enables market participants to make an informed judgment about the soundness of its liquidity risk management framework and liquidity position.

The Role of Supervisors

Principle 14

Supervisors should regularly perform a comprehensive assessment of a bank's overall liquidity risk management framework and liquidity position to determine whether they deliver an adequate level of resilience to liquidity stress given the bank's role in the financial system.

Principle 15

Supervisors should supplement their regular assessments of a bank's liquidity risk management framework and liquidity position by monitoring a combination of internal reports, prudential reports, and market information.

Principle 16

Supervisors should intervene to require effective and timely remedial action by a bank to address deficiencies in its liquidity risk management processes or liquidity position.

Principle 17

Supervisors should communicate with other supervisors and public authorities, such as central banks, both within and across national borders, to facilitate effective cooperation regarding the supervision and oversight of liquidity risk management. Communication should occur regularly during normal times, with the nature and frequency of the information sharing increasing as appropriate during times of stress.

Liquidity (Risk) Management: A Concept for All Banks?

Liquidity (risk) management should be conducted by financial institutions; the subject is a key element of prudent banking / risk management. Institutions of all sizes should adhere to Bank for International Settlements (BIS) principles.

Key Takeaways

- The Basel Committee introduced its Principles for Sound Liquidity Risk Management and Supervision in September 2008.
- The principles focus on key risk issues, such as governance, measurement, management, and disclosure.
- Banks of any size should adhere to the principles.

Liquidity Coverage Ratio

The liquidity coverage ratio (LCR) is an important part of the Basel III liquidity standards, as the reform defines how much liquid assets have to be held by financial institutions. Independent of regulatory requirements, the LCR is a necessary indicator for most banks in the world, independent of size.

Objective of the LCR

This standard aims to ensure that a bank maintains an adequate level of unencumbered, high-quality liquid assets (HQLA) that can be converted into cash at little or no loss of value in private markets to meet its liquidity needs for a 30-calendar-day time horizon under a significantly severe liquidity stress scenario specified by supervisors. At a minimum, the stock of unencumbered HQLA should enable the bank to survive until day 30 of the stress scenario, by which time it is assumed that appropriate corrective actions can be taken by management and supervisors, or that the bank can be resolved in an orderly way. Furthermore, it gives the central bank time to take appropriate measures. The LCR builds on traditional liquidity "coverage ratio" methodologies used internally by banks to assess exposure to contingent liquidity events.

Definition of the LCR

The stress scenario for this standard entails a combined idiosyncratic and market-wide shock that would result in:

- The run-off of a proportion of retail deposits;
- A partial loss of unsecured wholesale funding capacity;
- A partial loss of secured, short-term financing with certain collateral and counterparties;
- Additional contractual outflows that would arise from a downgrade in the bank's public credit rating by up to and including three notches, including collateral posting requirements;
- Increases in market volatilities that impact the quality of collateral or potential future exposure of derivative positions and thus require larger collateral haircuts or additional collateral, or lead to other liquidity needs;

▨ Unscheduled draws on committed but unused credit and liquidity facilities that the bank has provided to its clients; and

▨ The potential need for the bank to buy back debt or honor non-contractual obligations in the interest of mitigating reputational risk.

The Basel Committee has announced that the stress scenario, as defined under Basel III, incorporates many of the shocks experienced during the crisis that started in 2007 into one significant stress scenario for which a bank would need sufficient liquidity on hand to survive for up to 30 calendar days.

The LCR has two components:

▨ Value of the stock of HQLA in stressed conditions; and

▨ Total net cash outflows, calculated according to the scenario parameters outlined below.

$$LCR = \frac{\text{Stock of high-quality liquid assets}}{\text{Total net cash outflows over the next 30 calendar days}} \geq 100\%$$

Definition of Liquidity and Funding Risk at HSBC:[41]

"The risk that we do not have sufficient financial resources to meet our obligations as they fall due or that we can only do so at excessive cost."

Stock of HQLA

The numerator of the LCR, the stock of unencumbered HQLA, is intended to serve as a defense against the potential onset of liquidity stress. During a period of financial stress, however, banks may use their stock of HQLA, thereby falling below 100 percent, as maintaining the LCR at 100 percent under such circumstances could produce undue negative effects on the bank and other market participants. In order to qualify as HQLA, assets must be liquid in markets during a time of stress and, ideally, be central bank eligible.

Assets are considered to be HQLA if they can be easily and immediately converted into cash at little or no loss of value. The liquidity of an asset depends on the underlying stress scenario, the volume to be monetized, and the timeframe considered.

HQLA must meet:

▨ Fundamental characteristics;

▨ Market-related characteristics; and

▨ Operational requirements.

Fundamental Characteristics of the HQLA

Low risk: Assets that are less risky tend to have higher liquidity. High credit standing of the issuer and a low degree of subordination increase an asset's liquidity. Low duration,

---

[41]HSBC Annual Report / Risk Report / Page 136.

low legal risk, low inflation risk, and denomination in a convertible currency with low foreign exchange risk all enhance an asset's liquidity.

Ease and certainty of valuation: An asset's liquidity increases if market participants are more likely to agree on its valuation. Assets with more-standardized, homogenous, and simple structures tend to be more fungible, promoting liquidity. The pricing formula of a high-quality liquid asset must be easy to calculate and not depend on strong assumptions. The inputs into the pricing formula must also be publicly available. In practice, this should rule out the inclusion of most structured or exotic products.

HQLA must have low correlation with risky assets: The stock of HQLA must not be subject to wrong-way (highly correlated) risk. For example, assets issued by financial institutions are more likely to be illiquid in times of liquidity stress in the banking sector.

HQLA must be listed on a developed and recognized exchange: Being listed increases an asset's transparency.

Market-Related Characteristics of the HQLA

Active and sizable market: The asset should have active outright sale or repo markets at all times. This means that:

- There should be historical evidence of market breadth and market depth. This could be demonstrated by low bid-ask spreads, high trading volumes, and a large and diverse number of market participants. Diversity of market participants reduces market concentration and increases the reliability of the liquidity in the market.
- There should be robust market infrastructure in place. The presence of multiple committed market makers increases liquidity as quotes will most likely be available for buying or selling HQLA.

Low volatility: Assets whose prices remain relatively stable and are less prone to sharp price declines over time will have a lower probability of triggering forced sales to meet liquidity requirements. Volatility of traded prices and spreads are simple proxy measures of market volatility. There should be historical evidence of relative stability of market terms (e.g., prices and haircuts) and volumes during stressed periods.

Flight to quality: Historically, the market has shown tendencies to move into these types of assets in a systemic crisis. The correlation between proxies of market liquidity and banking system stress is one simple measure that could be used.

Operational Requirements

All assets in the stock should be unencumbered. "Unencumbered" means free of legal, regulatory, contractual, or other restrictions on the ability of the bank to liquidate, sell, transfer, or assign the asset. An asset in the stock should not be pledged.

The bank must have the operational capability to monetize the assets to meet outflows during the stress period. Monetization of the asset must be executable, from an operational perspective, in the standard settlement period for the asset class in the relevant jurisdiction.

The stock should be under the control of the function charged with managing the liquidity of the bank, most likely the treasurer, meaning the function has the continuous authority, and legal and operational capability.

Potential Portfolio Composition of the HQLA

Figure 18.1 describes the two main categories of assets that can be included in the stock of HQLA. "Level 1" assets can be included without limit, while "Level 2" assets can only comprise up to 40 percent of the stock. Supervisors may also choose to include within Level 2 an additional class of assets, i.e., "Level 2B assets." If included, these assets should comprise no more than 15 percent of the total stock of HQLA. They must also be included within the overall 40 percent cap on Level 2 assets. As a consequence, the stock of HQLA breaks up into three categories:

- Level 1 assets;
- Level 2A assets;
- Level 2B assets.

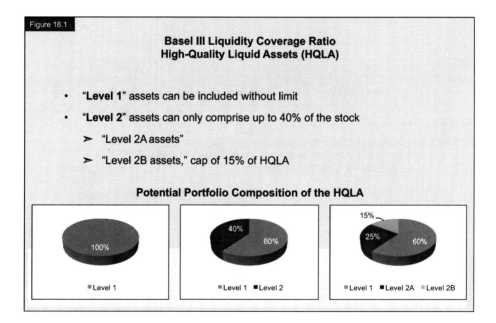

Figure 18.1

**Basel III Liquidity Coverage Ratio
High-Quality Liquid Assets (HQLA)**

- "**Level 1**" assets can be included without limit

- "**Level 2**" assets can only comprise up to 40% of the stock

  ➤ "Level 2A assets"

  ➤ "Level 2B assets," cap of 15% of HQLA

Potential Portfolio Composition of the HQLA

Definition of HQLA and Haircuts Applied

Basel III has clearly defined what assets comprise levels 1, 2A, and 2B. The reform requires the application of haircuts, which can be further tightened, if necessary, by supervisors within national discretion.

Definition of Haircut:

The percentage by which an asset's market value is reduced for the purpose of calculating risk, liquidity, capital adequacy, margin, and collateral levels. Haircuts endeavor to cover market volatility, i.e., the reduction of price, especially in a stressed market. For example, a blue chip stock on the Dow Jones Industrial Index worth $100 will be reduced by $30 to cover the market volatility of this particular stock; hence, the haircut applied for this particular stock would be 30 percent.

Level 1 Assets and Haircuts Applied

Level 1 assets can comprise an unlimited share of the pool and are not subject to a haircut under the LCR. However, national supervisors may wish to require haircuts for Level 1 securities based on, among other things, their duration, credit and liquidity risk, and typical repo haircuts.

Level 1 assets are limited to the assets as described in Figure 18.2.

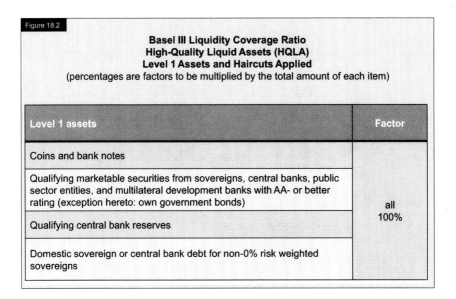

Figure 18.2

Basel III Liquidity Coverage Ratio
High-Quality Liquid Assets (HQLA)
Level 1 Assets and Haircuts Applied
(percentages are factors to be multiplied by the total amount of each item)

Level 1 assets	Factor
Coins and bank notes	
Qualifying marketable securities from sovereigns, central banks, public sector entities, and multilateral development banks with AA- or better rating (exception hereto: own government bonds)	all 100%
Qualifying central bank reserves	
Domestic sovereign or central bank debt for non-0% risk weighted sovereigns	

Level 2A Assets and Haircuts Applied

Level 2 assets comprising Level 2A assets and any Level 2B assets permitted by supervisors can be included in the stock of HQLA, subject to the requirement that they comprise no more than 40 percent of the overall stock after haircuts have been applied.

A 15 percent haircut is applied to the current market value of each Level 2A asset held in the stock of HQLA. Level 2A assets are limited to the assets as described in Figure 18.3:

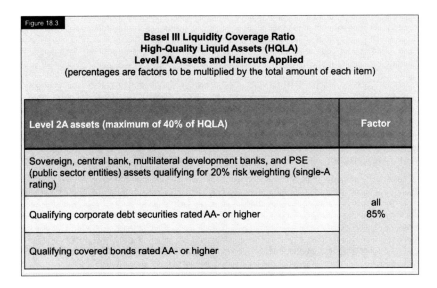

Figure 18.3

Basel III Liquidity Coverage Ratio
High-Quality Liquid Assets (HQLA)
Level 2A Assets and Haircuts Applied
(percentages are factors to be multiplied by the total amount of each item)

Level 2A assets (maximum of 40% of HQLA)	Factor
Sovereign, central bank, multilateral development banks, and PSE (public sector entities) assets qualifying for 20% risk weighting (single-A rating)	all 85%
Qualifying corporate debt securities rated AA- or higher	
Qualifying covered bonds rated AA- or higher	

Level 2B Assets and Haircuts Applied

Certain additional assets—Level 2B assets—can be included in Level 2 at the discretion of national authorities. In choosing to include these assets in Level 2 for the purpose of the LCR, supervisors are expected to ensure that such assets fully comply with the qualifying criteria. Supervisors are also expected to ensure that banks have appropriate systems and measures to monitor and control the potential risks (e.g., credit and market risks) that banks could be exposed to in holding these assets.

A larger haircut is applied to the current market value of each Level 2B asset held in the stock of HQLA. Level 2B assets are limited to the assets as described in Figure 18.4:

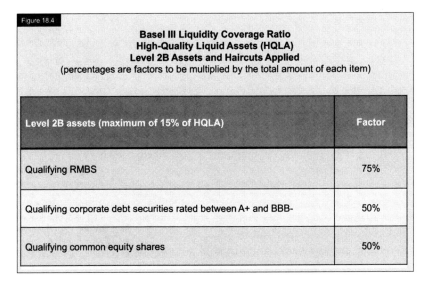

Figure 18.4

Basel III Liquidity Coverage Ratio
High-Quality Liquid Assets (HQLA)
Level 2B Assets and Haircuts Applied
(percentages are factors to be multiplied by the total amount of each item)

Level 2B assets (maximum of 15% of HQLA)	Factor
Qualifying RMBS	75%
Qualifying corporate debt securities rated between A+ and BBB-	50%
Qualifying common equity shares	50%

Total Net Cash Outflows

The term total net cash outflows is defined as the total expected cash outflows minus total expected cash inflows in the specified stress scenario for the subsequent 30 calendar days. Total expected cash outflows are calculated by multiplying the outstanding balances of various categories or types of liabilities and off-balance-sheet commitments by the rates at which they are expected to run off or be drawn down. Where applicable, cash inflows and outflows should include interest that is expected to be received and paid during the 30-day time horizon.

Total expected cash inflows are calculated by multiplying the outstanding balances of various categories of contractual receivables by the rates at which they are expected to flow in under the scenario up to an aggregate cap of 75 percent of total expected cash outflows.

> **Total net cash outflows over the next 30 calendar days =**
> **Total expected cash outflows – Min**
> **{total expected cash inflows; 75% of total expected cash outflows}**

Cash Outflows

The definition of the stress scenario in the denominator of the liquidity coverage ratio (LCR)—and therefore the levels of cash outflows and the effect on a bank's liability—is a major challenge for both bank managers and regulatory authorities. At the end, the scenario will be a reflection of customers' behavior in a bank run. Of course, the liability side of a bank is very diverse in terms of customer groups, structures, and maturities. Customers include:

- **Retail customers,** usually small and medium-sized savers and depositors, of which some can be effectively net borrowers; this customer group also includes small business owners, i.e., convenience store /small shops owners (such as a bakery or delicatessen), hairdressers, lawyers, accountants, restaurant owners, photographers, small-scale manufacturers, online business owners, web designers, programmers, etc.
- **Asset/wealth management customers,** i.e., private individuals, high net worth individuals (HNWI) and ultra-high net worth individuals (UHNWI).
- **Banks of all sizes,** both foreign and domestic, including regional and community banks (i.e., below $10 billion in consolidated assets), medium-sized banks (i.e., between $10 billion and $50 billion in consolidated assets), and large banks (i.e., $50 billion and above).
- **Other financial institutions,** including rating-sensitive market players, broker / dealers, hedge funds, pension funds, mutual funds, and insurance companies.
- **Non-financial** corporations, including small and midsize enterprises, large caps, and multinational corporations.
- **Sovereigns, central banks, municipalities, multilateral development banks, and other public sector entities.**

A bank run can be described as a situation when a large number of customers withdraw their deposits from a financial institution at the same time and either demand cash or transfer those funds into government bonds, gold, or a safer institution because they believe that the financial institution is, or might become, insolvent.

There are many causes and triggers to such customer behavior, which can be classified into both institute-specific and market-specific categories, including the danger of losses due to nonexisting market liquidity / market disruptions. Institution-specific problems may have different causes; examples include:

- **Credit risk/delay of receivables:** Non-performing loans are increasing due to deterioration in the general economy, i.e., an increase in the level of unemployment.
- **Concentration risk:** unexpected credit, e.g., the largest customer defaults.
- **Market risk:** an unexpected significant loss from (proprietary) trading activities.
- **Operational risk:** an unexpected significant operational loss, i.e., from a rogue trader or cybercrime activity.

Bank run:

Bank runs are not new; some go back hundreds of years. The Great Depression of the 1930s is not only a good example of how far the world's economy can decline; it also triggered prevention and mitigation tools. The Great Depression had devastating effects in rich and poor countries. International trade plunged, corporate revenues were hit hard, and personal income plunged as unemployment rose dramatically. A run on banks was the natural consequence as customers simply wanted to protect their money. One of the main systemic techniques derived from that experience was the concept of deposit insurance, mainly with the formation of the Federal Deposit Insurance Corporation (FDIC) in the United States in June 1933. Today, the FDIC preserves and promotes public confidence in the U.S. financial system by insuring deposits in banks and thrift institutions for at least $250,000; by identifying, monitoring, and addressing risks to the deposit-insurance funds; and by limiting the effect on the economy and the financial system when a bank or thrift institution fails.

As a bank run progresses, it generates its own momentum, in a kind of self-fulfilling prophecy (or positive feedback loop): As more people withdraw their deposits, the likelihood of default increases, thus triggering further withdrawals. This can destabilize the bank to the point where it runs out of cash and thus faces sudden bankruptcy.

a) Cash Outflows – Retail Deposits

Savings represent one of the fundamental pillars of economic and financial life. Deposits are a cornerstone of our economic system. Deposits are generally the primary source of funding for banks in Europe. Figure 18.5 specifies the LCR cash outflows for retail deposits under Basel III.

Figure 18.5

Basel III Liquidity Coverage Ratio
Cash Outflows
Retail Deposits

Retail Deposits	Cash Outflows
Demand deposits and term deposits (less than 30 days maturity)	
▪ Stable deposits (deposit insurance scheme)	3%
▪ Stable deposits	5%
▪ Less stable retail deposits	10%
Term deposits with residual maturity greater than 30 days	0%

b) Cash Outflows – Wholesale Funding

Wholesale funding is a method that banks use in addition to core demand deposits to finance operations and manage risk. Wholesale funding sources include, but are not limited to, federal funds, public funds, brokered deposits, and deposits obtained through the Internet or other listing services.

Wholesale funding providers are generally sensitive to changes in the credit risk profile of the institutions to which they provide these funds and to the interest rate environment. For instance, such providers closely track the institution's financial condition and may be likely to curtail such funding if other investment opportunities offer more attractive interest rates. As a result, an institution may experience liquidity problems due to lack of wholesale funding availability when needed.

Figure 18.6 specifies the cash outflows for unsecured wholesale funding under Basel III.

Figure 18.6

Basel III Liquidity Coverage Ratio
Cash Outflows
Unsecured Wholesale Funding

Unsecured Wholesale Funding	Cash Outflows
Demand and term deposits (less than 30 days maturity) provided by small business customers:	
▪ Stable deposits	5%
▪ Less stable deposits	10%
Operational deposits generated by clearing, custody, cash management activities	25%
▪ Portion covered by deposit insurance	5%
Cooperative banks in an institutional network	25%
Corporations, sovereigns, central banks, MDBs, and PSEs	40%
If the entire amount is fully covered by deposit insurance scheme	20%
Other legal entity customers	100%

c) Cash Outflows – Secured Funding

Secured funding provides an alternative source of term liquidity for a bank's balance sheet. Institutions therefore issue asset-backed securities (ABS) and covered bonds that are secured primarily over high-quality customer loans and advances, such as corporate loans, credit cards, and residential mortgage loans.

Figure 18.7 specifies the LCR cash outflows for secured funding under Basel III.

Figure 18.7 **Basel III Liquidity Coverage Ratio Cash Outflows Secured Funding**	
Secured Funding	**Cash Outflows**
Secured funding transactions with a central bank counterparty or backed by Level 1 assets with any counterparty.	0%
Secured funding transactions backed by Level 2A assets, with any counterparty	15%
Secured funding transactions backed by non-Level 1 or non-Level 2A assets, with domestic sovereigns, multilateral development banks, or domestic PSEs as a counterparty	25%
Backed by RMBS eligible for inclusion in Level 2B	25%
Backed by other Level 2B assets	50%
All other secured funding transactions	100%

d) Derivatives Outflows

The sum of all net cash outflows receives a 100 percent factor. Banks must calculate, in accordance with their existing valuation methodologies, expected contractual derivative cash inflows and outflows. Cash flows should be calculated on a net basis (i.e., inflows can offset outflows) by counterparty only where a valid master netting agreement exists. Banks should exclude from such calculations those liquidity requirements that would result from increased collateral needs due to market value movements or declines in value of collateral posted. Options should be assumed to be exercised when they are "in the money" to the option buyer. Where derivative payments are collateralized by high-quality liquid assets, cash outflows should be calculated net of any corresponding cash or collateral inflows that would result, all other things being equal, from contractual obligations for cash or collateral to be provided to the bank (if the bank is legally entitled and operationally capable to re-use the collateral in new cash-raising transactions once the collateral is received).

e) Downgrading Triggers

Usually, contracts governing derivatives and other transactions have clauses that require the posting of additional collateral, drawdown of contingent facilities, or early repayment of existing liabilities upon the bank's downgrade by a recognized credit rating organization. The scenario therefore requires that for each contract in which "downgrade triggers" exist, the bank assumes that 100 percent of this additional collateral or cash outflow will have to be posted for any downgrade up to and including a three-notch downgrade of the bank's long-term credit rating. Triggers linked to a bank's short-term rating should be assumed to be triggered at the corresponding long-term rating in accordance with published ratings criteria.

f) Other Outflows

In the stress scenario of the LCR, banks need to consider additional outflows; these include:

- Increased liquidity needs related to the potential for valuation changes on posted collateral securing derivative and other transactions;
- Increased liquidity needs related to excess non-segregated collateral held by the bank that could contractually be called at any time by the counterparty;
- Increased liquidity needs related to contractually required collateral on transactions for which the counterparty has not yet demanded the collateral be posted;
- Increased liquidity needs related to contracts that allow collateral substitution to non-HQLA assets;
- Increased liquidity needs related to market valuation changes on derivative or other transactions;
- Loss of funding on asset-backed-securities-covered bonds and other structured financing instruments;
- Loss of funding on asset-backed commercial paper, conduits, securities investment vehicles, and other such financing facilities;
- Drawdowns on committed credit and liquidity facilities.

Cash Inflows

When considering its available cash inflows, the bank should only include contractual inflows (including interest payments) from outstanding exposures that are fully performing and for which the bank has no reason to expect a default within the 30-day time horizon. Contingent inflows are not included in total net cash inflows.

In order to prevent banks from relying solely on anticipated inflows to meet their liquidity requirement, and also to ensure a minimum level of HQLA holdings, the amount of inflows that can offset outflows is capped at 75 percent of total expected cash outflows as calculated in the standard. This requires that a bank must maintain a minimum amount of stock of HQLA equal to 25 percent of the total cash outflows.

LCR Phase-in Arrangements

a) Under Basel III

Under Basel III, the LCR was introduced on January 1, 2015, at a level of 60 percent, and was set to rise in equal annual steps of 10 percentage points to reach 100 percent on January 1, 2019.

	2015	2016	2017	2018	2019
Minimum LCR requirement	60%	70%	80%	90%	100%

Of course, the LCR standard establishes a minimum level of liquidity for internationally active banks. Banks are expected to meet this standard as well as adhere to the Sound Principles as described in Chapter 24.

b) Under the Capital Requirements Directive IV (CRD IV) in the European Union

For the EU, the treatment of liquidity is seen as fundamental, both for the stability of banks as well as for their role in supporting wider economic recovery. Therefore, to highlight this importance, the co-legislators there decided to advance full implementation of the LCR by one year so that a 100 percent LCR will already apply in 2018.

	2015	2016	2017	2018
Minimum LCR requirement	60%	70%	80%	100%

However, if appropriate—and in light of a report to be prepared by the European Banking Association (EBA) taking into account the economic situation as well as European specificities and international regulatory developments—the commission is empowered to defer the 100 percent phasing-in of the LCR until 2019 and apply in 2018 a 90 percent LCR, in line with the Basel schedule.

Frequency of Calculation and Reporting

The LCR must be used on an ongoing basis to help monitor and control liquidity risk. The LCR must therefore be reported to supervisors at least monthly, with the operational capacity to increase the frequency to weekly or even daily in stressed situations at the discretion of bank supervisors. The time lag in reporting should be as short as feasible and ideally should not surpass two weeks.

Banks are expected to inform supervisors of their LCR and their liquidity profile on an ongoing basis. Banks should also notify supervisors immediately if their LCR has fallen, or is expected to fall, below 100 percent.

Does That Mean There Were No Liquidity Rules until 2015?

No. In order to underline the importance of avoiding liquidity mismatches, from the date of its adoption the regulation already established a general requirement that institutions need to hold liquid assets to cover their net cash outflows in stressed conditions over a 30-day period. However, this was a general requirement and not a detailed ratio requirement as when the LCR entered into force in 2015.

Is an Institution Always Obliged to Have an LCR Ratio above 100 Percent?

No. In a stressed situation an institution is obliged to make use of its liquid assets with the result that its LCR ratio (temporarily) falls below 100 percent. Of course, banks should then immediately notify the authorities and submit a plan for the timely restoration of the LCR ratio to above 100 percent.

The LCR: A Concept for all Banks?

The management of liquidity is essential to (most) banking institutions of all sizes in retaining the confidence of stakeholders and financial markets and ensuring that the business is sustainable. The LCR typically plays a key role in a bank's liquidity risk framework and has been designed to meet the following primary objectives:

- To maintain liquidity resources that are sufficient in both quality and quantity in a stress situation;
- To maintain market confidence in the bank's name;
- To set an early warning indicator to identify immediately the emergence of increased liquidity risk or vulnerabilities including events that would impair access to liquidity resources.

Further, the LCR concept is used, even today, by credit analysts, investors, and rating agencies world-wide. A bank's LCR has a direct influence on a bank's rating, and therefore, on its funding costs and eventually its net income and profitability.

Key Takeaways

- The LCR aims to ensure that a bank maintains an adequate level of unencumbered, high-quality liquid assets (HQLA) that can be converted into cash at little or no loss of value in private markets to meet its liquidity needs for a 30-calendar-day time horizon under a significantly severe liquidity stress scenario specified by examiners.
- The total net cash outflows for the stress scenario are to be calculated for 30 calendar days into the future. The standard requires that the value of the ratio be no lower than 100 percent, i.e., the stock of high-quality liquid assets should at least equal total net cash outflows.
- Banks are expected to meet the LCR requirement continuously and hold a stock of unencumbered, high-quality liquid assets as a defense against the potential onset of severe liquidity stress. The stock of HQLA must meet fundamental characteristics, market-related characteristics, and operational requirements.
- The LCR was introduced January 1, 2015, at a level of 60 percent, and is set to rise in equal annual steps of 10 percentage points to reach 100 percent on January 1, 2019.
- The management of liquidity is essential to banking institutions of all sizes in retaining the confidence of stakeholders and financial markets and ensuring that the business is sustainable.
- The LCR concept is used, even today, by credit analysts, investors, and rating agencies world-wide. A bank's LCR has a direct influence on a bank's rating, and therefore on its funding costs and eventually its net income and profitability.
- Banks of any size should implement the LCR.

Net Stable Funding Ratio

The net stable funding ratio (NSFR) is another important part of the Basel III liquidity standards and aims to ensure banks are able to survive an extended closure of wholesale funding markets.

Objective of the NSFR

The net stable funding ratio was developed to promote more medium- and long-term funding of the assets and activities of banking organizations. This metric establishes a minimum acceptable amount of stable funding based on the liquidity characteristics of an institution's assets and activities over a one-year horizon. The standard is designed to act as a minimum enforcement mechanism to complement the liquidity coverage ratio (LCR, Chapter 18) and reinforce other supervisory efforts by promoting structural changes in the liquidity risk profiles of institutions away from short-term funding mismatches and toward more stable, longer-term funding of assets and business activities.

In particular, the NSFR standard is structured to ensure that long-term assets are funded with at least a minimum amount of stable liabilities in relation to their liquidity risk profiles. Most importantly, the NSFR aims to limit over-reliance on short-term wholesale funding during times of buoyant market liquidity and encourage better assessment of liquidity risk across all on- and off-balance-sheet items.

Definition of the NSFR

The NSFR standard is structured to ensure that long-term assets are funded with at least a minimum amount of stable liabilities in relation to their liquidity risk profiles; consequently, available stable funding must be greater than the required stable funding.

$$\text{NSFR} = \frac{\text{Available stable funding}}{\text{Required stable funding}} > 100\%$$

157

> *Stable Funding / Basel Committee on Banking Supervision:*
>
> *"Stable funding" is defined as the portion of those types and amounts of equity and liability financing expected to be reliable sources of funds over a one-year time horizon under conditions of extended stress.*

Available Stable Funding

Available stable funding (ASF) is defined by Basel III as the total amount of a bank's capital; preferred stock with maturity equal to or greater than one year; liabilities with effective maturities of one year or greater; the portion of non-maturity deposits and/or term deposits with maturities of less than one year that would be expected to stay with the institution for an extended period in an idiosyncratic stress event; and the portion of wholesale funding with maturities of less than a year that is expected to stay with the institution for an extended period in an idiosyncratic stress event. Extended borrowing from central bank lending facilities outside regular open market operations are not considered in this ratio, in order to not create a reliance on the central bank as a source of funding.

To calculate the ASF, the carrying value of an institution's equity and liabilities is multiplied by an ASF factor, the maximum value for which depends on the type of funding.

Table 19.1 enlists available stable funding sources—equity and liabilities—including the relevant ASF factors for the different balance sheet items.

Table 19.1 Components of Available Stable Funding and Associated ASF Factors	
Components of ASF Category (Equity and Liabilities)	ASF Factor
• Tier 1 & 2 capital requirements • Other preferred shares and capital instruments in excess of tier 2 allowable amount having an effective maturity of one year or greater • Other liabilities with an effective maturity of one year or greater	100%
• Stable deposits of retail and small business customers • (non-maturity or residual maturity < one year)	90%
• Less-stable deposits of retail and small business customers (non-maturity maturity < one year)	80%
• Wholesale funding provided by non-financial corporate customers, sovereign central banks, multilateral development banks and PSEs (non- maturity or residual maturity < one year)	50%
• All other liabilities and equity not included above	0%

Required Stable Funding

The required stable funding (RSF) factors assigned to various types of assets are parameters intended to approximate the amount of a particular asset that could not be monetized through sale or use as collateral in a secured borrowing on an extended basis during a liquidity event lasting one year. Under this standard such amounts are expected to be supported by stable funding.

Table 19.2 enlists required stable funding elements including the relevant RSF factors for the different balance sheet items, all of them being assets.

Table 19.2 **Composition of Asset Categories and Associated RSF Factors**	
Components of ASF Category (Equity and Liabilities)	RSF Factor
• Cash (immediately available)	0%
• Unencumbered short-term unsecured instruments and transactions with outstanding maturities of less than one year	
• Unencumbered securities with stated remaining maturities of less than one year with no embedded options that would increase the expected maturity to more than one year	
• Unencumbered securities held where the institution has an offsetting reverse repurchase transaction when the security on each transaction has the same unique identifier (e.g., ISIN number)	
• Unencumbered loans to financial entities with effective remaining maturities of less than one year that are not renewable and for which the lender has an irrevocable right to call	
• Unencumbered marketable securities with residual maturities of one year or greater representing claims on or claims guaranteed by sovereigns, central banks, the BIS, the IMF, the EC, non-central government PSEs, or multilateral development banks that are assigned a 0% risk-weight under the Basel II standardized approach, provided that active repo or sale-markets exist for these securities	5%
• Unencumbered corporate bonds or covered bonds rated AA- or higher with residual maturities of one year or greater satisfying all of the conditions for Level 2 assets in the LCR	20%
• Unencumbered marketable securities with residual maturities of one year or greater representing claims on or claims guaranteed by sovereigns, central banks, and non-central government PSEs that are assigned a 20% risk-weight under the Basel II standardized approach, provided that they meet all of the conditions for Level 2 assets in the LCR	
• Unencumbered gold	50%
• Unencumbered equity securities, not issued by financial institutions or their affiliates, listed on a recognized exchange and included in a large-cap market index	
• Unencumbered corporate bonds and covered bonds (conditions apply)	
• Unencumbered loans to non-financial corporate clients, sovereigns, central banks, and PSEs having a remaining maturity of less than one year	
• Unencumbered residential mortgages of any maturity that would qualify for the 35% or lower risk weight under the Basel II Standardized Approach for credit risk	65%
• Other unencumbered loans, excluding loans to financial institutions, with a remaining maturity of one year or greater, that would qualify for the 35% or lower risk weight under the Basel II Standardized Approach for credit risk	
• Unencumbered loans to retail customers (i.e., natural persons) and small business customers (as defined in the LCR) having a remaining maturity of less than one year (other than those that qualify for the 65% RSF above)	85%
• All other assets	100%

When Will the Net Stable Funding Requirement Come into Force?

Work on the NSFR has not progressed as far as that on the LCR and there is still a very considerable amount of development work to be carried out by the Basel Committee. Therefore, in light of the results of the observation period and reports to be prepared by supervisors, regulators will prepare, most likely and if appropriate, a legislative proposal by December 31, 2016, to ensure that institutions use stable sources of funding, taking full account of the diversity of the respective banking sector(s).

Does That Mean There Are No NSFR Rules until 2018?

No, at least within the European Union. Several years before any binding minimum standards for net stable funding requirements may be specified under EU law, the regulation already establishes the general rule from January 1, 2016, that institutions shall ensure that long-term obligations are adequately met with a diversity of stable funding requirements under both normal and stressed conditions.

The NSFR: A Concept for All Banks?

The management of liquidity is essential to banking institutions of all sizes in retaining the confidence of stakeholders and financial markets and ensuring that the business is sustainable. Complementary to the LCR, the NSFR plays a key role in a bank's liquidity risk framework and has been designed to meet the following primary objectives to:

- Maintain stable funding sources, especially shareholders' equity and deposits from retail customers;
- Diversify its funding source;
- Limit the institution's over-reliance on short-term wholesale funding, especially during times of buoyant market liquidity, and encourage better assessment of liquidity risk across all on- and off-balance-sheet items;
- Maintain market confidence in the bank's name.

Together with the LCR, the NSFR concept is used, even today, by credit analysts, investors, and rating agencies world-wide. A bank's NSFR has a direct influence on a bank's rating, and therefore, on its funding costs and eventually its net income and profitability. As a consequence, banks are working hard on increasing their stable funding sources, mainly shareholders' equity and deposits from retail customers and high net worth individuals (HNWIs).

Funding Profiles of Large Banks

Figure 19.1 illustrates how U.S. banks have managed to increase their deposits. In the time period 1Q2013 to end of FY2013, the 20 largest institutions increased deposits by $329 billion, or 5.3 percent.

Figure 19.1

Top 20 U.S. Based Depositories As of 1Q2013 and FY2013 in USD Billion

	Institution	1Q2013	FY2013
1.	JPMorgan Chase & Co.	1,203	1,288
2.	Bank of America Corporation	1,095	1,119
3.	Wells Fargo & Company	1,011	1,079
4.	Citigroup Inc.	934	968
5.	U.S. Bancorp	248	262
6.	Bank of New York Mellon Corporation	240	261
7.	PNC Financial Services Group	212	221
8.	Capital One Financial Group	212	205
9.	State Street Corporation	155	182
10.	Sun Trust Banks, Inc.	130	130
11.	BB&T Corporation	131	127
12.	Morgan Stanley	81	112
13.	Fifth Third Bancorp	92	99
14.	Charles Schwab Corporation	82	93
15.	Regions Financial Corporation	94	92
16.	Northern Trust Corporation	76	84
17.	Goldman Sachs Group, Inc.	73	71
18.	KeyCorp	65	69
19.	M&T Bank Corporation	65	65
20.	Comerica Incorporated	52	53
Sum		**6,251**	**6,580**

Source: Morgan Stanley, 1Q2014 Fixed Investor Update, 14-May-2014
Remark: excludes U.S. subsidiaries of foreign based banks

Large banks in particular have worked hard in order to increase their deposits and to improve their loans-to-deposits ratios. Barclays, for example, improved the loans-to-deposits ratio from 138 percent at the end of 2008 to 101 percent at the end of 2013, as illustrated in Figure 19.2. The loans-to-deposits ratio is a major indicator for funding and is closely tracked by regulators, rating agencies, and investors (see also Chapter 27).

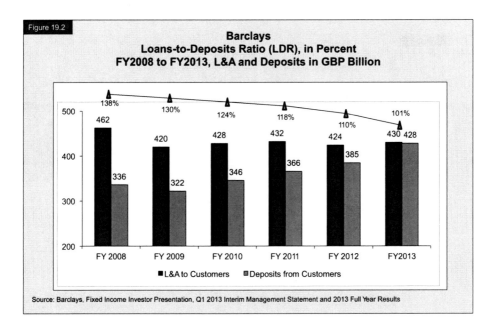

Figure 19.2

**Barclays
Loans-to-Deposits Ratio (LDR), in Percent
FY2008 to FY2013, L&A and Deposits in GBP Billion**

■ L&A to Customers   ▩ Deposits from Customers

Source: Barclays, Fixed Income Investor Presentation, Q1 2013 Interim Management Statement and 2013 Full Year Results

Some large banks have relatively small deposit volumes compared to total assets as a consequence of their business models, i.e., investment banks. Goldman Sachs and Morgan Stanley are reviewing their business models in order to generate more stable funding sources such as fiduciary deposits. Figure 19.3 illustrates Morgan Stanley's plan to increase deposits significantly over time.

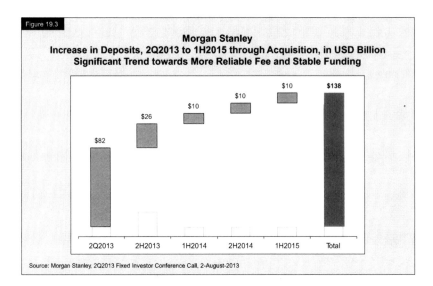

Figures 19.4 and 19.5 describe the funding profile of UBS, the largest Swiss bank, as of FY2013. The portfolio is well diversified in terms of products and currencies.

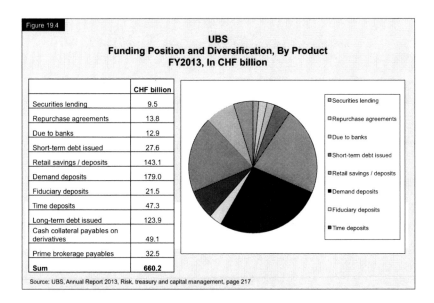

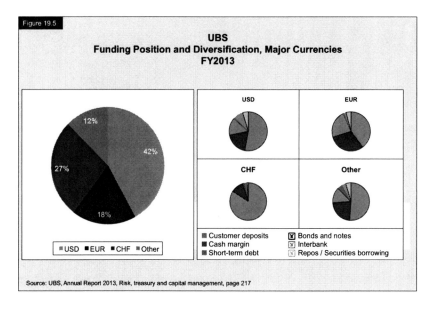

Figure 19.5

UBS
Funding Position and Diversification, Major Currencies
FY2013

USD   EUR   CHF   Other

USD

EUR

CHF

Other

Customer deposits ▢ Bonds and notes
Cash margin ▢ Interbank
Short-term debt ▢ Repos / Securities borrowing

Source: UBS, Annual Report 2013, Risk, treasury and capital management, page 217

Key Takeaways

- The net stable funding ratio (NSFR) aims to ensure banks are able to survive an extended closure of wholesale funding markets. It establishes a minimum acceptable amount of stable funding based on the liquidity characteristics of an institution's assets and activities over a one-year horizon.
- The NSFR is defined as the available amount of stable funding to the amount of required stable funding. This ratio must be greater than 100 percent.
- The NSFR standard is structured to ensure that long-term assets are funded with at least a minimum amount of stable liabilities in relation to their liquidity risk profiles.
- The NSFR aims to limit over-reliance on short-term wholesale funding during times of buoyant market liquidity and encourage better assessment of liquidity risk across all on- and off-balance-sheet items.

Liquidity Risk – Monitoring Tools

In addition to key liquidity ratios—the liquidity coverage ratio (LCR, Chapter 18) and the net stable funding ratio (NSFR, Chapter 19)—monitoring tools make up another important section of the Basel III reform. These metrics capture specific information related to a bank's cash flows, balance sheet structure, available unencumbered collateral, and certain market indicators.

These metrics provide the cornerstone of information that aid supervisors in assessing the liquidity risk of a bank. In utilizing these metrics, supervisors will take action when potential liquidity difficulties are signaled through a negative trend in the metrics, when a deteriorating liquidity position is identified, or when the absolute result of the metric identifies a current or potential liquidity problem. The Basel III metrics / monitoring tools include the following:

- Contractual maturity mismatch;
- Concentration of funding;
- Available unencumbered assets;
- LCR by significant currency; and
- Market-related monitoring tools.

Contractual Maturity Mismatch Profile

Objective

The contractual maturity mismatch profile identifies the gaps between the contractual inflows and outflows of liquidity for defined time bands. These maturity gaps indicate how much liquidity a bank would potentially need to raise in each of these time bands if all outflows occurred at the earliest possible date. This metric provides insight into the extent to which the bank relies on maturity transformation under its current contracts.

Definition

Contractual cash and security inflows and outflows from all on- and off-balance-sheet items mapped to defined time bands based on their respective maturities.

164

A bank must report contractual cash and security flows in the relevant time bands based on their residual contractual maturity. Supervisors in each jurisdiction will determine the specific template, including required time bands, by which data must be reported. Supervisors should define the time buckets so as to be able to understand the bank's cash flow position. Possibilities include requesting the cash flow mismatch to be constructed for the overnight, 7-day, 14-day, 1-, 2-, 3-, 6-, and 9-month, and 1-, 2-, 3-, 5-, and beyond 5-years buckets.

Concentration of Funding

Concentration risk can be defined as any single (direct and/or indirect) exposure or group of exposures with the potential to produce losses large enough to threaten an institution's health or its ability to maintain its core business. Concentration risk mainly arises from a bank's:

- Loan portfolio, i.e., large credit exposures to individual borrowers, entire industries, geographic regions, or sovereigns;
- Funding strategy, i.e., over-reliance on certain funding sources. Figure 1.5 in Chapter 1 describes how Northern Rock's funding distribution before the start of the financial crisis was heavily reliant on both capital markets funding via securitizations and wholesale funding sources (in total 75 percent of the overall funding profile), which turned out to be a liquidity concentration that eventually damaged the institution.

Objective

This metric is meant to identify those sources of wholesale funding that are of such significance that withdrawal of this funding could trigger liquidity problems. The metric thus encourages the diversification of funding sources. A bank should establish a funding strategy that provides effective diversification in both the sources and tenor of funding. It should maintain an ongoing presence in its chosen funding markets and strong relationships with funds providers to promote effective diversification of funding sources. A bank should regularly gauge its capacity to raise funds quickly from each source. It should identify the main factors that affect its ability to raise funds and monitor those factors closely to ensure that estimates of fundraising capacity remain valid.

Definitions

Significant counterparties: Funding liabilities sourced from each significant counterparty as a percentage of total liabilities, i.e., a major market player in the interbank money markets. A "significant counterparty" is defined as a single counterparty or group of connected or affiliated counterparties accounting in aggregate for more than 1 percent of the bank's total balance sheet.

Significant product/instrument: Funding liabilities sourced from each significant product/instrument as a percentage of total liabilities, i.e., reliance on capital markets funding via securitizations. A "significant instrument/product" is defined as a single instrument/product or group of similar instruments/products that in aggregate amount to more than 1 percent of the bank's total balance sheet.

List of asset and liability amounts by significant currency: A currency is considered "significant" if the aggregate liabilities denominated in that currency amount to 5 percent or more of the bank's total liabilities.

Available Unencumbered Assets

Objective

These metrics provide supervisors with data on the quantity and key characteristics, including currency denomination and location, of banks' available unencumbered assets. These assets have the potential to be used as collateral to raise additional HQLA or secured funding in secondary markets or are eligible at central banks and as such may potentially be additional sources of liquidity for the bank.

Definitions

> *Available unencumbered assets that are marketable as collateral in secondary markets*
>
> *and*
>
> *Available unencumbered assets that are eligible for central banks' standing facilities*

LCR by Significant Currency

Objective

While the LCR is required to be met in one single currency, in order to better capture potential currency mismatches, banks and supervisors should also monitor the LCR in significant currencies. This will allow the bank and the supervisors to track potential currency mismatch issues that could arise.

Definition

> **Foreign Currency LCR = Stock of HQLA in each significant currency/ Total net cash outflows over a 30-day time period in each significant currency**
> *(Note: Amount of total net foreign exchange cash outflows should be net of foreign exchange hedges)*

The definition of the stock of high-quality foreign exchange assets and total net foreign exchange cash outflows should mirror those of the LCR for common currencies. A currency is considered "significant" if the aggregate liabilities denominated in that currency amount to 5 percent or more of the bank's total liabilities.

Market-Related Monitoring Tools

Objective

High frequency market data with little or no time lag can be used as early warning indicators in monitoring potential liquidity difficulties at banks.

Definition

While there are many types of data available in the market, supervisors can monitor data at the following levels to focus on potential liquidity difficulties:

1. Market-wide information;
2. Information on the financial sector;
3. Bank-specific information.

Market-wide information:

Supervisors can monitor information both on the absolute level and direction of major markets and consider their potential impact on the financial sector and the specific bank. Market-wide information is also crucial when evaluating assumptions behind a bank's funding plan. Valuable market information to monitor includes, but is not limited to: equity prices (i.e., overall stock markets and sub-indices in various jurisdictions relevant to the activities of the supervised banks); debt markets (money markets, medium-term notes, long-term debt, derivatives, government bond markets, credit default spread indices, etc.); and foreign exchange markets, commodities markets, and indices related to specific products, such as for certain securitized products.

Information on the financial sector:

To track whether the financial sector as a whole is mirroring broader market movements or is experiencing difficulties, information to be monitored includes equity and debt market information for the financial sector broadly and for specific subsets of the financial sector, including indices.

Bank-specific information:

To monitor whether the market is losing confidence in a particular institution or has identified risks at an institution, it is useful to collect information on equity prices, credit default swap (CDS) spreads, money-market trading prices, the situation of rollovers and prices for various lengths of funding, and the price/yield of a bank debenture or subordinated debt in the secondary market.

Key Takeaways

- Five key monitoring tools supplement the key liquidity ratios (LCR and NSFR): contractual maturity mismatch, concentration of funding, available unencumbered assets, LCR by significant currency, and market-related monitoring tools.

Articles/Sources Used

- *Basel III: The Liquidity Coverage Ratio and Liquidity Risk Monitoring Tools,* Basel Committee on Banking Supervision, Bank for International Settlements, January 2013

Stress Testing – Best Practices for Banks

Stress Testing Principles

The Basel Committee on Banking Supervision has issued principles for sound stress testing practices and supervision.[42] Stress testing is a critical tool used by banks as part of their internal risk management and capital planning. The guidance sets out a comprehensive set of principles for the sound governance, design, and implementation of stress testing programs at banks. The principles address the weaknesses in such programs that were highlighted by the financial crisis. Stress testing also is a key component of the supervisory assessment process that assists supervisors in identifying vulnerabilities and evaluating banks' capital adequacy. The principles therefore establish expectations for the role and responsibilities of supervisors when evaluating firms' stress testing practices.

A stress test, in financial terminology, is an analysis or simulation designed to determine the ability of a given financial instrument, portfolio, or financial institution to deal with an economic crisis. Instead of doing financial projection on a "best estimate" basis, an institution or its regulators may do stress testing where they look at how robust an institution is in certain extreme market situations, i.e., a crash or contagion.

Stress testing is an important risk management tool that is used by banks as part of their internal risk management and, through the Basel II capital adequacy framework, is promoted by supervisors. Stress testing alerts bank management to adverse unexpected outcomes related to a variety of risks and provides an indication of how much capital might be needed to absorb losses should large shocks occur. A bank stress test is a simulation based on an examination of the balance sheet of that institution. Large international banks began using internal stress tests in the early 1990s. In 1996, the Basel Capital Accord was amended to require banks and investment firms to conduct stress tests to determine their ability to respond to market events. However, up until 2007, stress tests were typically performed only by the banks themselves, for internal self-assessment. Beginning in 2007, governmental regulatory bodies became interested in conducting their own stress tests to insure the effective operation of financial institutions. Since then, stress tests have been routinely performed by financial regulators in different countries or regions, to insure that the banks under their authority

---

[42]"Principles for Sound Stress Testing and Supervision," Basel Committee on Banking Supervision, Bank for International Settlements, May 2009.

are engaging in practices likely to avoid negative outcomes. In October 2012, U.S. regulators unveiled new rules expanding this practice by requiring the largest American banks to undergo stress tests twice per year, once internally and once conducted by the regulators.

While stress tests provide an indication of the appropriate level of capital necessary to endure deteriorating economic conditions, a bank alternatively may employ other actions in order to help mitigate increasing levels of risk. Stress testing is a tool that supplements other risk management approaches and measures. It plays a particularly important role in:

- Providing forward-looking assessments of risk;
- Overcoming limitations of models and historical data;
- Supporting internal and external communication;
- Feeding into capital and liquidity planning procedures;
- Informing the setting of a bank's risk tolerance; and
- Facilitating the development of risk mitigation or contingency plans across a range of stressed conditions.

Principles for Banks

a) Use of Stress Testing and Integration in Risk Governance

Principle 1

Stress testing should form an integral part of the overall governance and risk management culture of the bank. Stress testing should be actionable, with the results from stress testing analyses impacting decision-making at the appropriate management level, including strategic business decisions of the board and senior management. Board and senior management involvement in the stress testing program is essential for its effective operation.

Principle 2

A bank should operate a stress testing program that promotes risk identification and control, provides a complementary risk perspective to other risk management tools, improves capital and liquidity management, and enhances internal and external communication.

Principle 3

Stress testing programs should take account of views from across the organization and should cover a range of perspectives and techniques.

Principle 4

A bank should have written policies and procedures governing the stress testing program. The operation of the program should be appropriately documented.

Principle 5

A bank should have a suitably robust infrastructure in place that is sufficiently flexible to accommodate different and possibly changing stress tests at an appropriate level of granularity.

Principle 6

A bank should regularly maintain and update its stress testing framework. The effectiveness of the stress testing program, as well as the robustness of major individual components, should be assessed regularly and independently. Areas for assessment should include:

- The effectiveness of the program in meeting its intended purposes;
- Documentation;
- Development work;
- System implementation;
- Management oversight;
- Data quality; and
- Assumptions used.

b) Stress Testing Methodology and Scenario Selection

Principle 7

Stress tests should cover a range of risks and business areas, including at the firm-wide level. A bank should be able to integrate effectively, in a meaningful fashion, across the range of its stress testing activities to deliver a complete picture of firm-wide risk. The impact of stress tests is usually evaluated against one or more measures. The particular measures used will depend on the specific purpose of the stress test, the risks and portfolios being analyzed, and the particular issue under examination. A range of measures may need to be considered to convey an adequate impression of the impact. Typical measures used are:

- Asset values;
- Accounting profit and loss;
- Economic profit and loss;
- Regulatory capital or risk-weighted assets (RWAs);
- Economic capital requirements; and
- Liquidity and funding gaps.

Principle 8

Stress testing programs should cover a range of scenarios, including forward-looking scenarios, and aim to take into account system-wide interactions and feedback effects.

Principle 9

Stress tests should feature a range of severities, including events capable of generating the most damage whether through size of loss or through loss of reputation. A stress testing program should also determine what scenarios could challenge the viability of the bank (reverse stress tests) and thereby uncover hidden risks and interactions among risks.

Principle 10

As part of an overall stress testing program, a bank should aim to take account of simultaneous pressures in funding and asset markets, and the impact of a reduction in market liquidity on exposure valuation. A bank should enhance its stress testing practices by considering important interrelations between various factors, including:

- Price shocks for specific asset categories;
- The drying-up of corresponding asset liquidity;
- The possibility of significant losses damaging the bank's financial strength;
- Growth of liquidity needs as a consequence of liquidity commitments;
- Taking on board-affected assets; and
- Diminished access to secured or unsecured funding markets.

c) Specific Areas of Focus

Principle 11

The effectiveness of risk mitigation techniques should be systematically challenged.

Principle 12

The stress testing program should explicitly cover complex and bespoke products such as securitized exposures. Stress tests for securitized assets should consider the underlying assets, their exposure to systematic market factors, relevant contractual arrangements and embedded triggers, and the impact of leverage, particularly as it relates to the subordination level in the issue structure.

Principle 13

The stress testing program should cover pipeline and warehousing risks. A bank should include such exposures in its stress tests regardless of their probability of being securitized.

Principal 14

A bank should enhance its stress testing methodologies to capture the effect of reputational risk. The bank should integrate risks arising from off-balance sheet vehicles and other related entities in its stress testing program.

Principle 15

A bank should enhance its stress testing approaches for highly leveraged counterparties in considering its vulnerability to specific asset categories or market movements and in assessing potential wrong-way risk related to risk-mitigating techniques.

Principles for Supervisors

Principle 16

Supervisors should make regular and comprehensive assessments of a bank's stress testing program.

Principle 17

Supervisors should require management to take corrective action if material deficiencies in the stress testing program are identified or if the results of stress tests are not adequately taken into consideration in the decision-making process. The range of remedial action should take into consideration the magnitude and likelihood of potential stress events and be proportionate to the severity of the impact of the stress test, the overall risk management framework, and other limiting or risk-mitigating policies. The measures undertaken by supervisors may involve:

- The review of limits;
- The recourse to risk-mitigation techniques;
- The reduction of exposures to specific sectors, countries, regions, or portfolios;
- The revision of bank policies, such as those that relate to funding or capital adequacy; and
- The implementation of contingency plans.

Principle 18

Supervisors should assess and if necessary challenge the scope and severity of firm-wide scenarios. Supervisors may ask banks to perform sensitivity analysis with respect to specific portfolios or parameters, use specific scenarios, or evaluate scenarios under which their viability is threatened (reverse stress testing scenarios).

Principle 19

Under Pillar 2 (supervisory review process) of the Basel II framework, supervisors should examine a bank's stress testing results as part of a supervisory review of both the bank's internal capital assessment and its liquidity risk management. In particular, supervisors should consider the results of forward-looking stress testing for assessing the adequacy of capital and liquidity.

Principle 20

Supervisors should consider implementing stress test exercises based on common scenarios.

Principle 21

Supervisors should engage in a constructive dialogue with other public authorities and the industry to identify systemic vulnerabilities. Supervisors should also ensure that they have the capacity and skills to assess a bank's stress testing program.

Stress Testing: A Concept for all Banks?

Yes. Stress Testing should be conducted by all financial institutions. It is without doubt a key element of prudent banking / risk management. Institutions of all sizes should adhere to the Bank for International Settlements (BIS) principles.

Key Takeaways

- The Basel Committee introduced its principles for sound stress testing practices and supervision in May 2009.
- The principles focus on key risk issues such as governance, methodology, coverage, and severities, and on simultaneous pressures in asset and funding markets.
- Banks of any size should adhere to the principles.

Comprehensive Capital Analysis and Review (CCAR) under Dodd-Frank: Methodology and Results

One of the key issues under Dodd-Frank is stress testing. As a result, the Federal Reserve expects large, complex bank holding companies (BHCs) to hold sufficient capital to continue lending to support real economic activity, even under adverse economic conditions. Stress testing is one tool that helps bank supervisors measure whether a BHC has enough capital to support its operations throughout periods of stress.

The Fed highlighted the use of stress tests as a means of assessing capital sufficiency under stress during the 2009 Supervisory Capital Assessment Program (SCAP) and the 2011, 2012, and 2013 Comprehensive Capital Analysis and Review (CCAR).[43]

CCAR is an annual exercise by the Federal Reserve to ensure that institutions have robust, forward-looking capital planning processes that account for their unique risks and sufficient capital to continue operations throughout times of economic and financial stress. As part of the CCAR, the Federal Reserve evaluates institutions' capital adequacy, internal capital adequacy assessment processes, and their plans to make capital distributions, such as dividend payments or stock repurchases. The CCAR includes a supervisory stress test to support the Federal Reserve's analysis of the adequacy of the firms' capital. Boards of directors of the institutions are required each year to review and approve capital plans before submitting them to the Federal Reserve.

The Dodd-Frank Act requires the Fed to conduct an annual stress test of large BHCs and all nonbank financial companies designated by the Financial Stability Oversight Council (FSOC) for Federal Reserve supervision to evaluate whether they have sufficient capital to absorb losses resulting from adverse economic conditions. The act also requires BHCs and other financial companies supervised by the Federal Reserve to conduct their own stress tests. Under the rules, 18 BHCs were part of the Dodd-Frank Act Stress Testing in 2013 (DFAST 2013). Table 22.1 lists the 30 BHCs required to participate and disclose their results as part of CCAR 2014, which was published in March 2014.

In the United States, the Federal Reserve's annual assessment of capital adequacy for U.S.-domiciled, top-tier bank holding companies with total consolidated assets of $50 billion or more includes consideration of a BHC's overall financial condition, risk profile, and capital adequacy on a forward-looking basis. Assessments will also be made on

---

[43]"Comprehensive Capital Analysis and Review 2014 – Summary Instructions and Guidance," Board of Governors of the Federal Reserve System, November 1,.2013.

the overall content of a capital plan and the strength of the BHC's capital adequacy process (CAP), including its capital policy. Pursuant to the capital plan rule, each BHC with total consolidated assets of $50 billion or more is required to submit a capital plan approved by the BHC's board of directors, or a committee thereof, for the Federal Reserve's annual CCAR, irrespective of whether the BHC intends to undertake any capital distributions over the planning horizon covered in its capital plan.

The supervisory review of a BHC's capital plan includes an assessment of:

- The comprehensiveness of the capital plan, including the suitability of the BHC scenarios, and the extent to which the risk measurement and other analysis underlying the plan capture and appropriately address potential risks stemming from all activities across the BHC under baseline and stressed operating conditions;
- The reasonableness of the BHC's assumptions and analysis underlying the capital plan and a review of the robustness of the BHC's overall CAP; and
- The BHC's capital policy.

Table 22.1

Participants CCAR 2014

Previous CCAR Participants, also Participants in 2014

- Ally Financial Inc.
- American Express Company
- Bank of America Corporation
- The Bank of New York Mellon Corporation
- BB&T Corporation
- Capital One Financial Corporation
- Citigroup Inc.
- Fifth Third Bancorp
- The Goldman Sachs Group, Inc.
- JPMorgan Chase & Co.
- KeyCorp
- Morgan Stanley
- The PNC Financial Services Group, Inc.
- Regions Financial Corporation
- State Street Corporation
- SunTrust Banks, Inc.
- U.S. Bancorp
- Wells Fargo & Company

Global Market Shock Participants, 2014

- Bank of America Corporation
- Citigroup Inc.
- The Goldman Sachs Group, Inc.
- JPMorgan Chase & Co.
- Morgan Stanley
- Wells Fargo & Company

Participants New to CCAR in 2014

- BMO Financial Corp.
- BBVA Compass Bancshares, Inc.
- Comerica Inc.
- Discover Financial Services
- HSBC North America Holdings Inc.
- Huntington Bancshares Inc.
- M&T Bank Corp.
- Northern Trust Corp.
- RBS Citizens Financial Group, Inc.
- Santander Holdings USA, Inc.
- UnionBanCal Corp.
- Zions Bancorporation

Counterparty Default Participants, 2014

- Bank of America Corporation
- The Bank of New York Mellon Corporation
- Citigroup Inc.
- The Goldman Sachs Group, Inc.
- JPMorgan Chase & Co.
- Morgan Stanley
- State Street Corporation
- Wells Fargo & Company

The capital plans must reflect the results of each BHC's company-run stress test using three scenarios that the Federal Reserve is providing under the Dodd-Frank Act stress test rules. The supervisory scenarios provided by the Fed are the baseline scenario, the adverse scenario, and the severely adverse scenario. In addition to three supervisory scenarios, each BHC must conduct a stress test based on its own scenarios, including at least one stress scenario (BHC stress scenario) and a baseline scenario (BHC baseline scenario). Each BHC must then submit the results of the BHC baseline scenario using the BHC's planned capital actions and the results of the BHC stress scenario(s) using any alternative capital actions (if applicable). As discussed further below, under certain conditions a BHC can choose to use the supervisory baseline scenario as its own baseline scenario.

In conducting its supervisory stress tests of BHCs under the DFAST rules, the Fed will use the same scenarios and assumptions as the BHCs are required to use under the DFAST rules to project revenues, losses, net income, and pro forma capital ratios, as illustrated in Figure 22.1. In addition, the Fed will independently project BHCs' balance sheet and risk-weighted assets over a nine-quarter planning horizon, using the same macroeconomic scenarios, to increase the comparability of supervisory stress test results across BHCs.

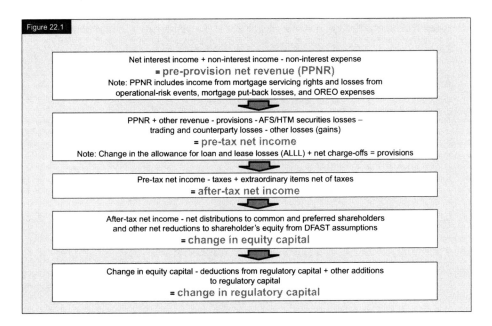

CCAR is a comprehensive assessment that takes into account all relevant risks to the BHC, such as estimates of potential losses and the impact of the stress scenarios. It is the responsibility of each BHC to capture all potential sources of losses from all on- and off-balance-sheet positions, as well as any other events that have the potential to impact capital in both baseline and stressful environments.

CCAR 2014

A BHC's submission of its pro forma, post-stress capital projections in its capital plan, inclusive of planned or alternative capital actions, must begin with data as of September 30, 2013 and span the nine-quarter planning horizon, beginning in the fourth quarter of the current year and concluding at the end of the fourth quarter, two years out.

For CCAR 2014, for example, the planning horizon commenced at the beginning of the fourth quarter of 2013 (October 1, 2013) and will conclude at the end of the fourth quarter of 2016 (December 31, 2016).

The Federal Reserve conducted qualitative and quantitative assessments of a firm's capital plan and either objected to, or provided a non-objection to, each of the 30 BHCs' capital plans. The qualitative assessment focused on the strength of the BHCs' capital plans and supporting practices. The Federal Reserve conducted its quantitative assessment based on the supervisory stress test conducted under the Fed's rules implementing the stress tests required under Dodd-Frank, combined with the BHCs' planned capital actions under the BHC baseline scenario.

Stress Testing Scenario Selection in CCAR 2014

For purposes of CCAR, BHCs will be required to submit the results of company-run stress tests based on three supervisory scenarios (DFA supervisory stress test scenarios), at least one stressed scenario developed by the BHC, and a BHC baseline scenario, as follows:

- BHC baseline: a BHC-defined baseline scenario.
- BHC stress: at least one BHC-defined stress scenario.
- Supervisory baseline: a baseline scenario provided by the Federal Reserve under the DFAST rules.
- Supervisory adverse: an adverse scenario provided by the Federal Reserve under the DFA stress test rules.
- Supervisory severely adverse: a severely adverse scenario provided by the Federal Reserve under the DFAST rules.

When constructing the BHC-defined baseline and stress scenarios, institutions need to take all relevant parameters for their respective balance sheets (including off-balance-sheet positions, of course) into account. The relevant parameters are a function of an institution's business lines and geographical reach.

For most banks all over the world, a deep recession in their respective economies, with a significant decline in GDP over time and a corresponding increase in unemployment is a major concern. Consequently, under the severely adverse scenario of CCAR 2014, banks needed to test their balance sheets and capital levels for the capacity to withstand the following items:

- Decline of 5 percent in real GDP;
- Jump in unemployment to 12 percent;
- A 50 percent drop in stock prices;
- A 20 percent fall in home prices.

Of course, other key economic indicators such as inflation, interest rates, and foreign exchange rates would be affected immediately, with consequences for yields on government and corporate bonds and mortgage rates.

Globalization certainly has an effect on large BHCs as they are usually inter-connected. Therefore, international scenarios must be taken into account, such as deep recessions in the Euro area or developing Asia.

Specialized institutions such as commercial real estate banks or ship-financing specialists need to look at additional parameters relevant for their business. Ship-financing banks, for example, closely track container freight rates, which depend on a number of indicators such as world GDP, international trade, fuel prices, number of vessels operating, and so on.

Main Results CCAR 2014 (Results from March 2014)[44]

The Federal Reserve approved the capital plans of 25 bank holding companies participating in CCAR. The Fed objected to the plans of the other five participating firms—four based on qualitative concerns and one because it did not meet a minimum post-stress capital requirement.

The Federal Reserve considered both qualitative and quantitative factors. These include a firm's capital ratios under severe economic and financial market stress and the strength of the firm's capital planning process.

The Federal Reserve did not object to the capital plans for Ally Financial Inc.; American Express Company; Bank of America Corporation; The Bank of New York Mellon Corporation; BB&T Corporation; BBVA Compass Bancshares Inc.; BMO Financial Corp.; Capital One Financial Corporation; Comerica Incorporated; Discover Financial Services; Fifth Third Bancorp; The Goldman Sachs Group Inc.; Huntington Bancshares Incorporated; JP Morgan Chase & Co.; Keycorp; M&T Bank Corporation; Morgan Stanley; Northern Trust Corporation; The PNC Financial Services Group Inc.; Regions Financial Corporation; State Street Corporation; SunTrust Banks Inc.; U.S. Bancorp; UnionBanCal Corporation; and Wells Fargo & Company.

Bank of America Corporation and The Goldman Sachs Group Inc., met minimum capital requirements after submitting adjusted capital actions.

Based on qualitative concerns, the Federal Reserve objected to the capital plans of Citigroup Inc.; HSBC North America Holdings Inc.; RBS Citizens Financial Group Inc.; and Santander Holdings USA Inc.

The Federal Reserve objected to the capital plan of Zions Bancorporation because the firm did not meet the minimum, post-stress tier 1 common ratio of 5 percent.

U.S. firms have substantially increased their capital since the first set of government stress tests in 2009. The aggregate tier 1 common equity ratio, which compares high-quality capital to risk-weighted assets, of the 30 bank holding companies in the 2014 CCAR had more than doubled from 5.5 percent in the first quarter of 2009 to 11.6 percent in the fourth quarter of 2013, reflecting an increase in tier 1 common equity of more than $511 billion to $971 billion during the same period.

---

[44]CCAR Press Release, Federal Reserve, March 26, 2014.

That Federal Reserve expects this trend to continue. All but two of the 30 participants in the 2014 CCAR were expected to build capital from the second quarter of 2014 through the first quarter of 2015. In the aggregate, the firms were expected to distribute 40 percent less than their projected net income during the same period. The 30 institutions in CCAR 2014 have a combined $13.5 trillion in assets, or approximately 80 percent of all U.S. bank holding company assets.

Stress Testing in the European Union[45]

The European Banking Authority (EBA) released in April 2014 its methodology and macroeconomic scenarios for the 2014 EU-wide stress test. While the extensive process of banks' balance sheet repair was already underway, the test, designed to assess banks' resilience to hypothetical external shocks, was to identify remaining vulnerabilities in the EU banking sector and provide a high level of transparency into EU banks' exposures.

The EBA 2014 EU-wide stress test came in the midst of the process of repair of EU banks' balance sheets and followed asset quality reviews (AQRs) undertaken by various competent authorities in the EU. The EBA's common methodology was used by all EU supervisory authorities to ensure that the main EU banks were all assessed against common assumptions, definitions, and approaches. It was to allow for results that were comparable across the EU, shedding further light on the EU banking sector, and facilitating the work of supervisors. The EBA also released the macroeconomic scenarios developed by the European Systemic Risk Board (ESRB) that were used to assess the impact that changes in the economic environment have on EU banks. These were relevant to the entire EU single market and consistent throughout.

Key Features of the EU Methodology and the Scenario

The common methodology and underlying assumptions covered a wide range of risks including: credit and market risks, exposures towards securitization, and sovereign and funding risks. To ensure consistency, the methodology was restrictive and rested on a number of key constraints. These included a static balance sheet assumption, which precluded any defensive actions by banks; prescribed approaches to market risk and securitization; and a series of caps and floors on net interest income, risk-weighted assets, and net trading income.

Other key methodological components were: (i) a sovereign shock that impacts banks' entire balance sheets including exposures held in the available-for-sale portfolio (AFS) via the internationally agreed gradual phase-out of prudential filters, and (ii) a shock to banks' funding costs that pass through to the asset and liability side in a conservative asymmetric fashion.

The adverse scenario designed by the ESRB reflected the systemic risks that are currently assessed as representing the most pertinent threats to the stability of the EU banking sector: (i) an increase in global bond yields amplified by an abrupt reversal in risk as-

---

[45]Press Release: "EBA Publishes Common Methodology and Scenario for 2014 EU-Banks Stress Test," European Banking Authority, April 29, 2014.

sessment, especially towards emerging market economies; (ii) a further deterioration of credit quality in countries with feeble demand; (iii) stalling policy reforms jeopardizing confidence in the sustainability of public finances; and (iv) the lack of necessary bank balance sheet repair to maintain affordable market funding.

The negative impact of the shocks, which also included stress in the commercial real estate sector, as well as a foreign exchange shock in Central and Eastern Europe, was substantially global. In the European Union, the scenario led overall to a cumulative deviation of EU GDP from its baseline level by -2.2 percent in 2014, by -5.6 percent in 2015, and -7.0 percent in 2016. The EU unemployment was higher than its baseline level, after a 0.6 percentage–point spread in 2014. The figure was 1.9 percentage points higher in 2015 and 2.9 percentage points higher in 2016.

For most advanced economies, including Japan and the U.S., the scenario resulted in a negative response of GDP ranging between 5-6 percent in cumulative terms compared to the baseline.

Process of the EU Stress Test

The EU-wide stress test was conducted on a sample of 124 EU banks that covered at least 50 percent of each national banking sector, and was run at the highest level of consolidation. The running of the exercise involved close cooperation between the EBA and the competent authorities (CAs) at the national level, including the European Central Bank (ECB). The EBA was and continues to be responsible for coordinating the exercise in cooperation with the ECB—in the case of Single Supervisory Mechanism (SSM) countries—and ensuring effective cooperation between home and host supervisors. Most importantly, the EBA acts as a data hub for the extensive transparency of the results of the common exercise. On the other hand, CAs bear responsibility for overseeing the exercise with the banks, checking the quality of the results, and identifying and implementing any necessary supervisory reaction measure.

Stress Testing: A Concept for all Banks?

Yes. Banks of any size should run an internal stress test regularly. The scenarios are different, as institutions' balance sheets vary. Large international banks are under severe scrutiny by regulators and have developed stress tests that are disclosed on their investor relations websites.

Small and midsize banks across the world should also look at stress situations. Stress scenarios for those institutions should involve a deep recession, i.e., a large decline in GDP; the corresponding increase in unemployment; a drop in both stock and housing markets; and changes in interest rates, foreign exchange rates, and commodities, e.g., oil and gas.

Key Takeaways

- ▦ The Comprehensive Capital Analysis and Review (CCAR) is an annual exercise by the Federal Reserve in the United States to ensure that institutions have robust, forward-looking capital-planning processes that account for their unique risks and sufficient capital to continue operations throughout times of economic and financial stress. As part of the CCAR, the Federal Reserve evaluates institutions' capital adequacy, internal capital adequacy assessment processes, and their plans to make capital distributions, such as dividend payments or stock repurchases.

- Under CCAR, bank holding companies (BHCs) will be required to submit the results of company-run stress tests based on three Dodd-Frank Act supervisory stress test scenarios, at least one stressed scenario developed by the BHC, and a BHC baseline scenario.
- The European Banking Authority (EBA) released in April 2014 its methodology and macroeconomic scenarios for the 2014 EU-wide stress test. While the extensive process of banks' balance sheet repair was already underway, the test, designed to assess banks' resilience to hypothetical external shocks, was to identify remaining vulnerabilities in the EU banking sector and provide a high level of transparency into EU banks' exposures.
- All financial institutions—independent of size—should conduct regular stress tests.

Bank-Internal Stress Testing

In banking institutions, stress testing and scenario analysis programs are central to the monitoring of top and emerging risks. In addition to regulatory requirements, banks therefore conduct a range of group-wide stress testing scenarios including, but not limited to, a severe economic downturn; country, sector, and counterparty failures; and a variety of projected major operational risk events. The outcomes of the stress testing are used to assess the potential demand for capital under the various scenarios.

In addition to the suite of risk scenarios considered at group level, major subsidiaries of banks usually conduct regular macroeconomic and event-driven scenario analyses specific to their region and business.

Stress testing is used across risk categories such as market risk, liquidity and funding risk, and credit risk to evaluate the potential impact of stress scenarios on portfolio values, structural long-term funding positions, income, or capital.

Concentration Risk

Concentration risk is one of the main possible causes of major losses in a credit institution. Events during the 2008-2009 financial crises have brought to light many examples of risk concentrations within institutions. Given that it can jeopardize the survival of an institution, this risk type requires special attention by both risk managers and supervisors.

Risk concentrations refer to a loss potential resulting from an unbalanced distribution of dependencies on specific risk drivers and can occur within specific risk types (inter-risk concentrations). They are encountered within and across counterparties, businesses regions, countries, legal entities, industries, and products impacting the aforementioned risks. The management of risk concentrations is usually integrated into the management of the individual risk types and monitored on a regular basis. The key objectives of managing risk concentrations is to avoid any undue concentrations in a bank's portfolio, which risk managers endeavor to control through a quantitative and qualitative approach, as follows:

- Intra-risk concentrations refer to risk concentrations that may arise from interactions between different risk exposures within a single risk category. They are assessed and monitored by the individual risk disciplines (credit risk, market risk, operational risk). This is supported by limit-setting on different levels according to risk type.

- Inter-risk concentration refers to risk concentrations that may arise from interactions between different risk exposures across different risk categories. The interactions between the different risk exposures may stem from a common underlying risk driver or from interacting risk drivers. These risks are often managed by quantitative, top-down stress testing and qualitative, bottom-up reviews identifying and assessing risk themes independent of any risk type and providing a holistic view across banks.

Examples of Risk Concentration

Examples of Inter-Risk Concentration – Description of Events of the Subprime Crisis of 2007-2008

The crisis clearly showed how inter-risk concentrations may arise within financial institutions as risks and losses steeply increased because of single or interacting risk drivers. The interactions between the risk exposures and the difficulty of measuring and managing risks under these conditions can give rise to the rapid growth of unexpected risk positions and losses. What follows is a short abstract of some of these experiences:

Severe doubts about the credit quality of U.S. subprime mortgages, coupled with valuation difficulties and uncertainties about the adequacy of credit-rating-agency ratings led to a severe drop in investor demand. This left originators and structures with the inability to transfer assets to the securitization markets and unexpectedly concentrated exposures to assets whose values were sensitive to market variables, credit quality, and asset liquidity changes. Due to the uncertainties about the underlying quality of the collateral the asset-backed commercial paper (ABCP) markets also seized up. The freezing of the ABCP markets led to some funding difficulties for certain financial institutions, forcing some to draw on their liquidity lines and/or shorten the maturity of their debt. These concentrated funding exposures to short-term horizons increased the fragility of the liquidity position. Large (sponsoring) institutions were faced with a build-up of exposures to structured credit assets and further pressure on liquidity positions. The increase in risk aversion, the steep rises in some reference interest rates, and credit and liquidity hoarding led to forced asset sales and subsequently to severe price decreases in multiple asset classes (equity, traded credit, corporate bonds, etc.). These falls in asset values often provoked additional collateral requirements leading to further deterioration in the liquidity situation of the credit institutions. This general liquidity squeeze, the uncertainties about the institutions' own contingent exposures, and heightened counterparty risk concerns brought the inter-bank market to a standstill. Hedging the credit and market risks proved extremely hard under these conditions and often less effective than expected, rendering the exposures to those risks much higher (basis risk). Through the losses and downgrading of the monoline insurance companies, the issue of (indirect) counterparty risk suddenly attracted much more attention, again, as hedges proved ineffective. Given the generally declining markets the number of litigation cases rose strongly. In addition institutions faced with, for instance, rogue trades found it much harder to close those positions without incurring severe losses.

Examples of Inter-Risk Concentration

- **Credit – liquidity risk:** failure of material counterparties impairs an institution's cash flow and its ability to meet commitments.
- **Credit – market risk:** where counterparties may be closely related, or the same, or where unsystematic or undiversifiable risk is considered. (Undiversifiable risk is the part of the market risk that derives not from general price movements but from specific ones due to, for example, changes in the perception of the inherent credit risk of an issuer.) The worsening credit quality of an issuer can be the source of inter-risk concentration between market risk and credit risk. This, for example, would be the case where an institution has given a loan or granted a credit facility in addition to investing in the equity of the same company. All these positions will be adversely affected by a deteriorating credit quality. Therefore the different types of risks cannot be measured independently and the risks cannot be seen as uncorrelated. This confirms the necessity for the adequate management of inter-risk concentrations.
- **Credit – operational risk:** exposure to credit risk may be related to potential operational risk drivers, or the credit quality of risk mitigants (e.g., insurance purchased) may affect the adequacy of operational risk buffers.
- **Market – liquidity risk:** interruptions, increased volatility, rapid changes in value, or the drying up of markets for certain instruments may negatively affect the liquidity of a given institution.

Market Risk Concentration and Inter-Risk Concentration Based on the Credit Quality of the Issuer as Risk Driver

The credit quality of an issuer is an example of a single risk driver that affects different types of risks and leads to market risk concentration. Deterioration of an issuer's credit-worthiness has a negative impact on its share price as well as on the prices of its bonds and it influences the prices of corresponding derivatives. The equity trading desk of an institution could have bought equity, the fixed-income desk bonds, and the derivatives desk could have sold credit protection on the same issuer. Since the prices of all instruments are dependent on the same risk driver, the correlations between these different instrument types are very high. This risk concentration should be taken into account because otherwise the risk situation would not be reflected correctly.

Market Risk Concentration and Inter-Risk Concentration Based on the Risk Aversion of Market Participants

Another cause of a market risk concentration is a change in the risk preference of market participants. Greater uncertainty about the economic outlook could lead to reluctance to buy risky positions. Risk premiums on all risky products will rise and their prices will fall. This increases the correlations between different asset classes. Some markets will possibly even dry up completely because market participants are no longer willing to buy those products. An institution, although holding a diversified portfolio, will suffer losses on all types of instruments. This risk concentration caused by a change in the risk premium and the accompanying change in correlations ("correlation breakdown") should be included in the risk management of an institution.

The rise in the risk premium could also be the source of an inter-risk concentration between market risk and liquidity risk. An institution can generate less liquidity by selling assets because of the lower prices. It is possible that some assets cannot be sold at acceptable prices if the markets are illiquid as a consequence of market participants' risk aversion. In addition the issuance of debt or equity is more expensive because the institution has to pay a higher risk premium itself. Here again the connection between different risk types demands appropriate management of risk concentrations.

Inter-Risk Concentration between Market Risk and Credit Risk Based on the FX Rate

Lending in foreign currency to domestic borrowers is exposed to both market (FX rate) and credit risk. When the domestic currency depreciates, the value of the loan in the domestic currency increases, which (by increasing the cost of installments) may reduce the ability of borrowers to repay. This effect becomes fairly non-linear at higher depreciation rates.

Examples of Inter-Relationships between Liquidity and Other Risk Factors

The institution's overall exposure to other risks and their possible influence on the level of liquidity risk should be analyzed in conjunction with the institution's funding profile.

Interrelationships between liquidity risk and other risks driven by the same factors can occur especially in times of stressed market conditions. Such dependencies can strengthen the effect of concentrations that exist in liquidity risk. Examples of such interrelationships may comprise:

- **Own-credit – liquidity risk:** a deterioration in market prices or a downgrade of a counterparty could trigger a margin call or lead to the obligation to deliver additional collateral;
- **Reputational – liquidity risk:** reputational difficulties may lead to a loss of trust in the institution on the part of counterparties and as a consequence a reduction in funds available to the institution, as well as to the withdrawal of funds;
- **Reputational – liquidity risk:** in order to maintain a good reputation and to avoid adverse market perceptions, institutions may wish to provide funding support to associated parties, even if not contractually obliged to, which leads to a deterioration in their liquidity position;

- **Operational – liquidity risk:** interruptions in the payment or settlement process may result in liquidity problems;
- **Legal – liquidity risk:** potential errors or inaccuracies existing in legal arrangements may make it impossible to enforce the fulfillment of counterparty contracts to provide financing. It may particularly threaten the liquidity of an institution if shortcomings exist in arrangements regarding contingency financing for times of market stress.

Credit Risk to Single Customers

Banks should manage large exposures for single customers—usually large multinational corporations or systemically important financial institutions (SIFIs)—very carefully, employing all modern risk management tools and techniques:

- **Modern rating tools / risk methodologies,** i.e., exposure at defaults (EADs), probability of defaults (PDs), and loss given defaults (LGDs);
- **Apply stringent limits,** which should be linked to the bank's risk strategy and risk appetite statements;
- Use **modern risk mitigation tools,** i.e., netting agreements, collateral agreements, covenants;
- **Actively manage/hedge risk** by buying protection in the derivatives markets, i.e., credit default swaps.

Industry Sector Risk

Banks are often heavily exposed to certain industry sectors, following the structure of their economies. For example, it is crucial for German banks to measure the impact of a downturn in the automobile industry on their respective solvencies. This is, of course, motivated by the important role the automobile industry plays in the German economy and its close ties to other industry sectors.

Regional Risk

Previous to the start of the financial crisis, foreclosure rates in the U.S. real estate / housing markets were very low (below 1 percent). The housing market in the U.S. was booming and eventually overheated, especially in certain U.S. states. A number of banks, e.g., Countrywide Financial (today part of Bank of America) and Washington Mutual (today part of JPMorgan Chase), had significant exposures in the housing market, especially in those states with significant levels of "underwater" mortgages. During the crisis, many mortgage holders found themselves underwater; that is, owing more than their homes were worth. Negative equity is an important predicator of default. When a borrower has negative equity, unemployment acts as a major catalyst, increasing the probability of default massively.

Figure 23.1 illustrates that levels of underwater mortgages have been quite uneven across regions in the United States. Levels were extremely high, for example, in Arizona, California, Florida, Michigan, and Nevada.

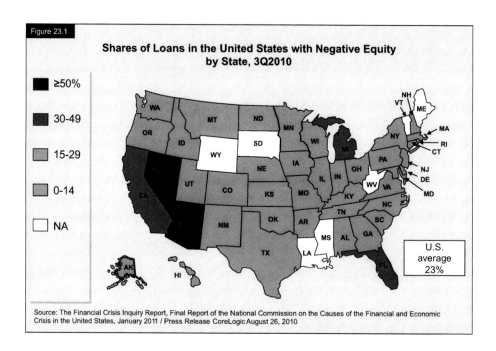

Figure 23.1

Shares of Loans in the United States with Negative Equity by State, 3Q2010

Source: The Financial Crisis Inquiry Report, Final Report of the National Commission on the Causes of the Financial and Economic Crisis in the United States, January 2011 / Press Release CoreLogic August 26, 2010

Sovereign Risk

Many banks have specialist arms for public finance business, sometimes linked with commercial real estate financing.

The public finance division of a large bank usually covers:

- Conventional public sector lending, i.e., central governments, states, and municipalities, or borrowers guaranteed by these;
- Financing and consulting for public-private partnership projects;
- Pfandbrief[46] refinancing and covered pool management.

Previous to the financial crisis, a number of banks had built up significant public exposures. European institutions had large exposures in the so-called GIIPS countries (Greece, Ireland, Italy, Portugal, Spain), which led to significant impairments later. Figure 23.2 illustrates how one institution, Deutsche Bank, has increased its efforts to reduce the bank's sovereign risk after the crisis; this effort is rather representative for other banks active in this particular business.

---

[46]The Pfandbrief is a debt security backed by cash flows from mortgages or public sector loans.

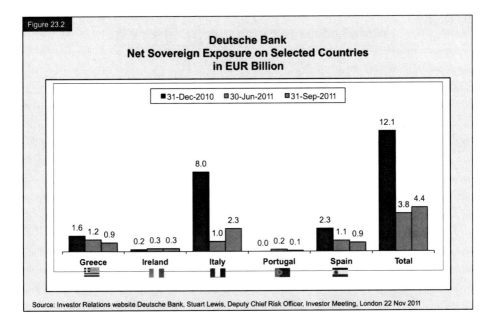

Figure 23.2

Deutsche Bank
Net Sovereign Exposure on Selected Countries
in EUR Billion

Source: Investor Relations website Deutsche Bank, Stuart Lewis, Deputy Chief Risk Officer, Investor Meeting, London 22 Nov 2011

Why Run Bank-Internal Stress Tests?

Institutions of all sizes should run bank-internal stress tests, specific to the exact portfolio composition and strategy of the institution. Banks must run regulatory stress tests, if so required; furthermore, banks should follow stress testing principles and guidelines as described in Chapter 21.

The difficulty with bank-internal stress tests is that they must be designed as individually as the institution itself, depending on the franchise set-up and the exact portfolio composition.

Systemically Important Financial Institutions (SIFIs)

Large international banks with commercial banking and investment banking activities need to consider a large variety of parameters and macroeconomic factors, both domestic and international. These include a large variety of indicators, mainly:

- Key economic drivers such as GDP, unemployment, consumer confidence, and inflation;
- Interest rates and related sovereign and corporate bond yields;
- Exchange rates;
- Family housing / real estate indices;
- Stock markets; and
- Commodity markets.

Further, SIFIs need to consider other issues that may influence the global economy and markets and test their resilience:

Table 23.1	World Economic Forum / Global Risks 2013

Economic risks

- Another major systemic financial failure
- Recurring liquidity crisis
- Chronic fiscal imbalances
- Fiscal crisis
- Slowing economy / recession in major economies
- Hard landing or slowing of an emerging economy
- Severe income disparity
- Chronic labor market imbalances
- Asset price collapse
- Oil price shock or spike
- Retrenchment from globalization
- Extreme volatility in energy and food prices

Environmental risks

- Rising greenhouse gas emissions
- Meteorological/climatological/hydrological catastrophes

Geopolitical risks

- War
- Terrorism
- Critical fragile states
- Regional instability
- Corruption
- Global governance gaps

Societal risks

- Rising religious fanaticism
- Mismanagement of population aging
- Unsustainable population growth
- Unmanaged migration
- Food shortage crisis
- Water supply crisis
- Pandemics / chronic disease

Technological risks

- Cyber attacks
- Massive incident of data fraud / theft
- Massive digital misinformation

Of course, the assessment of global risks listed in Table 23.1 creates tremendous challenges for institutions / risk managers world-wide:

▓ The understanding of those risks is challenging by itself and requires significant human resources, i.e., research analysts with experience and know-how;

▓ To derive an outcome where impacts and likelihood are derived is further challenging;

▓ As the world is complex, there are significant interdependencies between the individual risk types;

▓ And, most importantly for banks, the scenarios need to be linked into bank specific parameters, i.e., probability of defaults (PDs) and their impact on capital, liquidity and funding, asset quality, and net income.

Table 23.2 illustrates HSBC's group stress scenario assumptions as specified in the 2012 annual report. While such scenarios are certainly relevant for some other SIFIs, they may not apply to other banks.

Table 23.2	**HSBC Stress Scenario Assumptions**[48]	
Scenario	**Mild scenario assumptions**	**Severe scenario assumptions**
Assumptions	• The situation in Greece worsens and there is an orderly default in Greece;	• A disorderly default in Greece, where the Eurozone governments are unable to ring-fence peripheral countries and their banks;
	• Greek banks also default and, with support from the EU and the International Monetary Fund, are bailed out;	• Default of Portugal and Ireland with increases in bond yields for high debt countries;
	• Increasing bond yields in Portugal, Ireland, Spain, and Italy trigger further fiscal austerity measures, and governments strive to disassociate their countries from Greece;	• The ensuing credit crunch together with declining business and consumer confidence more than offset any relief gained from the depreciation of the euro;
	• Through financial and trade linkages, an orderly default in Greece results in the spread of contagion to the rest of the world;	• Investors become increasingly uncomfortable with the U.S. and the UK's fiscal positions, with the severe scenario resulting in a global slowdown; and
	• The UK, U.S., and emerging markets are adversely affected, albeit to varying degrees; and	• Emerging economies are less affected by the financial shock.
	• Slower global demand curbs growth and increases the risk premium on interest rates as well as commodity prices.	

As already mentioned in the liquidity chapters in Part 6, stress testing needs to be looked at from the liquidity and funding side.

---

[48]HSBC Holdings plc, Annual Report and Accounts 2012.

Regional and Community Banks

Regional banks and community banks continue to play an important role in many economies, i.e., the United States and the European Union, especially in Germany.

As former Federal Reserve Chairman Ben S. Bernanke said: "Community banks remain a critical component of our financial system and our economy. They help keep their local economies vibrant and growing by taking on and managing the risks of local lending, which larger banks may be unwilling or unable to do. They often respond with greater agility to lending requests than their national competitors because of their detailed knowledge of the needs of their customers and their close ties to the communities they serve."[49]

Community banks face difficult challenges, e.g., competition with larger banks (pricing advantage of larger institutions due to large scale), specialization (i.e., commercial real estate), and diversification of revenue sources and risk.

Like larger banks, community banks are also being affected by the state of the national economy. However, balance sheets—and therefore risks—of smaller and mid-size banks are less complex than those of large bank holding companies or even global systemically important financial institutions (G-SIFIs). For most regional and community banks, the loan book is by far the biggest risk. Naturally, institutions' close ties to local economies are, on balance, a source of strength, but a drawback of those ties is that the fortunes of communities and their banks tend to rise and fall together. This particular issue must be the main driver in defining stress scenarios.

Figure 23.3 illustrates the loan book of First Midwest Bancorp Inc., an Itasca, Illinois,[50] headquartered bank with a balance sheet of $8.25 billion as of December 31, 2013. The bank operates from almost 100 Midwest locations across Illinois, northwest Indiana, and eastern Iowa. Its loan business breaks down into five major elements:

- Commercial and industrial loans (32.8 percent of total loans);
- Agricultural loans (5.8 percent);
- Commercial real estate (48.0 percent);
- Family mortgages (4.9 percent);
- Consumer loans (8.5 percent).

Obviously, stress testing the loan book in regional/community banks must focus on key parameters / economic indicators for that particular region/community and mainly include:

- Real GDP, GDP growth;
- Disposable income;
- Unemployment;
- Interest rates / mortgage rates;
- House price index;
- Commercial real estate price index.

The stress scenarios then need to be translated into corporate insolvency rates, personal bankruptcies, foreclosures, and impact on the main credit parameters of exposure at default, probability of default, and loss given default.

---

[49]From a Bernanke speech at the Independent Community Bankers of America National Convention and Techworld, Nashville, Tennessee, March 14, 2012.
[50]A suburb of Chicago, Illinois

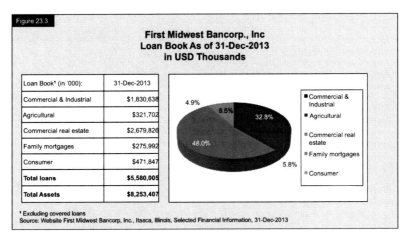

Figure 23.3

First Midwest Bancorp., Inc
Loan Book As of 31-Dec-2013
in USD Thousands

Loan Book¹ (in '000):	31-Dec-2013
Commercial & Industrial	$1,830,638
Agricultural	$321,702
Commercial real estate	$2,679,826
Family mortgages	$275,992
Consumer	$471,847
Total loans	**$5,580,005**
Total Assets	**$8,253,407**

¹ Excluding covered loans
Source: Website First Midwest Bancorp, Inc., Itasca, Illinois, Selected Financial Information, 31-Dec-2013

In addition, regional and community banks need to apply stress testing from a liquidity perspective and consider positions in money market / capital market products.

Specialized Institutions

Specialized banks are institutions with a specific expertise and experience. In order to cater to the wide customer needs, the offerings span quite wide and include foreign exchange banks, industrial banks, development banks, export-import banks, and specialized-asset institutions such as shipping financing houses. These banks provide financial services in their core business to industries, corporations, heavy turnkey projects, and foreign trade. Of course, specialized business can also be part of a large banking group, i.e., as a division. Let's explore one example:

Figure 23.4 illustrates HSH Nordbank's shipping portfolio, which had a default risk of €24.6 billion (€9.4 billion thereof defined as in the restructuring unit, i.e., non-core business), broken down by segment and geography.[51]

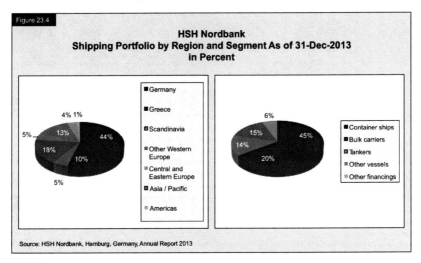

Figure 23.4

HSH Nordbank
Shipping Portfolio by Region and Segment As of 31-Dec-2013
in Percent

Source: HSH Nordbank, Hamburg, Germany, Annual Report 2013

---

[51]HSH Nordbank, Hamburg, Germany, Annual Report 2013, page 89.

The global shipping industry is one of the biggest industries of today's times. Its risk analysis, and stress testing in particular, needs to consider the following specialized indicators in addition to some of the global indicators (Table 23.1) as discussed above:

- Number of vessels on the ocean (supply);
- OPEC[52] production levels (demand);
- Other goods shipped (demand);
- Supply-demand relationship and its effect on charter rates and prices for containers, i.e., twenty-foot equivalent unit.

TEU

The twenty-foot equivalent unit (often TEU or teu) is an inexact unit of cargo capacity often used to describe the capacity of container ships and container terminals. It is based on the volume of a 20-foot-long (6.1 m) intermodal container, a standard-sized metal box which can be easily transferred between different modes of transportation, such as ships, trains, and trucks.[53]

Modeling Stress Scenarios – What All Banks Should Do

It is essential to involve senior management and obtain buy-in for the scenarios from decision makers. All scenarios should be discussed at risk committee and/or management board levels and should be disclosed to non-executive directors and supervisors.

Figure 23.5 illustrates a modeling path for stress scenarios that can be applied by banks of all sizes. The starting point is the institution's identification of major risk driv-

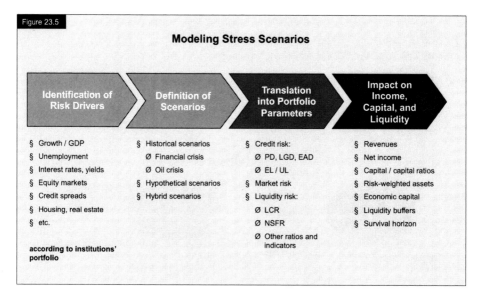

Figure 23.5

Modeling Stress Scenarios

Identification of Risk Drivers	Definition of Scenarios	Translation into Portfolio Parameters	Impact on Income, Capital, and Liquidity
§ Growth / GDP	§ Historical scenarios	§ Credit risk:	§ Revenues
§ Unemployment	Ø Financial crisis	Ø PD, LGD, EAD	§ Net income
§ Interest rates, yields	Ø Oil crisis	Ø EL / UL	§ Capital / capital ratios
§ Equity markets	§ Hypothetical scenarios	§ Market risk	§ Risk-weighted assets
§ Credit spreads	§ Hybrid scenarios	§ Liquidity risk:	§ Economic capital
§ Housing, real estate		Ø LCR	§ Liquidity buffers
§ etc.		Ø NSFR	§ Survival horizon
		Ø Other ratios and indicators	
according to institutions' portfolio			

---

[52]Organization of the Petroleum Exporting Countries.
[53]Wikipedia

ers as described above, i.e., the economy itself (GDP) and unemployment rates. These depend largely on the bank's balance sheet and risk profile. The next step is the definition of the relevant scenarios, i.e., unemployment up from current levels of x_{to} to the level of x_{t+n} over a given time period t. Scenarios used by banks are often historical, hypothetical, or a hybrid of both. Probably the biggest challenge is the transformation of the defined scenarios into the relevant bank parameters, which must link into the management "dashboard". For most banks, credit risk and liquidity risk are the most imminent risk types. However, banks must not forget market risk and should never underestimate or even ignore operational risk. The last step is running the scenario / calculating the impact on the bank's key risk and performance indicators, i.e., net income and capital.

How Often to Run Stress Tests

Stress tests should be run regularly but not too often. After all, stress scenarios must have—by default—low probabilities and impacts. If scenarios are reported too often, a Cassandra effect will take place and this powerful risk management tool is wasted.

Cassandra

From ancient Greek myth, Cassandra was the daughter of King Priam of Troy. She was given the gift of prophecy but once she spurned Apollo's love, she was cursed to have no one ever believe her. She foretold the fall of Troy and knew the Trojan Horse contained Greek soldiers, but no one heeded her words.

Wikipedia describes the Cassandra effect as "when a person believes he or she knows the future happening of a catastrophic event, having already seen it in some way, or even experienced it first hand; however, the person knows there is nothing that can be done to stop the event from happening and that nobody will believe it even if he or she tries to tell others. For example, in finance, the more you warn your colleagues about the tail risks—the rare but devastating events that can bring the bank down—the more they roll their eyes, give a yawn, and change the subject. This eventually leads to self-censorship."[54]

Key Takeaways

- Banks of all sizes should run stress tests on a regular basis.
- Concentration risks are those risks that could have catastrophic consequences in a stress situation. Institutions must define and manage concentration risk and closely link it to stress testing.
- When managing concentrations, banks should look at both intra-risk and inter-risk concentrations.
- Stress testing is a unique exercise that needs to be defined by each institution individually, taking the balance sheet composition and risk profile into account.
- Banks should model stress scenarios—indentify risk drivers, define scenarios, translate those into the key bank parameters—and generate the impact on capital, net income, and liquidity.

---

[54]Wikipedia

Governance and Risk Management

Corporate Governance

The Financial Crisis Inquiry Report in the United States[55] concluded that dramatic failures of corporate governance and risk management at many systemically important financial institutions (SIFIs) were a key cause of the financial crisis. For example:

- "Institutions acted recklessly, taking on too much risk, with too little capital, and with too much dependence on short-term funding."
- "Particularly the large investment banks and bank holding companies focused their activities increasingly on risky trading activities that produced hefty profits."
- "Compensation systems…too often rewarded the quick deal, the short-term gain."
- "Our examination revealed stunning instances of governance breakdowns and irresponsibility."

Ethical behavior in many large financial firms simply collapsed; in fact, any sense of fiduciary responsibility to the ultimate client faded or even completely disappeared.

Of course, ethical behavior alone does not guarantee success, i.e., net profits and subsequently distributions to shareholders, management, and staff. However, ethical behavior ensures that firms will obey the law, treat employees respectfully, be honest in public disclosures, honor commitments, be good citizens in the communities where they operate, and so on. But when a corporation, or an entire industry, behaves badly, we have no idea what to expect. The fact is, financial firms, much more than other firms, live and die on trust.

In the *Harvard Business Review*,[56] Max H. Bazerman and Ann E. Tenbrunsel write: "The vast majority of managers mean to run ethical organizations, yet corporate corruption is widespread. Part of the problem, of course, is that some leaders are out-and-out crooks, and they direct the malfeasance from the top. But that is rare. Much more often, we believe, employees bend or break ethics rules because those in charge are blind to unethical behavior and may even unknowingly encourage it."

OECD Principles of Corporate Governance of 2004

The OECD Principles of Corporate Governance were originally developed in response to a call by the Organization for Economic Co-Operation and Development (OECD) Council Meeting at Ministerial Level in April 1998 to develop—in conjunction with national gov-

---

[55]"The Financial Crisis Inquiry Report, Final Report of the National Commission on the Causes of the Financial and Economic Crisis in the United States," January 2011.
[56]"Ethical Breakdowns," Harvard Business Review, April 2011.

ernments, other relevant international organizations, and the private sector—a set of corporate governance standards and guidelines. Since the principles were agreed to in 1999, they have formed the basis for corporate governance initiatives in both OECD and non-OECD countries alike (Figure 24.1 shows the OECD member countries).

Moreover, they have been adopted as one of the 12 Key Standards for Sound Financial Systems by the Financial Stability Forum. Accordingly, they form the basis of the corporate governance component of the World Bank / International Monetary Fund (IMF) Reports on the Observance of Standards and Codes (ROSC).

The OECD Council Meeting at Ministerial Level in 2002 agreed to survey developments in OECD countries and to assess the principles in light of developments in corporate governance. This task was entrusted to the OECD Steering Group on Corporate Governance, which comprised representatives from OECD countries. In addition, the World Bank, the Bank for International Settlements (BIS), and the International Monetary Fund were observers to the group. For the assessment, the steering group also invited the Financial Stability Forum, the Basel Committee, and the International Organization of Securities Commissions (IOSCO) as ad hoc observers.

The principles focused on the following key issues:

- Ensuring the basis for an effective corporate governance framework;
- The rights of shareholders and key ownership functions;
- The equitable treatment of shareholders;
- The role of stakeholders;
- Disclosure and transparency;
- The responsibilities of the board.

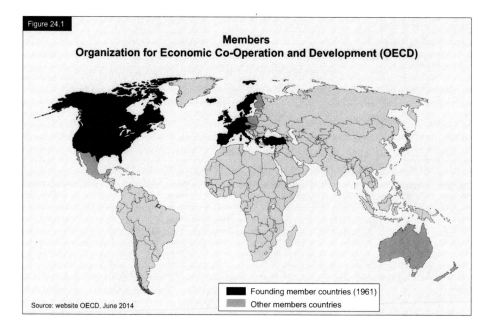

Figure 24.1

**Members
Organization for Economic Co-Operation and Development (OECD)**

Founding member countries (1961)
Other members countries

Source: website OECD, June 2014

Consequently, members developed individual governance codes—in general based on the OECD requirements—in their respective countries. Examples include the United Kingdom Corporate Governance Code, a set of principles of good corporate governance aimed at companies listed on the London Stock Exchange or the Deutscher Corporate Governance Kodex in Germany.

BIS Principles for Enhancing Corporate Governance

Sadly, the financial industry—in particular the large international banks and investment banks—relies on the regulatory community, in particular the BIS, to define appropriate governance standards. As a result of the financial crisis, the Basel Committee therefore published its "Principles for Enhancing Corporate Governance" in October 2010. Naturally, the committee's guidance drew largely from principles of corporate governance that were published in 2004 by the OECD.

From a banking industry perspective, corporate governance involves the allocation of authority and responsibilities, i.e., the manner in which the business and affairs of a bank are governed by its board and senior management, including how they:

- Set the bank's strategy and objectives;
- Determine the bank's risk tolerance/appetite;
- Operate the bank's business on a day-to-day basis;
- Protect the interests of depositors, meet shareholder obligations, and take into account the interests of other recognized stakeholders; and
- Align corporate activities and behavior with the expectation that the bank will operate in a safe and sound manner, with integrity and in compliance with applicable laws and regulations.

A. Board Practices / Board's Overall Responsibilities

Principle 1

The board has overall responsibility for the bank, including approving and overseeing the implementation of the bank's strategic objectives, risk strategy, corporate governance, and corporate values. The board is also responsible for providing oversight of senior management.

Of course, the board has ultimate responsibility for the bank's business, risk strategy, and financial soundness, as well as for how the bank organizes and governs itself. Accordingly, the board must:

- Approve and monitor the overall business strategy of the bank, taking into account the bank's long-term financial interests, its exposure to risk, and its ability to manage risk effectively; and
- Approve and oversee the implementation of the bank's overall risk strategy (including its risk tolerance/appetite); its policies for risk, risk management, and compliance; its internal controls system; the corporate governance framework, principles, and corporate values (including a code of conduct or comparable document); and the compensation system.

A demonstrated corporate culture that supports and provides appropriate norms and incentives for professional and responsible behavior is an essential foundation of good governance. In this regard, the board should take the lead in establishing the "tone at the top" and in setting professional standards and corporate values that promote integrity for itself, senior management, and other employees. A bank's code of conduct, or comparable policy, should articulate acceptable and unacceptable behaviors. It is especially important that such a policy clearly disallows behavior that could result in the bank engaging in any improper or illegal activity, such as financial misreporting, money laundering, fraud, bribery, or corruption. It should also discourage the taking of excessive risks as defined by internal corporate policy.

Further, the bank's corporate values should recognize the critical importance of timely and frank discussion and elevation of problems/risks to higher levels within the organization. In this regard, employees should be encouraged and able to communicate, with protection from reprisal, legitimate concerns about illegal, unethical, or questionable practices.

Oversight of Senior Management

The board should select and, when necessary, replace senior management and have in place an appropriate plan for succession. The board should provide oversight of senior management as part of the bank's checks and balances. In doing so the board should:

- Monitor that senior management's actions are consistent with the strategy and policies approved by the board, including the risk tolerance/appetite;
- Meet regularly with senior management;
- Question and review critically explanations and information provided by senior management;
- Set formal performance standards for senior management consistent with the long-term objectives, strategy, and financial soundness of the bank, and monitor senior management's performance against these standards; and
- Ensure that senior management's knowledge and expertise remain appropriate given the nature of the business and the bank's risk profile.

Board Qualifications

Principle 2

Board members should be and remain qualified, including through training, for their positions. They should have a clear understanding of their role in corporate governance and be able to exercise sound and objective judgment about the affairs of the bank.

The board should possess, both as individual board members and collectively, appropriate experience, competencies, and personal qualities, including professionalism and personal integrity.

Board's Own Practices and Structures

> *Principle 3*
>
> *The board should define appropriate governance practices for its own work and have in place the means to ensure that such practices are followed and periodically reviewed for ongoing improvement.*

The board should exemplify through its own practices sound governance principles. These practices help the board carry out its duties more effectively. At the same time, they send important signals internally and externally about the kind of enterprise the bank aims to be.

The board should maintain, and periodically update, organizational rules, by-laws, or other similar documents setting out its organization, rights, responsibilities, and key activities.

The board should structure itself in a way—including in terms of size, frequency of meetings, and the use of committees—that promotes efficiency; sufficiently deep review of matters; and robust, critical challenge and discussion of issues.

To support board performance, it is a good practice for the board to carry out regular assessments of both the board as a whole and of individual board members. Assistance from external facilitators in carrying out board assessments can contribute to the objectivity of the process. Where the board has serious reservations about the performance or integrity of a board member, the board should take appropriate actions. Either separately or as part of these assessments, the board should periodically review the effectiveness of its own governance practices and procedures, determine where improvements may be needed, and make any necessary changes.

Role of the Chair

The chair of the board plays a crucial role in the proper functioning of the board. He or she provides leadership to the board and is responsible for the board's effective overall functioning, including maintaining a relationship of trust with board members. The chair should possess the requisite experience, competencies, and personal qualities in order to fulfill these responsibilities.

The chair should ensure that board decisions are taken on a sound and well-informed basis. He or she should encourage and promote critical discussion and ensure that dissenting views can be expressed and discussed within the decision-making process.

To achieve appropriate checks and balances, an increasing number of banks require the chair of the board to be a non-executive, except where otherwise required by law. Where a bank does not have this separation and particularly where the roles of the chair of the board and chief executive officer (CEO) are vested in the same person, it is important for the bank to have measures in place to minimize the impact on the bank's checks and balances of such a situation (such as, for example, by having a lead board member, senior independent board member, or a similar position).

Board Committees

To increase efficiency and allow deeper focus in specific areas, boards in many jurisdictions establish certain specialized board committees. The number and nature of committees depends on many factors, including the size of the bank and its board, the nature of the business areas of the bank, and its risk profile.

Each committee should have a charter or other instrument that sets out its mandate, scope, and working procedures. In the interest of greater transparency and accountability, a board should disclose the committees it has established, their mandates, and their composition (including members who are considered to be independent). To avoid undue concentration of power and to promote fresh perspectives, it may be useful to consider occasional rotation of membership and chairmanship of such committees, provided that doing so does not impair the collective skills, experience, and effectiveness of these committees.

Committees should maintain appropriate records (e.g., meeting minutes or summary of matters reviewed and decisions taken) of their deliberations and decisions. Such records should document the committees' fulfillment of their responsibilities and help in the assessment by those responsible for the control functions or the supervisor of the effectiveness of these committees.

1. Audit Committee

Banks, in particular large banks and internationally active banks, must have an audit committee or equivalent. Typically, the audit committee is responsible for the financial reporting process; providing oversight of the bank's internal and external auditors; approving, or recommending to the board or shareholders for their approval, the appointment, compensation, and dismissal of external auditors; reviewing and approving the audit scope and frequency; receiving key audit reports; and ensuring that senior management is taking necessary corrective actions in a timely manner to address control weaknesses, and non-compliance with policies, laws and regulations, and other problems identified by auditors. In addition, the audit committee should oversee the establishment of accounting policies and practices by the bank.

2. Risk Committee

It is also appropriate for many banks, especially large banks and internationally active banks, to have a board-level risk committee or equivalent that is responsible for advising the board on the bank's overall current and future risk tolerance/appetite and strategy, and for overseeing senior management's implementation of that strategy. This should include strategies for capital and liquidity management, as well as for credit, market, operational, compliance, reputational, and other risks of the bank. To enhance the effectiveness of the risk committee, it should receive formal and informal communication from the bank's risk management function and chief risk officer (CRO) and should, where appropriate, have access to external expert advice, particularly in relation to proposed strategic transactions, such as mergers and acquisitions.

3. Compensation Committee

The compensation committee oversees the compensation system's design and operation, and ensures that compensation is appropriate and consistent with the bank's culture, long-term business and risk strategy, and performance and control environment, as well as with any legal or regulatory requirements.

4. Nominations / Human Resources / Governance Committee

The nominations / human resources / governance committee provides recommendations to the board for new board members and members of senior management; may be involved in assessment of board and senior management effectiveness; and may be involved in overseeing the bank's personnel or human resource policies.

5. Ethics/Compliance Committee

The ethics/compliance committee focuses on ensuring that the bank has the appropriate means for promoting proper decision-making and compliance with laws, regulations, and internal rules; and provides oversight of the compliance function.

Conflicts of Interest

Conflicts of interest may arise as a result of the various activities and roles of the bank (e.g., where the bank extends loans to a firm while its proprietary trading function buys and sells securities issued by that firm), or between the interests of the bank or its customers and those of the bank's board members or senior managers (e.g., where the bank enters into a business relationship with an entity in which one of the bank's board members has a financial interest). Conflicts of interest may also arise when a bank is part of a broader group. For example, where the bank is part of a group, the flow of information and reporting lines between the bank, its parent company, and/or other subsidiaries can lead to the emergence of conflicts (e.g., sharing of potential proprietary, confidential, or otherwise sensitive information from different entities). The board should ensure that policies to identify potential conflicts of interest are developed and implemented and, if these conflicts cannot be prevented, are appropriately managed (based on the permissibility of relationships or transactions under sound corporate policies consistent with national law and supervisory standards).

The board should have a formal, written conflicts-of-interest policy and an objective compliance process for implementing the policy. The policy should include:

- A member's duty to avoid to the extent possible activities that could create conflicts of interest or the appearance of conflicts of interest;
- A review or approval process for members to follow before they engage in certain activities (such as serving on another board) so as to ensure that such activity will not create a conflict of interest;
- A member's duty to disclose any matter that may result, or has already resulted, in a conflict of interest;
- A member's responsibility to abstain from voting on any matter where the member may have a conflict of interest or where the member's objectivity or ability to properly fulfill duties to the bank may be otherwise compromised;
- Adequate procedures for transactions with related parties to be made on an arms-length basis; and
- The way in which the board will deal with any non-compliance with the policy.

Controlling Shareholders

Where there are controlling shareholders with power to appoint board members, the board should exercise corresponding caution. In such cases, it is useful to bear in mind that the board members have responsibilities to the bank itself, regardless of who appoints them. In cases where there are board members appointed by a controlling shareholder, the board may wish to set out specific procedures or conduct periodic reviews to ensure the appropriate discharge of responsibilities by all board members.

Group Structures

Principle 4

In a group structure, the board of the parent company has the overall responsibility for adequate corporate governance across the group and ensuring that there are governance policies and mechanisms appropriate to the structure, business, and risks of the group, and its entities.

Board of Parent Company

In the discharge of its corporate governance responsibilities, the board of the parent company should be aware of the material risks and issues that might affect both the bank as a whole and its subsidiaries. It should therefore exercise adequate oversight over subsidiaries, while respecting the independent legal and governance responsibilities that might apply to regulated subsidiary boards.

In order to fulfill its corporate governance responsibilities, the board of the parent company should:

- Establish a governance structure that contributes to the effective oversight of subsidiaries and that takes into account the nature, scale, and complexity of the different risks to which the group and its subsidiaries are exposed;
- Assess the governance structure periodically to ensure that it remains appropriate in light of growth, increased complexity, geographic expansion, etc;
- Approve a corporate governance policy at the group level for its subsidiaries that includes the commitment to meet all applicable governance requirements;
- Ensure that enough resources are available for each subsidiary to meet both group standards and local governance standards;
- Understand the roles and relationships of subsidiaries to one another and to the parent company; and
- Have appropriate means to monitor that each subsidiary complies with all applicable governance requirements.

Board of a Regulated Subsidiary

In general, the board of a regulated banking subsidiary should adhere to the corporate values and governance principles espoused by its parent company. In doing so the board should take into account the nature of the business of the subsidiary and the legal requirements that are applicable.

The board of a regulated banking subsidiary should retain and set its own corporate governance responsibilities, and should evaluate any group-level decisions or practices to ensure that they do not put the regulated subsidiary in breach of applicable legal or regulatory provisions or prudential rules.

The board of the regulated banking subsidiary should also ensure that such decisions or practices are not detrimental to:

- The sound and prudent management of the subsidiary;
- The financial health of the subsidiary; or
- The legal interests of the subsidiary's stakeholders.

B. Senior Management

Principle 5

Under the direction of the board, senior management should ensure that the bank's activities are consistent with the business strategy, risk tolerance/appetite, and policies approved by the board.

Senior management consists of a core group of individuals who are responsible and should be held accountable for overseeing the day-to-day management of the bank. These individuals should have the necessary experience, competencies, and integrity to manage the businesses under their supervision as well as have appropriate control over the key individuals in these areas.

Senior management contributes substantially to a bank's sound corporate governance through personal conduct (e.g., by helping to set the "tone at the top" along with the board); by providing adequate oversight of those they manage; and by ensuring that the bank's activities are consistent with the business strategy, risk tolerance/appetite, and policies approved by the bank's board.

Senior management is responsible for delegating duties to the staff and should establish a management structure that promotes accountability and transparency. Senior management should remain cognizant of its obligation to oversee the exercise of such delegated responsibility and its ultimate responsibility to the board for the performance of the bank.

Senior management should implement, consistent with the direction given by the board, appropriate systems for managing the risks—both financial and non-financial—to which the bank is exposed. This includes a comprehensive and independent risk management function and an effective system of internal controls.

C. Risk Management & Internal Controls

Principles 6 – 9

These principles are covered in detail in Chapter 25.

D. Compensation

Compensation systems contribute to bank performance and risk-taking, and should therefore be key components of a bank's governance and risk management. In practice, however, risk has not always been taken into account in determining compensation practices, with the result that some long-term risks may have been exacerbated by compensation incentives, such as those to boost short-term profits. In recognition of this, the Financial Stability Board (FSB) issued the FSB principles in April 2009 and the accompanying FSB standards in September 2009 to assist in their implementation. In addition, the committee issued in January 2010 its "Compensation Principles and Standards Assessment Methodology" document. Banks should fully implement the FSB principles and standards, or the applicable national provisions that are consistent with the FSB principles and standards.

Principle 10

The board should actively oversee the compensation system's design and operation, and should monitor and review the compensation system to ensure that it operates as intended.

The board is responsible for the overall design and operation of the compensation system for the entire bank. As such, those board members who are most actively involved in the design and operation of the compensation system (e.g., as members of the board's compensation committee) should be independent, non-executive members with substantial knowledge about compensation arrangements and the incentives and risks that can arise from such arrangements. Compensation should be aligned with risk, i.e., via risk-adjusted performance measurement tools; therefore, an understanding of the firm's risk measurement and management, and of how different compensation practices can impact the firm's risk profile, is important as well.

In addition to establishing the compensation system, the board should monitor and review outcomes to ensure that the compensation system is operating as intended. For example, the board should ensure that lower risk-adjusted income in a business line will result in reduced compensation.

The compensation of the control function (e.g., CRO and risk management staff) should be structured in a way that is based principally on the achievement of their objectives and does not compromise their independence (e.g., compensation should not be substantially tied to business line revenue).

Principle 11

An employee's compensation should be effectively aligned with prudent risk taking; compensation should be adjusted for all types of risk; compensation outcomes should be symmetric with risk outcomes; compensation payout schedules should be sensitive to the time horizon of risks; and the mix of cash, equity, and other forms of compensation should be consistent with risk alignment.

Since employees can generate equivalent short-term revenues while taking on vastly different amounts of risk in the longer term, a bank should ensure that variable compensation is adjusted to take into account the risks an employee takes. This should consider all types of risk over a timeframe sufficient for risk outcomes to be revealed. It is appropriate to use both quantitative risk measures and human judgment in determining risk adjustments. Where firms make such adjustments, all material risks should be taken into account, including difficult-to-measure risks (e.g., reputational risk) and potentially severe risk outcomes.

In addition to ex ante risk adjustments, banks should take other steps to better align compensation with prudent risk taking. One characteristic of effective compensation outcomes is that they are symmetric with risk outcomes, particularly at the bank or business line level. That is, the size of the bank's variable compensation pool should vary in response to both positive and negative performance. Variable compensation should be diminished or eliminated when a bank or business line incurs substantial losses.

Compensation should be sensitive to risk outcomes over a multi-year horizon. This is typically achieved through arrangements that defer compensation until risk outcomes have been realized, and may include so-called "malus" or "clawback" provisions whereby compensation is reduced or reversed if employees generate exposures that cause the bank to perform poorly in subsequent years or if the employee has failed to comply with internal policies or legal requirements.

"Golden parachute" arrangements under which terminated executives or staff receive large payouts irrespective of performance are generally not consistent with sound compensation practice.

The mix of cash, equity, and other forms of compensation (e.g., options) should be consistent with risk alignment and will likely vary across employees, depending on their position and role in the bank.

Bonus Restrictions

One major new regulation in Europe under the Capital Requirements Directive IV (CRD IV) is a cap on a banker's bonus, which is automatically set at the level of annual salary. That ceiling can be raised to twice base pay if the bank's shareholders vote in favor. If at least half of shareholders turn out to vote, then 66 percent need to vote in favor for the cap to be raised. If fewer turn out, then 75 percent need to vote in favor of lifting the cap.

Deutsche Bank asked its shareholders at the annual general meeting on May 22, 2014, to pay out pay out a bonus ration between fixed salary and variable compensation of 1:2 to selected staff members: "Pursuant to § 25a (5) sentence 2 German Banking Act in the version applicable since January 1, 2014, the variable compensation of employees of credit institutions in principle must not exceed 100 percent of the fixed compensation (i.e. a 1:1 ratio). § 25a (5) sentence 5 German Banking Act allows that the General Meeting may approve a higher ratio of variable compensation, which however must not exceed 200 percent of the fixed compensation (i.e., a 1:2 ratio) for the respective employee."[58]

E. Complex or Opaque Corporate Structures

Principle 12

The board and senior management should know and understand the bank's operational structure and the risks that it poses (i.e., "know-your-structure").

Some banks create structures for legal, regulatory, fiscal, or product-offering purposes in the form of units, branches, subsidiaries, or other legal entities that can considerably increase the complexity of the organization. The sheer number of legal entities, and in partic-

---

[58]Deutsche Bank Annual General Meeting, May 22, 2014: "Compensation for employees and for members of management bodies of subsidiaries ."

ular the interconnections and intra-group transactions among such entities, can lead to challenges in identifying, overseeing, and managing the risks of the organization as a whole, which is a risk in and of itself.

The board and senior management should understand the structure and the organization of the group, i.e., the aims of its different units/entities and the formal and informal links and relationships among the entities and with the parent company. This includes understanding the legal and operational risks and constraints of the various types of intra-group exposures and transactions and how they affect the group's funding, capital, and risk profile under normal and adverse circumstances. Sound and effective measures and systems should be in place to facilitate the generation and exchange of information among and about the various entities, to manage the risks of the group as a whole, and for the effective supervision of the group. In this regard, senior management should inform the board regarding the group's organizational and operational structure and the key drivers of the group's revenues and risks.

Another governance challenge arises when banks establish business or product line management structures that do not match the bank's legal entity structure. While this is a quite common practice, it nevertheless introduces additional complexity. Apart from ensuring the appropriateness of these matrix structures, the board or senior management as appropriate should ensure that all products and their risks are captured and evaluated on an individual entity and group-wide basis.

The board should approve policies and clear strategies for the establishment of new structures and should properly guide and understand the bank's structure, its evolution, and its limitations. Moreover, senior management, under the oversight of the board, should:

- Avoid setting up unnecessarily complicated structures;
- Have a centralized process for approving and controlling the creation of new legal entities based on established criteria, including the ability to monitor and fulfill on an ongoing basis each entity's requirements (e.g., regulatory, tax, financial reporting, governance);
- Understand and be able to produce information regarding the bank's structure, including the type, charter, ownership structure, and businesses conducted for each legal entity;
- Recognize the risks that the complexity of the legal entity structure itself may pose, including lack of management transparency, operational risks introduced by interconnected and complex funding structures, intra-group exposures, trapped collateral, and counterparty risk; and
- Evaluate how the aforementioned risks of the structure and legal entity requirements affect the group's ability to manage its risk profile and deploy funding and capital under normal and adverse circumstances.

Principle 13

Where a bank operates through special-purpose or related structures or in jurisdictions that impede transparency or do not meet international banking standards, its board and senior management should understand the purpose, structure, and unique risks of these operations. They should also seek to mitigate the risks identified (i.e., "understand your structure").

F. Disclosure & Transparency

Principle 14

The governance of the bank should be adequately transparent to its shareholders, depositors, other relevant stakeholders, and market participants.

Transparency is essential for sound and effective corporate governance. The objective of transparency in the area of corporate governance is to provide these parties, consistent with national law and supervisory practice, with key information necessary to enable them to assess the effectiveness of the board and senior management in governing the bank.

Although transparency may be less detailed for non-listed banks, especially those that are wholly owned, these institutions can nevertheless pose the same types of risk to the financial system as publicly traded banks through various activities, including their participation in payments systems and acceptance of retail deposits.

The bank should disclose relevant and useful information that supports the key areas of corporate governance. Such disclosure should be proportionate to the size, complexity, structure, economic significance, and risk profile of the bank.

Chapter 27, "Key Risk and Performance Indicators," has been specifically dedicated to this subject.

Examples of Corporate Governance in Large Banks Today

UBS/Switzerland

Figure 24.2 illustrates the committees of the board of directors of Switzerland's largest bank, UBS. The bank operates—as suggested by modern corporate governance codes and required by Basel—with a structure of five different committees: audit committee, corporate responsibility committee, governance and nominating committee, human resources and compensation committee, and risk committee.[59]

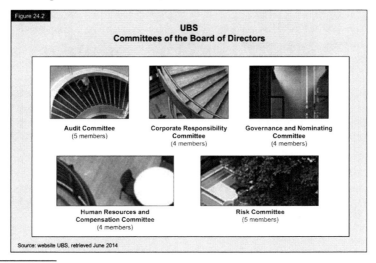

Figure 24.2

UBS
Committees of the Board of Directors

Audit Committee
(5 members)

Corporate Responsibility Committee
(4 members)

Governance and Nominating Committee
(4 members)

Human Resources and Compensation Committee
(4 members)

Risk Committee
(5 members)

Source: website UBS, retrieved June 2014

---

[59]http://www.ubs.com/global/en/about_ubs/corporate-governance/board-of-directors/committees.html

Deutsche Bank / Germany

Deutsche Bank has given the subject of responsibility a top management priority. In fact, the subject can be found as a major rider on the firm's corporate website.

Home	Company	Investor Relations	Media	Responsibility	Careers

On its website, Deutsche Bank says that it wants to create sustainable value for clients, employees, shareholders, and society. It further states, "Our goal is clear: Our high-performance culture must go hand-in-hand with a culture of responsibility."

The firm gathers comprehensive data to measure performance against economic, environmental, and social goals. Facts and figures are disclosed on the website in 11 areas. For example, in the area of "Corporate Governance and Compliance," the bank states the following:[60]

Compliance

"We ensure compliance with laws and regulations with the aid of special programs and structures:

- Anti-Financial Crime Committee (AFCC): Group-wide oversight and governance body aimed at curbing financial crime.
- Anti-money laundering program.
- Anti-corruption guideline: System of rules for combating corruption and bribery.
- Global Compliance Core Principles: Set of principles that commits the employees and senior managers to uphold principles of integrity, accountability, responsibility, fairness, and considerateness.
- Know-Your-Customer (KYC) Policy: System of rules for the KYC process, i.e., scrutiny of clients that is mandatory for banks in order to combat money laundering.
- Compliance Control Framework.
- Red Flag Monitoring System: Monitoring system that reports all violations of compliance requirements. The results of the monitoring are integrated into management and reporting structures and taken into account in performance assessments
- Regulatory Contact Offices: Offices of Deutsche Bank in Frankfurt am Main, London, and New York that manage contacts and communication with domestic and foreign supervisory authorities

International Standards and Initiatives
- "Our approach to corporate governance conforms to general legal regulations as well stock exchange law; its essential foundations are:
- The German Stock Corporation Act [Aktiengesetz].
- The German Corporate Governance Code.
- The U.S. capital market laws.
- The rules of the Securities and Exchange Commission (SEC) and the New York Stock Exchange."

Deutsche Bank

---

[60]https://www.db.com/cr/en/datacenter/facts-and-figures.htm

JPMorgan Chase / United States

JPMorgan Chase has published its internal code of ethics.[61]

"This Code of Ethics applies to the Chief Executive Officer, President, Chief Financial Officer, and Chief Accounting Officer of JPMorgan Chase & Co. (the "firm") and to all other professionals of the firm worldwide serving in a finance, accounting, corporate treasury, tax or investor relations role.

The purpose of this Code of Ethics is to promote honest and ethical conduct and compliance with the law, particularly as related to the maintenance of the firm's financial books and records and the preparation of its financial statements. The obligations of this Code of Ethics supplement, but do not replace, the firm's Code of Conduct. As a finance professional of the firm, you are expected to:

- Engage in and promote ethical conduct, including the ethical handling of actual or apparent conflicts of interest between personal and professional relationships, and to disclose to the Office of the Secretary any material transaction or relationship that reasonably could be expected to give rise to such a conflict.
- Carry out your responsibilities honestly; in good faith; and with integrity, due care, and diligence, exercising at all times the best independent judgment.
- Assist in the production of full, fair, accurate, timely, and understandable disclosure in reports and documents that the firm and its subsidiaries file with, or submit to, the Securities and Exchange Commission and other regulators and in other public communications made by the firm.
- Comply with applicable government laws, rules, and regulations of federal, state, and local governments and other appropriate regulatory agencies.
- Promptly report (anonymously, if you wish to do so) to the Audit Committee of the Board of Directors any violation of this Code of Ethics or any other matters that would compromise the integrity of the firm's financial statements. You may contact the Audit Committee by mail, by phone, or by e-mail....
- Never ... take, directly or indirectly, any action to coerce, manipulate, mislead, or fraudulently influence the firm's independent auditors in the performance of their audit or review of the firm's financial statements.

Compliance with this Code of Ethics is a term and condition of your employment. The firm will take all necessary actions to enforce this Code, up to and including immediate dismissal. Violations of this Code of Ethics may also constitute violations of law, which may expose both you and the firm to criminal or civil penalties."

JPMorgan Chase

Barclays / United Kingdom

Barclays publishes the following board responsibilities on its corporate website:[62]

"The Board's principal duty is to create and deliver sustainable shareholder value through setting Barclays' strategy and overseeing its implementation.

In doing so, we pay due regard to matters that will affect the future of Barclays, such as the effect the Board's decisions may have on our employees, the environment, our communities, and relationships with suppliers.

(continued)

---

[61]http://www.jpmorganchase.com/corporate/About-JPMC/code-of-ethics.htm
[62]http://www.barclays.com/about-barclays/barclays-corporate-governance/board-responsibilities.html

The Board also ensures Barclays' management team achieves the right balance between promoting long-term growth and delivering short-term objectives.

Members of the Board are also responsible for maintaining an effective system of internal control that provides assurance of efficient operations and for ensuring that Barclays' management team maintains an effective risk management and oversight process across the company.

Summary of Matters Rreserved to the Board:

1. Risk Appetite, Capital, and Liquidity
- Changes relating to capital structure or status as a PLC
- Approval of annual capital plan
- Approval of risk appetite and liquidity risk appetite

2 Financial results and dividends
- Approval of interim and final financial statements, dividends, and any significant change in accounting policies or practices
- Any share dividend alternative

3. Strategy
- Approval of Barclays' strategy, medium-term, and short-term plans
- Monitoring delivery of the strategy and performance against plan
- Major acquisitions, mergers or disposals
- Major capital investments and projects

4. Board Membership
- Board appointments and removals
- Succession planning for key positions on the board
- Role profiles of key positions on the board

5. Remuneration
- Approval of the framework for determining the policy and specific remuneration of executive directors
- Approval of non-executive director remuneration
- Major changes in employee share schemes

6. Governance
- Authorization for directors' conflicts or possible conflicts of interest
- Remuneration of auditors and recommendations for appointment or removal of auditors
- Approval of all circulars, prospectuses, and significant press releases
- Principal regulatory filings with stock exchanges
- Approval of allotment of shares
- Rules and procedures for dealing in Barclays securities
- Terms of reference and membership of board committees
- Approval of board's and board committees' performance-evaluation process
- Determination of independence of non-executive directors
- Approval of corporate governance framework
- Approval of division of responsibilities between the chairman and chief executive
- Appointment (or removal) of company secretary and chief risk officer

Key Takeaways

- Following the financial crisis, there has been renewed interest in the corporate governance practices of modern corporations, in particular banks. The Basel Committee published its "Principles for Enhancing Corporate Governance"—applicable to banks—in October 2010.
- Key focus areas include the overall governance framework, codes and rules, the roles and responsibilities of top management (both board of directors and executive committee), organization, compensation, risk management and controls, audit independence, and transparency/disclosure.
- In response, financial institutions have upgraded their governance infrastructures.
- In order to improve the fractured relationship with society, banks need to continue their efforts and investments in the corporate governance area.
- Customers/society request from banks that they go back to their roots and carry out their responsibilities in line with basic human morals and ethics, i.e., honesty, good faith, integrity, due care/diligence, and independent judgment.

Risk Management

The Financial Crisis Inquiry Report in the United States[63] concluded that dramatic failures of corporate governance and risk management at many systemically important financial institutions (SIFIs) were a key cause of the financial crisis. With regards to risk management, the report found:

- "Financial institutions [and credit rating agencies] embraced mathematical models as reliable predictors of risk, replacing judgment in too many instances. Too often, risk management became risk justification."
- "Collapsing mortgage lending standards" and "irresponsible lending."
- "Uncontrolled leverage; lack of transparency, capital, and collateral requirements; concentrations of risk [in the OTC markets]."

Plenty of other problems in risk management existed, e.g., over-the-counter (OTC) derivatives, securitization, data problems in core bank business lines (probability of default, loss-given-default, default correlations), liquidity risk, concentration risk, and—possibly most important of all—tail risk.

Even banks with top-rated risk management infrastructures failed.

Of course, risk management in a financial institution and the institution's risk management team or division are in fact two different things. Banking and insurance business is risk business, so risk management starts at the top of the institution and trickles down to both front- (business) and back-office (support, control) units. Risk management must never be a silo in the institution. Risk management must be an interactive process between risk officers and business divisions, which must complement each other in the best way possible. Risk management is like good defense in sports. In major team sports—including baseball, basketball, [American] football, ice hockey, and soccer—"offense wins games, but defense wins championships." Some statisticians or sports enthusiasts may claim that this statement is a myth; however, no one would argue that it takes both good offense and de-

---

[63]"The Financial Crisis Inquiry Report, Final Report of the National Commission on the Causes of the Financial and Economic Crisis in the United States," January 2011

fense to win the World Series, the NBA title, the Super Bowl, the Stanley Cup, or the UEFA Champions League.

This entire book is about risk management, every single chapter. This particular chapter is therefore "only" a summary and an overview of the most critical risk management issues, from a governance perspective.

Bank for International Settlements (BIS) Principles for Enhancing Corporate Governance – Risk Management and Internal Controls

The principles have been designed for large banks, mainly:

- A bank should have a risk management function, including a chief risk officer (CRO) or equivalent for large banks and internationally active banks, a compliance function, and an internal audit function, each with sufficient authority, stature, independence, resources, and access to the board;
- Risks should be identified, assessed, and monitored on an ongoing firm-wide and individual entity basis;
- An internal controls system which is effective in design and operation should be in place;
- The sophistication of a bank's risk management, compliance, and internal control infrastructures should keep pace with any changes to its risk profile (including its growth) and to the external risk landscape; and
- Effective risk management requires frank and timely internal communication within the bank about risk, both across the organization and through reporting to the board and senior management.

Principle 6

Banks should have an effective internal controls system and a risk management function (including a chief risk officer or equivalent) with sufficient authority, stature, independence, resources, and access to the board.

Risk Management vs. Internal Controls

Risk management generally encompasses the process of:

- Identifying key risks to the bank;
- Assessing these risks and measuring the bank's exposures to them;
- Monitoring the risk exposures and determining the corresponding capital needs (i.e., capital planning) on an ongoing basis;

▪ Monitoring and assessing decisions to accept particular risks, risk mitigation measures, and whether risk decisions are in line with the board-approved risk tolerance/appetite and risk policy; and

▪ Reporting to senior management and the board as appropriate.

Internal controls are designed, among other things, to ensure that each key risk has a policy, process, or other measure, as well as a control to ensure that such policy, process, or other measure is being applied and works as intended. As such, internal controls help ensure process integrity, compliance, and effectiveness. Internal controls help provide comfort that financial and management information is reliable, timely, and complete and that the bank is in compliance with its various obligations, including applicable laws and regulations. In order to avoid actions beyond the authority of the individual or even fraud, internal controls also place reasonable checks on managerial and employee discretion. Even in very small banks, key management decisions should be made by more than one person ("four eyes principle"). Internal control reviews should also determine the extent of an institution's compliance with company policies and procedures, as well as with legal and regulatory policies.

Chief Risk Officer (CRO) or Equivalent

Large banks and internationally active banks, and others depending on their risk profile and local governance requirements, should have an independent senior executive with distinct responsibility for the risk management function and the institution's comprehensive risk management framework across the entire organization. This executive is commonly referred to as the CRO. Since some banks may have an officer who fulfills the function of a CRO but has a different title, reference in this guidance to the CRO is intended to incorporate equivalent positions. Whatever the title, at least in large banks, the role of the CRO should be distinct from other executive functions and business line responsibilities, and there generally should be no "dual hatting" (i.e., the chief operating officer, CFO, chief auditor, or other senior management should not also serve as the CRO).

Formal reporting lines may vary across banks, but regardless of these reporting lines, the independence of the CRO is paramount. While the CRO may report to the CEO or other senior management, the CRO should also report and have direct access to the board and its risk committee without impediment. Also, the CRO should not have any management or financial responsibility with respect to any operational business lines or revenue-generating functions. Interaction between the CRO and the board should occur regularly and be documented adequately. Non-executive board members should have the right to meet regularly—in the absence of senior management—with with the CRO.

The CRO should have sufficient stature, authority, and seniority within the organization. This will typically be reflected in the ability of the CRO to influence decisions that affect the bank's exposure to risk. Beyond periodic reporting, the CRO should thus have the ability to engage with the board and other senior management on key risk issues and to access such information as the CRO deems necessary to form his or her judgment. Such interactions should not compromise the CRO's independence.

If the CRO is removed from his or her position for any reason, this should be done with the prior approval of the board and generally should be disclosed publicly. The bank should also discuss the reasons for such removal with its supervisor.

Scope of Responsibilities, Stature, and Independence of the Risk Management Function

The risk management function is responsible for identifying, measuring, monitoring, controlling or mitigating, and reporting on risk exposures. This should encompass all risks to the bank—on- and off-balance-sheet and at a group-wide, portfolio, and business-line level—and should take into account the extent to which risks overlap (e.g., lines between market and credit risk and between credit and operational risk are increasingly blurred). This should include a reconciliation of the aggregate level of risk in the bank to the board-established risk tolerance/appetite.

The risk management function—both firm-wide and within subsidiaries and business lines—under the direction of the CRO should have sufficient stature within the bank such that issues raised by risk managers receive the necessary attention from the board, senior management, and business lines. Business decisions by the bank typically are a product of many considerations. By properly positioning and supporting its risk management function, a bank helps ensure that the views of risk managers will be an important part of those considerations.

While it is not uncommon for risk managers to work closely with individual business units and, in some cases, to have dual reporting lines, the risk management function should be sufficiently independent of the business units whose activities and exposures it reviews.

While such independence is an essential component of an effective risk management function, it is also important that risk managers are not so isolated from business lines—geographically or otherwise—that they cannot understand the business or access necessary information. Moreover, the risk management function should have access to all business lines that have the potential to generate material risk to the bank. Regardless of any responsibilities that the risk management function may have to business lines and senior management, its ultimate responsibility should be to the board.

Resources

A bank should ensure through its planning and budgeting processes that the risk management function has adequate resources (in both number and quality) necessary to assess risk, including personnel; support; and access to information technology systems, systems development resources, and internal information. These processes should also explicitly address and provide sufficient resources for internal audit and compliance functions. Compensation and other incentives (e.g., opportunities for promotion) of the CRO and risk management staff should be sufficient to attract and retain qualified personnel.

Qualifications

Risk management personnel should possess sufficient experience and qualifications, including market and product knowledge as well as mastery of risk disciplines. Staff should have the ability and willingness to challenge business lines regarding all aspects of risk arising from the bank's activities.

Principle 7

Risks should be identified and monitored on an ongoing firm-wide and individual entity basis, and the sophistication of the bank's risk management and internal control infrastructures should keep pace with any changes to the bank's risk profile (including its growth), and to the external risk landscape.

Risk Methodologies and Activities

Risk analysis should include both quantitative and qualitative elements. While risk measurement is a key component of risk management, excessive focus on measuring or modeling risks at the expense of other risk management activities may result both in overreliance on risk estimates that do not accurately reflect real exposures and in insufficient action to address and mitigate risks. The risk management function should ensure that the bank's internal risk measurements cover a range of scenarios, are not based on overly optimistic assumptions regarding dependencies and correlations, and include qualitative firm-wide views of risk relative to return and to the bank's external operating environment. Senior management and, as applicable, the board should review and approve scenarios that are used in the bank's risk analysis and should be made aware of assumptions and potential shortcomings embedded in the bank's risk models.

As banks make use of certain internal and external data to identify and assess risk, make strategic or operational decisions, and determine capital adequacy, the board should give special attention to the quality, completeness, and accuracy of the data it relies on to make risk decisions.

As part of its quantitative and qualitative analysis, the bank should also utilize forward-looking stress tests and scenario analysis to better understand potential risk exposures under a variety of adverse circumstances. These should be key elements of a bank's risk management process, and the results should be communicated to, and given appropriate consideration by, the relevant business lines and individuals within the bank. A forward-looking approach to risk management should include ongoing monitoring of existing risks as well as identifying new or emerging risks.

In addition to these forward-looking tools, banks should also regularly review actual performance after the fact relative to risk estimates (i.e., backtesting) to assist in gauging the accuracy and effectiveness of the risk management process and making necessary adjustments.

The risk management function should promote the importance of senior management and business line managers in identifying and assessing risks critically, rather than relying excessively on external risk assessments. While external assessments such as external credit ratings or externally purchased risk models can be useful as an input into a more comprehensive assessment of risk, the ultimate responsibility for assessing risk lies solely with the bank. For example, in the case of a purchased credit or market risk model, the bank should take the steps necessary to validate the model and calibrate it to the bank's individual circumstances to ensure accurate and comprehensive capture and analysis of risk. In any case, banks should avoid over-reliance on any specific risk methodology or model.

In the case of subsidiary banks, a similar approach is necessary. The board and management of a subsidiary remain responsible for effective risk management processes at the subsidiary. While parent companies should conduct strategic, group-wide risk management and prescribe corporate risk policies, subsidiary management and boards should have appropriate input into their local or regional adoption and to assessments of local risks. If group risk management systems and processes are prescribed, subsidiary management, with subsidiary board oversight, is responsible for assessing and ensuring that those systems and processes are appropriate, given the nature of the operations of the subsidiary. Furthermore, adequate stress testing of subsidiary portfolios should occur, based not only on the subsidiaries' economic and operating environments, but also based on the ramifications of potential stress on the parent company (e.g., liquidity, credit, reputational risk, etc). In some cases, such evaluations may be accomplished through joint head office and subsidiary teams. Local management and those responsible for the control functions are accountable for prudent risk management at the local level. Parent companies should ensure that adequate tools and authorities are provided to the subsidiary and that the subsidiary understands what reporting obligations it has to the head office.

In addition to identifying and measuring risk exposures, the risk management function should evaluate possible ways to manage these exposures. In some cases, the risk management function may direct that risk be reduced or hedged to limit exposure. In other cases, the risk management function may simply report risk positions and monitor these positions to ensure that they remain within the bank's framework of limits and controls. Either approach may be appropriate provided the independence of the risk management function is not compromised.

The sophistication of the bank's risk management and internal control infrastructures—including, in particular, a sufficiently robust information technology infrastructure—should keep pace with developments such as balance sheet and revenue growth, increasing complexity of the bank's business or operating structure, geographic expansion, mergers and acquisitions, or the introduction of new products or business lines. Strategic business planning, and periodic review of such plans, should take into account the extent to which such developments have occurred and the likelihood that they will continue going forward.

Banks should have approval processes for new products. These should include an assessment of the risks of new products, significant changes to existing products, the introduction of new lines of business, and entry into new markets. The risk management function should provide input on risks as a part of such processes. This should include a full and frank assessment of risks under a variety of scenarios, as well as an assessment of potential shortcomings in the ability of the bank's risk management and internal controls to effectively manage associated risks. In this regard, the bank's new-product approval process should take into account the extent to which the bank's risk management, legal and regulatory compliance, information technology, business line, and internal control functions have adequate tools and the expertise necessary to manage related risks. If adequate risk management processes are not yet in place, a new product offering should be delayed until such time that systems and risk management are able to accommodate the relevant activity. There should also be a process to assess risk and performance relative to initial projections, and to adapt the risk management treatment accordingly, as the business matures.

Mergers and acquisitions can pose special risk management challenges to the bank. In particular, risks can arise from conducting insufficient due diligence that fails to identify risks that arise post-merger or activities that conflict with the bank's strategic objectives or risk tolerance/appetite. The risk management function should therefore be actively involved in assessing risks that could arise from mergers and acquisitions, and should report its findings directly to the board and/or its relevant specialized committee.

While the risk management function plays a vital role in identifying, measuring, monitoring, and reporting on risk exposures, other units in the bank also play an important role in managing risk. In addition to business lines, which should be accountable for managing risks arising from their activities, the bank's treasury and finance functions should promote effective firm-wide risk management not only through supporting financial controls but also through applying robust internal pricing of risk especially at large banks and internationally active banks. A business unit's internal cost of funds should reflect material risks to the bank arising from its activities. Failure to do so may result in greater investment in high-risk activities than would be the case if internal pricing were risk-adjusted.

Although the risk management function has a key leadership and coordinating role on risks, the operational responsibility for making operational decisions on risks and managing risk rests with management and ultimately extends to other employees of the bank. The bank's risk management framework should be clear and transparent regarding staff and organizational responsibilities for risk.

Principle 8

Effective risk management requires robust internal communication within the bank about risk, both across the organization and through reporting to the board and senior management.

Sound corporate governance is evidenced, among other things, by a culture where senior management and staff are expected and encouraged to identify risk issues as opposed to relying on the internal audit or risk management functions to identify them. This expectation is conveyed not only through bank policies and procedures, but also through the "tone at the top" established by the board and senior management.

The bank's risk exposures and strategy should be communicated throughout the bank with sufficient frequency. Effective communication, both horizontally across the organization and vertically up the management chain, facilitates effective decision-making that fosters safe and sound banking and helps prevent decisions that may result in amplifying risk exposures.

Information should be communicated to the board and senior management in a timely, complete, understandable, and accurate manner so that they are equipped to make informed decisions. This is particularly important when a bank is facing financial or other difficulties and may need to make prompt, critical decisions. If the board and senior management have incomplete or inaccurate information, their decisions may magnify risks rather than mitigate them. Serious consideration should be given by the board to instituting periodic reviews of the amount and quality of information the board receives or should receive.

In ensuring that the board and senior management are sufficiently informed, management and those responsible for the control functions should strike a balance between communicating information that is accurate and "unfiltered" (i.e., that does not hide potentially bad news) and not communicating so much extraneous information that the sheer volume of information becomes counterproductive.

Risk reporting to the board requires careful design in order to ensure that firm-wide and individual portfolio and other risks are conveyed in a concise and meaningful manner. Reporting should accurately communicate risk exposures and results of stress tests or scenario analyses, and should provoke a robust discussion of, for example, the bank's current and prospective exposures (particularly under stressed scenarios), risk/return relationships, risk tolerance/appetite, etc. In addition to internal measurement and assessment of bank risks, reporting should include information about the external environment to identify market conditions and trends that may have a bearing on the bank's current or future risk profile.

Risk reporting systems should be dynamic, comprehensive, and accurate, and should draw on a range of underlying assumptions. Risk monitoring and reporting should occur not only at the disaggregated level (including risk residing in subsidiaries that could be considered significant), but should also be aggregated upward to allow for a firm-wide or consolidated picture of risk exposures. Risk-reporting systems should be clear about any deficiencies or limitations in risk estimates, as well as any significant embedded assumptions (e.g., regarding risk dependencies or correlations). These systems should not only aggregate information to provide a firm-wide, integrated perspective on risk (geographically and by risk type), but should also highlight emerging risks that have the potential to become significant and may merit further analysis.

In this regard, organizational "silos" can impede effective sharing of information across a bank and can result in decisions being made in isolation from the rest of the bank. Overcoming information-sharing obstacles posed by silo structures may require the board and senior management to review or rethink established practices in order to encourage greater communication. Some firms have found it useful to create risk management committees—distinct from the board's risk committee—that draw members from across the firm (e.g., from business lines and the risk management function) to discuss issues related to firm-wide risks.

Principle 9

The board and senior management should effectively utilize the work conducted by internal audit functions, external auditors, and internal control functions.

The board should recognize and acknowledge that independent, competent, and qualified internal and external auditors, as well as other internal control functions (including the compliance functions), are vital to the corporate governance process in order to achieve a number of important objectives. Senior management should also recognize the importance of the effectiveness of these functions to the long-term soundness of the bank.

The board and senior management can enhance the ability of the internal audit function to identify problems with a bank's governance, risk management, and internal control systems by:

- Encouraging internal auditors to adhere to national and international professional standards, such as those established by the Institute of Internal Auditors;

- Requiring that audit staff have skills that are commensurate with the business activities and risks of the firm;
- Promoting the independence of the internal auditor, for example by ensuring that internal audit reports are provided to the board and the internal auditor has direct access to the board or the board's audit committee;
- Recognizing the importance of the audit and internal control processes and communicating their importance throughout the bank;
- Requiring the timely and effective correction of identified internal audit issues by senior management; and
- Engaging internal auditors to judge the effectiveness of the risk management function and the compliance function, including the quality of risk reporting to the board and senior management, as well as the effectiveness of other key control functions.

The board and senior management are responsible for the preparation and fair presentation of financial statements—unless the law says otherwise—in accordance with applicable accounting standards in each jurisdiction, and for the establishment of effective internal controls related to financial reporting. The board and senior management can also contribute to the effectiveness of external auditors by including in engagement letters the expectation that the external auditor will be in compliance with applicable domestic and international codes and standards of professional practice.

Non-executive board members should have the right to meet regularly—in the absence of senior management—with the external auditor and the heads of the internal audit and compliance functions. This can strengthen the ability of the board to oversee senior management's implementation of the board's policies and to ensure that a bank's business strategies and risk exposures are consistent with risk parameters established by the board.

The bank should maintain sound control functions, including an effective compliance function that, among other things, routinely monitors compliance with laws, corporate governance rules, regulations, codes, and policies to which the bank is subject, and ensures that deviations are reported to an appropriate level of management and, in case of material deviations, to the board.

Senior management should promote strong internal controls and should avoid activities and practices that undermine their effectiveness. Examples of problematic activities or practices include failing to ensure that there is effective segregation of duties where conflicts could arise; not exercising effective control over employees in key business positions (even apparent "star" employees); and failing to question employees who generate revenues or returns out of line with reasonable expectations (e.g., where supposedly low-risk, low-margin trading activity generated unexpectedly high returns) for fear of losing either revenue or the employees.

Examples of Risk Disclosure in Large Banks Today

Deutsche Bank / Germany

In its 2013 annual report, Germany's largest bank dedicates 170 out of a total of 572 pages (30 percent) to risk; the bank's risk report covers all key areas and is structured in the following way:

Deutsche Bank – Structure Risk Report / Annual Report, Pages 55 – 225

(continued)

Key Takeaways

- Following the financial crisis, there has been renewed interest in the corporate governance practices and risk management of modern corporations, in particular banks. The Basel Committee published its "Principles for Enhancing Corporate Governance"—applicable to banks—in October 2010.
- Banks should have an effective internal controls system and a risk management function, including a chief risk officer or equivalent, with sufficient authority, stature, independence, resources, and access to the board.
- Risks should be identified and monitored on an ongoing firm-wide and individual-entity basis. The sophistication of the bank's risk management and internal control infrastructures should keep pace with any changes to the bank's risk profile (including its growth), and to the external risk landscape.
- Effective risk management requires robust internal communication within the bank about risk, both across the organization and through reporting to the board and senior management.
- The board and senior management should effectively utilize the work conducted by internal audit functions, external auditors, and internal control functions.

Sound Capital Planning Process

Capital planning is a dynamic and ongoing process that, in order to be effective, is forward looking in incorporating changes in a bank's strategic focus, risk tolerance levels, business plans, operating environment, or other factors that materially affect capital adequacy.

The Internal Capital Adequacy Assessment Process (ICAAP) requires banks to identify and assess risks, maintain sufficient capital to face these risks, and apply appropriate risk management techniques to maintain adequate capitalization on an ongoing and forward looking basis, i.e., internal capital supply to exceed internal capital demand. Banks, at a group level, typically maintain compliance with the ICAAP as required under Pillar 2 of Basel II and its local implementation—in Germany, the Minimum Requirements for Risk Management (MaRisk)—through a group-wide risk management and governance framework, methodologies, processes, and infrastructure.

Capital planning is very much in the focus of regulators and institutions as it helps the bank's board of directors and senior management to:

- Identify risks, improve their understanding of the bank's overall risks, set risk tolerance levels, and assess strategic choices in longer-term planning.
- Identify vulnerabilities such as concentrations and assess their impact on capital.
- Integrate business strategy, risk management, and capital and liquidity planning decisions, including due diligence for a merger or acquisition.
- Have a forward-looking assessment of the bank's capital needs, including capital needs that may arise from rapid changes in the economic and financial environment.

The most effective capital planning considers both short- and longer-term capital needs and is coordinated with a bank's overall strategy and planning cycles, usually with a forecast horizon of at least two years. Banks need to factor events that occur outside of the normal capital planning cycle into the capital planning process; for example, a natural disaster could have a major impact on future capital needs.

The capital planning process should be tailored to the overall risk, complexity, and corporate structure of the bank. The bank's range of business activities, overall risks, and operating environment have a significant impact on the level of detail needed in a bank's capital planning. A more-complex institution with higher overall risk is expected to have a more-detailed planning process than an institution with less-complex operations and lower risks. The corporate structure is also a factor.

Fundamental Components

The Bank for International Settlements (BIS) has defined fundamental components of a sound capital planning process:

1. Internal control and governance;
2. Capital policy and risk capture;
3. Forward-looking view;
4. Management framework for preserving capital.

1. Internal Control and Governance

There is considerable variation in how banks structure their capital planning processes. At some banks, the various responsibilities associated with capital planning are divided along functional lines. For example, experts assigned to a business unit have responsibility for establishing capital targets and managing their business in relation to them. Those estimates are aggregated to arrive at a firm-wide view of capital adequacy. Other banks rely on a more centralized model. In this model, a central group develops assumptions to be used firm-wide and has the authority and responsibility to review and challenge the estimates produced by individual areas of the bank. Irrespective of how a bank's capital planning process is oriented, it should aim at the sound practice of producing an internally consistent and coherent view of a bank's current and future capital needs.

It is important that a capital planning process reflects the input of different experts from across a bank, including but not limited to staff from business, risk, finance, and treasury departments. There should be a strong link between the capital planning, budgeting, and strategic planning processes within a bank. Collectively, these experts provide a view of the bank's current strategy, the risks associated with that strategy, and an assessment of how those risks contribute to capital needs as measured by internal and regulatory standards. Otherwise, banks may run the risk of developing capital plans that do not accurately reflect the strategy individual business lines are pursuing or that are incomplete in their scope, resulting in capital targets at the group level that may be overly optimistic.

Banks with sound capital planning processes have a formal process in place to identify situations where competing assumptions are made. In this context, differences in strategic planning and capital allocation across the bank are escalated for discussion and approval by senior executives. More concretely, this may include, for example, whether it is acceptable for one business unit to anticipate a rapid growth in loan balances while a complementary business unit may assume a sharp decline in such balances.

As a general matter, both senior management and the board of directors are involved in the capital planning process. Sound practice typically involves a management committee or similar body that works under the auspices of a bank's board of directors and guides and reviews efforts related to capital planning. Typically, the board of directors sets forth the principles that underpin the capital planning process. Those principles may include the forward strategy for the bank, an expression of risk appetite, and a perspective on striking the right balance between reinvesting capital in the bank's operations and providing returns to shareholders.

Banks with strong governance of the capital planning process require the board of directors or one or more committees thereof to review and approve capital plans at least annually. Those same bodies are also required to consider the outcome of the capital planning process when appraising business developments and strategy. The analysis captured in a capital plan informs the capital actions contemplated by the board of directors including, for example, whether to reconfirm or change a common stock dividend or common stock repurchase plan and/or issue regulatory capital instruments. In cases where this decision-making has been delegated to one or more committees of a board of directors, approval of the capital plan typically falls within the remit of the board's risk committee.

2. Capital Policy and Risk Capture

A capital policy is a written document agreed to by the senior management of a bank. It specifies the principles that management will follow in making decisions about how to deploy a bank's capital.

Leading practice among banks is for a board of directors to hold a management team accountable for demonstrating that adherence to a capital policy will allow the bank to maintain ready access to funding; meet its obligations to creditors and other counterparties; and continue to serve as a credit intermediary before, during, and after a stressful scenario. Implicitly, this means that a sound capital policy also details the range of strategies management is able to employ to address anticipated and unexpected capital shortfalls.

Typically, a capital policy will reference a suite of capital- and performance-related metrics against which management monitors the bank's condition. As described in Part 2, banks focus on the common equity tier 1 ratio and on ensuring that enough capital is retained to meet future requirements—for example, buffers set by regulators. Non-regulatory based metrics tend to focus on returns. Some of the more common return measures employed by banks include return on equity (ROE), return on risk-adjusted capital (RORAC), and risk-adjusted return on capital (RAROC).

Leading banks use economic capital as another complementary view of a bank's condition. This is an example of how management teams employing sound capital planning practices seek to evaluate their capital adequacy from many different perspectives. A bank employing this practice aggregates economic capital need—inclusive of any risk diversification benefits and capital cushions for model risks, cyclicality, or other factors—and compares it to the available financial resources.

It is important for a monitoring framework to be in place and complemented by a clear and transparent formal escalation protocol for those situations when a trigger or limit is approached and/or breached, at which point a timely decision needs to be taken.

An important input to a capital policy is an expression of risk tolerance by management and the board of directors. A risk tolerance statement is approved by the board of directors and renewed at least annually. It directly informs the bank's business strategy and capital management, including through the establishment of return targets, risk limits, and incentive compensation frameworks at the group and business unit levels.

As a general matter, the credibility of a bank's capital planning can be questioned if the process does not adequately reflect material risks, some of which may be difficult to quantify. Banks routinely quantify and hold capital against those risks that are specified in the minimum requirements or Pillar 1 of the Basel II and Basel III frameworks. Those risks typically include credit, counterparty, market, and operational risk. Banks with better practices have a comprehensive process in place to regularly and systematically identify, and understand the limitations of, their risk quantification and measurement methods. In addition, banks seek to capture in their capital plans those risks for which an explicit regulatory capital treatment is not present, such as, but not limited to, positions that result in concentrated exposures to a type of counterparty, industry, or country or reputational risk and strategic risk. It is also important to establish clear links between capital and liquidity monitoring, considerations that banks did not feature as prominently in past evaluations of capital adequacy.

For risks that are more difficult to quantify, carefully validated assumptions made in the estimation process are widely discussed and understood by senior management to ensure the potential for these to negatively impact a bank is not underestimated. Risks arising from the application of a model that is unable to capture embedded risks of a complex portfolio, for example, from limitations in data and/or quantification methods, may fall within this category.

3. Forward-Looking View

As described in Part 7, another key element of a sound capital-planning process is stress testing or scenario analyses. These techniques are often used to obtain a forward view on the sufficiency of a bank's capital base.

An effective capital-planning process requires a bank both to assess the risks to which it is exposed and to consider the potential impact on earnings and capital from an assumed economic downturn. In other words, stress testing needs to be an integral component of the capital-planning process.

4. Management Framework for Preserving Capital

For a capital-planning process to be meaningful, a bank's senior management and directors should rely on it to provide them with views of the degree to which a bank's business strategy and capital position may be vulnerable to unexpected changes in conditions.

Sound practice entails senior management and the board of directors ensuring that the capital policy and associated monitoring and escalation protocols remain relevant alongside an appropriate risk reporting and stress testing framework. In addition, they are responsible for prioritizing and quantifying the capital actions available to them to cushion against unexpected events.

In practice, those actions include reductions in or cessation of common stock dividends, equity raises, and/or balance sheet reductions. This last set of potential actions could include the disposition of capital markets inventory, monetizing business units, or reducing credit origination. It is critical that management teams assess the feasibility of the proposed contingent actions under stress, including potential benefits and long-term costs, and have a high degree of confidence that such actions can be executed as described. Otherwise, they should not be captured in a bank's capital plan.

Banks exhibiting sound practice have also developed guiding principles for determining the appropriateness of particular actions under different scenarios, which take into account relevant considerations, such as economic value added, costs and benefits, and market conditions.

In summary, it is important that actions to maintain capital are clearly defined in advance and that the management process allows for plans to be updated swiftly to allow for better decision-making in changing circumstances.

Key Takeaways

- Today, the main stakeholders view capital planning as a necessary complement to a robust regulatory framework. Sound capital planning is critical for determining the prudent amount, type, and composition of capital that is consistent with a longer-term strategy of being able to pursue business objectives, while also withstanding a stressful event.
- A sound capital-planning process is a formal practice that includes the following fundamental components: internal control and governance, capital policy and risk capture, forward-looking view, and management framework for preserving capital.
- The process must include stress testing scenarios.

Issues and Implications

Key Risk and Performance Indicators in Banks

Basel III and other banking reforms present a key challenge for banks. The new regulations claim to make the banking system safer by resolving many of the flaws that became visible in the crisis. Improving the quality and quantity of capital and introducing a framework for liquidity management is intended to motivate banks to improve their risk management capabilities. The rationale is that ultimately, if banks better control their risks, that should be good for their business and hence for consumers, investors, staff members, and governments.

Of course, stakeholders and markets will require much more from banking institutions than regulatory compliance; banks need to manage their businesses in a successful and profitable manner.

The literature on bank management, bank profitability, risk management, key management ratios, and key performance indicators is extensive. In addition, Basel III requires enhanced disclosures on capital, risk-weighted assets (RWAs), and liquidity. However, the experience has demonstrated the relevance of the topic for banking institutions.

So, what should we look for in a successful and profitable banking institution? First of all, key risk and performance indicators have emerged as vital navigation instruments used by CEOs, CFOs, CROs, and other managers to understand whether their firm is on a successful voyage or whether it is moving off the prosperous course. Without the right indicators, managers are sailing blind. Of course, not every indicator is equally important. Just like in the cockpits of our automobiles, some indicators are omnipresent; others only come on when a certain pre-defined threshold has been reached.

Effective managers understand the risk and performance indicators of all key dimensions of their respective business and use them to transport strategy and objectives to their operative units, i.e., business divisions, regional entities, or subsidiaries. Further, market analysts and investors—just like regulators—require standardized indicators, which can be benchmarked to industry peers.

One last comment before actually looking at important bank risk and performance indicators: If successfully implemented at different levels throughout an organization, they represent a powerful early warning tool. And that is most important in modern risk management. Risk identification is an essential first step for removing or alleviating risks. In some cases, however, it is not possible to remove risks in advance. Early warning indicators are pre-defined and quantified triggers that alert individuals responsible for risk management that an identified risk is imminent. This enables the most thorough and prepared approach to handling the situation.

Basic Characteristics of a Good Bank

- Well-capitalized.
- Diversified asset base (with a low level of impairments and a high coverage ratio).
- Experienced management.
- Quality income stream with solid ROE.
- Liquid.
- Well-matched funding.

Key Risk and Performance Indicators: Deutsche Bank

In December 2009, Dr. Josef Ackermann, chairman of the management board at Deutsche Bank, presented a "new set of performance metrics better reflecting key shareholder value drivers" in his concluding remarks at the Deutsche Bank Investor Day[64] (Figure 27.1). The metrics represent a best practice representation about both risk and performance of the institution; further, they integrate strategy in an exceptional way.

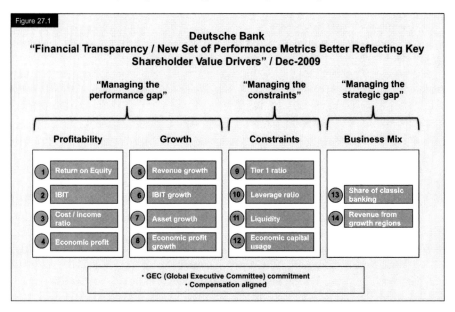

The (then) new metrics are remarkable in a number of ways. Some observations:

- The metrics represent a management cockpit from the chief's perspective. Indicators can be easily broken down to organizational units, i.e., business divisions, risk types, or regions, and to their respective sub-units.

---

[64]Dr. Josef Ackermann (chair of Deutsche Bank management board), "Strategy for a New Era," (presentation at Deutsche Bank Investor Day, Frankfurt, December 14, 2009

▓ The bank's strategy has been embedded into the metrics. For example, the firm's aspiration to grow in Asia—"focus on Asia as a key driver of revenue growth"[65]—can be broken down in individual indicators in all four buckets listed in Figure 27.1: profitability, growth, constraints, and business mix.

▓ It is not surprising that profitability indicators rank from No. 1 to No. 4. These include standard performance indicators that have been widely used in the industry: return on equity (ROE), income before income taxes (IBIT), cost/income ratio, and economic profit. Profitability remains the No. 1 objective, of course.

▓ The second bucket—indicators 5 through 8—sets objectives in terms of growth: revenue growth, IBIT growth, asset growth, and economic profit growth.

▓ The third bucket—indicators 9 to 12—is most relevant from a Basel III perspective. The term "constraints" is interesting, representing a limitation or restriction. Key areas for top management attention are tier 1 capital, the leverage ratio, liquidity, and economic capital usage.

▓ Other major risk indicators such as non-performing loans, loan loss provisions, expected loss, or risk density (exposure at default divided by expected loss, in basis points) are directly or indirectly integrated in other indicators, i.e., IBIT.

▓ Dr. Ackermann and his colleagues in the Global Executive Committee commit clearly to the metrics. Management buy-in at the helm is most crucial.

▓ Probably most important, compensation is aligned to the metrics. After all, it is a money business.

Other Important Indicators Not (Directly or Obviously) Enclosed in the Metrics:

▓ The **credit rating** of the institution. Credit ratings are determined by credit ratings agencies. The credit rating represents the credit rating agency's evaluation of qualitative and quantitative information for a company or government, including non-public information obtained by the credit rating agencies' analysts. Nevertheless, the large credit rating agencies base their ratings on the indicators enlisted, mainly profitability, capital and risk (asset quality), and liquidity.

▓ **Stress Testing.** The indicators are somewhat unclear regarding which levels of risk are likely to be presented. Risk professionals agree on a typical loss profile of a (large) banking institution, which breaks down into expected loss, unexpected loss, and an institution's stress level as illustrated in Figure 27.2. Most likely, the metrics cover both expected loss (covered under profitability) and unexpected loss (covered under constraints only). Of course, Deutsche Bank has an internal stress testing infrastructure, which includes scenario definition, risk calculation, reporting, and management discussion.

▓ Other key risks that cannot easily be quantified, e.g., reputational risk.

---

[65]Dr. Josef Ackermann (chair of Deutsche Bank management board), "Strategy for a New Era," (presentation at Deutsche Bank Investor Day, Frankfurt, December 14, 2009.

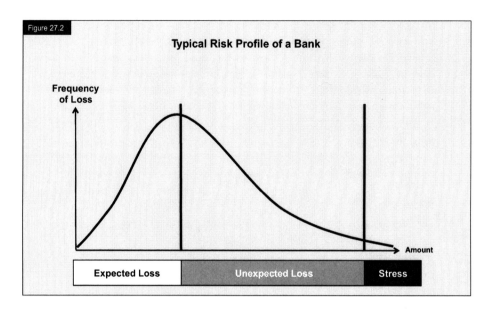

Figure 27.2 — Typical Risk Profile of a Bank

Focus of the Credit Rating Agencies – Key Indicators[66]

When analyzing a banking institution, large credit-rating agencies focus on the following key areas and indicators:.

11. Operating Environment
- Stability and structure of the bank's economy of operation, including weighting if the bank has operations in multiple economies;
- Credit risk of economic participants—mainly households and enterprises;
- Competitive dynamics or the competitive landscape and performance, financial products and practices, and the role of nonbank financial institutions;
- Funding through the debt markets or government, including the role of the central bank and government;
- Legal system;
- Integrity and corruption.

12. Regulatory Environment
- Independence of the regulators;
- Regulatory standards;
- Health of the banking system.

13. Franchise Value / Business Position
- Market share, stability, and sustainability;
- Geographical diversification;

---

[66]Moody's Consolidated Global Bank Rating Methodology, June 2012 / Standard & Poor's Bank Rating Methodology, November 2011.

- Corporate strategy;
- Management;
- Corporate governance;
- Vulnerability to event risk.

14. Profitability / Earnings Quality
- Net income;
- Income before income tax;
- Provision for credit losses;
- Return on equity (ROE);
- Quality of earnings / net interest income, fees and commissions, trading revenues;
- Earnings stability and diversification;
- Other.

15. Capital / Balance Sheet
- Total assets;
- Core tier 1 capital ratio, total tier 1 capital ratio;
- Debt-to-equity;
- Leverage ratio;
- Derivatives, in relation to total assets.

16. Efficiency
- Cost-to-income ratio.

17. Asset Quality / Risk Position
- Proportion of high-risk / moderate-risk / high-risk business;
- Rating profile / investment grade versus non-investment grade;
- Growth and changes in exposures;
- RWA / total assets;
- Impairments / problem loans / coverage ratio;
- Volume collateralized or risk mitigated, i.e., through guarantees, hedges, or loan loss allowances;
- Derivatives / counterparty risk / complexity;
- Concentrations, i.e., exposure to industries or countries;
- Sensitivity to market risk;
- Operational risk;
- Legal risk / litigation;
- Risks not covered by risk-adjusted capital framework.

18. Liquidity & Funding
- Liquidity reserves;
- Ability to finance itself under stress / short-term liquidity coverage;
- Stable funding sources and profile / access to market funding (interbank, fixed-income securities, derivatives) / loans-to-deposits ratio;
- Contingency plan.

EBA Risk Dashboard / KRI Heatmap[67]

The European Banking Authority lists the following key risk indicators (KRIs) and respective thresholds:

1. Solvency

Number	KRI	Threshold	Evaluation
1	**Tier 1 capital ratio**	>12%	Best
		9% - 12%	Intermediate
		<9%	Worst
2	**Tier 1 ratio** (excluding hybrid instruments)	>10%	Best
		5% - 10%	Intermediate
		<5%	Worst

2. Credit Risk & Asset Quality

Number	KRI	Threshold	Evaluation
3	**Impaired loans and Past due (>90 days) loans to total loans**	<5%	Best
		5% - 10%	Intermediate
		>10%	Worst
4	**Coverage ratio** (all allowances for loans and debt instruments to total gross impaired loans and debt instruments)	>50%	Best
		25% - 50%	Intermediate
		<25%	Worst
5	**Accumulated impairments on financial assets to total** (gross) **assets**	<1%	Best
		1% - 2%	Intermediate
		>2%	Worst
6	**Impairments on financial assets to total operating income**	<5%	Best
		5% - 20%	Intermediate
		>20%	Worst

3. Earnings

Number	KRI	Threshold	Evaluation
7	**Return on Equity**	>16%	Best
		8% - 16%	Intermediate
		<8%	Worst
8	**Cost-to-Income**	<33%	Best
		33% - 66%	Intermediate
		>66%	Worst

---

[67]"Risk Dashboard" (data of Q42013). European Banking Authority. http://www.eba.europa.eu/risk-analysis-and-data/risk-dashboard.

4. Balance Sheet Structure

Number	KRI	Threshold	Evaluation
9	**Loan-to-deposit ratio**	<100%	Best
		100% - 150%	Intermediate
		>150%	Worst
10	**Tier 1 capital (total assets – intangible assets)**	>7%	Best
		4% - 7%	Intermediate
		<4%	Worst
11	**Debt-to-equity ratio**	<10x	Best
		10x – 20x	Intermediate
		>20x	Worst
12	**Off-balance sheet items to total assets**	<10%	Best
		10% - 20%	Intermediate
		>20%	Worst

Key Takeaways

- A good bank is well capitalized, and has a diversified asset base (with low levels of impairments and a high coverage ratio), an experienced management, a quality income stream (with solid ROE), is liquid, and has well-matched funding.
- Financial institutions should look at the three levels of risk: expected risk, unexpected risk, and risk in a stress scenario.
- Rating agencies and regulators will track the same key risk indicators, focusing on solvency (capital adequacy), asset quality / risks (all risk types), earnings (stability and volatility) and profitability, efficiency (ROE), and balance sheet structure.

Basel III – Issues and Implications

As described in Chapter 2, Basel III is a comprehensive set of reform measures to strengthen the regulation, supervision, and risk management of the banking sector.

These measures have two main objectives:

- To strengthen global capital and liquidity regulations with the goal of promoting a more resilient banking sector.
- To improve the banking sector's ability to absorb shocks arising from financial and economic stress, which, in turn, would reduce the risk of a spillover from the financial sector to the real economy.

The objectives are significant and therefore must, more or less by default, generate issues and have implications.

Implications for the Financial System

1. Reduced Risk of Another Systemic Banking Crisis

The enhanced capital and liquidity buffers together with the focus on enhanced risk management standards and capability should lead to reduced risk of individual bank failure and also reduced interconnectivity between institutions. The combination of capital reform, liquidity standards, systemic risk issues, and governance and risk management topics will make banks stronger, and, subsequently, reduce the risk of another systemic banking crisis. However, a systemic banking crisis can be triggered by many areas, as described in Part 7 on stress testing. Basel III is a great reform, especially from a consumer or taxpayer perspective. But are the measures enough to even state that it "eliminated risk of another systemic banking crisis"? The reality is that no one in the world would underwrite this particular statement. As a consequence, regulators and central bankers, in particular the FSB, have a monumental task to ensure that the system does not become distressed. The governments' risk management system, i.e., the early warning tool, needs to function at any time. Never say never.

2. Reduced Number of Banks in the European Union and the United States

In theory, investors should be less attracted by bank debt or equity issuance given that dividends are likely to be reduced to allow firms to rebuild capital bases. In reality, though, large banks have raised hundreds of billion dollars of additional capital over the past few years. Some issuances were even oversubscribed. However, there are simply too many banks that need to raise capital to comply with the new regulations; and, of course, capital is scarce. As Figure 28.1 illustrates, the number of banks in both the EU and the U.S. has declined significantly since 2007. It is highly likely that this general trend will continue.

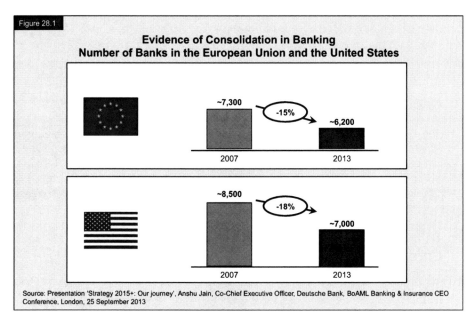

Figure 28.1

Evidence of Consolidation in Banking
Number of Banks in the European Union and the United States

Source: Presentation 'Strategy 2015+: Our journey', Anshu Jain, Co-Chief Executive Officer, Deutsche Bank, BoAML Banking & Insurance CEO Conference, London, 25 September 2013

3. Inconsistent Implementation of Basel III

Inconsistent implementation of Basel III in different jurisdictions may—similarly to implementation issues under Basel I and Basel II—create instability in the financial system. Institutions will consider options to optimize their cost for regulatory capital.

4. Reduced Lending Capacity Affecting the Real Economy

Going forward, CFOs and CROs in banks will analyze the utilization of capital intensively. Capital is a scarce resource and must be deployed in an optimal cost/benefit relationship. In its commercial lending portfolio—which is still the main business for most banks in the world—an institution must earn, at least, the equivalent to the sum of operating cost, funding cost, risk, and capital cost. In theory, risk and capital cost increase exponentially as the borrower rating decreases. Weaker firms—in particular small- and medium-sized enterprises (SMEs) that need the money the most—will face significantly higher interest rate charges, if the lender underwrites the loan in the first place. Possibly, this may lead to a real problem for corporations, especially SMEs. This subject is also described in Chapter 29, "Impact of Basel III on Small- and Medium-Sized Enterprises."

Issues and Implications for Financial Institutions

1. Reputation

In a number of developed economies, the banking industry today has a seriously fractured relationship with society; customers' trust in banks has eroded notably and is far from being intact. In fact, the industry's reputation is at the bottom of the table. This issue is particularly a concern for institutions in the European Union. According to the Edelman Trust Barometer,[68] German and Irish institutions have the lowest international levels, at just 23 percent. Chinese banks have the highest level at 76 percent, while those in the U.S. are at 50 percent.

2. Capital Issuance

One way to increase a bank's capital ratio is to increase the capital level—the numerator of the capital ratio formula. Large, globally active bank holding companies have raised hundreds of billion dollars in the past few years. One example: Deutsche Bank raised €3 billion in 2Q2013 and an astonishing additional €8 billion in 2Q2014. In order to subscribe successfully, banks need to present credible business strategies and good key risk and performance indicators to existing shareholders and potential new investors.

3. Dilution for Shareholders of Large Bank Holding Companies

When banks issue additional shares, this reduces an existing investor's proportional ownership in that firm, i.e., dilution. The effect is that the value of existing shares takes a hit.

4. Reduction of Risk-Weighted Assets (RWAs)

For banks, the other alternative to increase capital ratios is to decrease levels of RWAs, the denominator of the capital ratio formula, by one or more of the following measures:

- Creation of a "bad bank," i.e., a corporate structure is created by a troubled bank to isolate illiquid and high-risk securities and, hence, reduce the balance sheet.
- Sale or closure of portfolios/activities/operations, both in commercial banking and investment banking. Of course, revenue will suffer from this measure.
- Improving the risk density or risk quality, i.e., the relation between expected loss (EL) and exposure at default (EAD). Maturing loans or trading positions that expose the bank to counterparty credit risk (CCR) are replaced with new positions with a better rating.

---

[68]"2014 Edelman Trust Barometer." Edelman. www.edelman.com

▓ Reduction of the maturity of transaction, especially in trading business (to reduce CCR).

5. Active Balance Sheet Management

Pressure on bank capital has driven focus onto active capital management and active portfolio management. Banks will closely manage single lines on the balance sheet, relating assets and liabilities where useful. For example, the ratio between loans and deposits will be actively managed, most likely with clear limits and/or thresholds. Risk positions will be macro-hedged, where and when necessary. For example, large corporate exposures will be hedged by using credit default swaps.

6. Review of Business Models

Institutions will review their business models and strategy. Business divisions need to prove that they are profitable, of course on a risk-adjusted basis.

It can be expected that a number of banks will reduce/close their capital markets activities because of the additional burden from the calculation of RWAs. Banks will re-focus on granular loan business, in particular consumer banking—i.e., mortgages, credit cards, and consumer loans—and lending to SMEs. Of course, banks need to have tools and resources to calculate return on risk-adjusted capital (RORAC), risk-adjusted return on capital (RAROC), or a similar indicator. Finally, banks will allocate capital dynamically, deciding for core portfolios—i.e.,business divisions—whether to a) invest, b) maintain/re-tool, c) turnaround, or d) exit.

7. Review of Organization

Changes to the treatment of minority interests and investments in financial institutions within the definition of capital may encourage firms to withdraw from certain entities, dispose of certain stakes, or buy out minority interest positions to optimize the capital calculation.

8. Risk Methodology and Data

Institutions will review their risk methodologies, including the underlying data, both in commercial banking and investment banking. Institutions with best practice methodology and sufficient data will have a competitive edge in optimizing capital utilization. Relevant data includes defaults (both corporate and consumer, to calculate probability of defaults), work-out results from intensive care (to calculate loss given defaults), information from credit bureaus, market data (interest rates, FX, stocks, other) to calculate market risk and counterparty credit risk, and internal and external operational losses (fraud, execution, technology, etc.). Risk methodology is further crucially important for pricing.

9. Collateralization and Netting

Banks will take advantage of incentives set by regulators to reduce their counterparty credit exposures. One area of concentration is on increasing the use of collateral for derivatives transactions, whenever possible. This refers to new transactions, but can also have significant impact on existing transactions. Banks will systematically review their netting and collateral contracts, in particular the commercial terms. Where possible, institutions will renegotiate in order to make these powerful mitigation tools most efficient.

10. Central Counterparties (CCPs) / Trade Repositories (TRs)

Banks will take advantage of incentives set by regulators to reduce their counterparty credit exposures. Transactions will be cleared via CCPs and reported to TRs, as required. However, the increased transparency on pricing (of derivatives) will erode margins.

11. Liquidity Coverage

The introduction of the liquidity coverage ratio (LCR) poses a significant problem for banks. The LCR will require banks to hold significantly more liquid, low-yielding assets to meet the LCR, which will have a negative impact on profitability. Banks will change their funding profile, which will lead to more demand for longer-term funding. This funding may not be available from institutional investors that generally seek to reduce their holdings in the financial sector.

12. Stable Funding

The net stable funding ratio (NSFR) is designed to encourage and incentivize banks to use stable sources to fund their activities to reduce the dependency on short-term wholesale funding. Banks will need to increase the proportion of wholesale and corporate deposits with maturities greater than one year, but currently the appetite for term debt is limited. Of course, the most stable funding is insured deposits from retail customers. Banks in many countries are working hard on increasing their market share in retail business by using different means, such as commercial advertisements and reduction of account fees. Funding sources should be well diversified, with no concentrations. The exact funding profile must be managed based on a firm's own rating; the lower the rating, the longer the tenor, with all the consequences for profitability.

13. Disclosure

The new standards promote greater consistency in the way banks disclose information about risks, as well as their risk measurement and management. The aim of the revisions is to enable market participants to compare banks' disclosures of key risk and performance indicators and to assess more effectively a bank's overall capital adequacy. The disclosures are also a particular response to concerns about the opacity of internal model-based approaches to determining RWA.

14. Values and Ethics

Successful banks operate with true ethics and make values central to the way they manage their staff. Of course, compensation must be realigned with best practice standards.

Impact of Basel III on Small- and Medium-Sized Enterprises

Since the onset of the global financial and economic crisis, small and medium-sized enterprises (SMEs) in many countries face a persistently challenging operating environment, due in part to reduced access to credit. Unlike larger businesses, SMEs have a limited capacity to raise external finance through equity or corporate bond issuance. They therefore rely heavily on intermediated finance from financial institutions for their working capital, new capital expenditures, and opportunities for overall expansion. With Basel III, as described in previous chapters, banks will have to hold extra cushions of capital and cash in reserve, meaning that they will be able to lend out less money compared to pre-crisis levels. With SMEs producing significant levels of the private sector output and employing over 50 percent of private sector workers in some countries, SMEs are going to be negatively affected by the Basel III regulatory restrictions.

Several countries are introducing initiatives for restoring growth, with special focus on SMEs. To name just a couple of examples, the Funding for Lending Scheme in the United Kingdom is designed to boost lending to the real economy, whereby participating banks can borrow at a lower cost than those which scale bank lending. The Term Asset-Backed Securities Loan Facility in the United States is expected to help market participants meet the credit needs of SMEs by supporting the issuance of asset-backed securities collateralized by loans of various types.

Ensuring SMEs have access to the finance they need to invest and grow is an important priority for many governments. There is currently much debate between governments, finance providers, SMEs, and their representative organizations on the availability of finance and what can be done to increase it.

Definition of SME[69]

Small and medium-sized enterprises or small- and medium-sized businesses (SMBs) are companies whose personnel numbers fall below certain limits. The abbreviation "SME" is used in the European Union and by international organizations such as the World Bank, the United Nations (UN), and the World Trade Organization (WTO). Small enterprises

---

[69]Wikipedia

outnumber large companies by a wide margin and also employ many more people. SMEs are also said to be responsible for driving innovation and competition in many economic sectors.

In the European Union, there are three broad parameters which define SMEs:

- Micro entities are companies with up to 10 employees;
- Small companies employ up to 50 workers;
- Medium-sized enterprises have up to 250 employees.

The European definition of SME is as follows: "The category of micro, small, and medium-sized enterprises (SMEs) is made up of enterprises which employ fewer than 250 persons and which have an annual turnover not exceeding €50 million, and/or an annual balance sheet total not exceeding €43 million." EU member states, however, have had individual definitions of what constitutes an SME.

In the United States, the Small Business Administration sets small business criteria based on industry, ownership structure, revenue, and number of employees, which in some circumstances may be as high as 1,500, although the cap is typically 500. Both the U.S. and the EU generally use the same threshold of fewer than 10 employees for small firms.

German Mittelstand: SMEs in Germany[70]

Mittelstand refers to SMEs in Germany and other German-speaking economies, such as Austria and Switzerland. The German Ministry of Economics and Technology (Bundesministerium für Wirtschaft und Technologie) typically calls the German Mittelstand the "engine of the German economy."

The German Mittelstand at a Glance:

- More than 99 percent of all German firms belong to the German Mittelstand.
- The German Mittelstand contributes almost 52 percent of total economic output.
- The German Mittelstand accounted for around 37 percent of the overall turnover of German companies; in 2011, that was approximately €2 trillion.
- The German Mittelstand employs roughly 15.5 million people. That equates to approximately 60 percent of all employees subject to social security contributions.
- The international turnover of the German Mittelstand has been growing for years, and stood at €186.1 billion in 2010.
- Almost all of Germany's SMEs are family owned (95 percent), and many are managed by their owners (85 percent).
- Mittelstand companies tend to take a particularly long-term approach to business, typically based on stable client relations, continuous human resources policies, and strong ties to their region.
- The German Mittelstand companies are some of the most innovative in Europe: 54 percent of them launched an innovation onto the market in the 2008-2010 period.

---

[70]"German Mittelstand: Engine of the German Economy," German Federal Ministry of Economics and Technology (BMWi). www.bmwi.de

■ The German Mittelstand relies on sound financing models; besides their own equity, firms rely mostly on bank loans (see Figure 29.2).

The Mittelstand is the Backbone of Germany's Economy

In 2010, the German Mittelstand contributed almost 52 percent of the value added by the German economy. It accounted for almost 37 percent of the total turnover of all German firms (2011 figure). In absolute figures, the total turnover of the German Mittelstand stood at around €2 trillion in 2011 (excluding turnover of foreign subsidiaries). In comparison, the turnover of the 30 companies listed on Germany's blue chip DAX stock market index (Deutscher Aktienindex) amounted to €1.19 trillion in 2011 (including foreign subsidiaries).

In the German labor force, the Mittelstand is particularly important, especially in the crucial area of youth employment; in fact, four-fifths of trainees—more than 1.29 million of the 1.56 million trainees in Germany—receive their training in the Mittelstand (as of end of 2011). Fortunately, and as illustrated by Figure 29.1, the German Mittelstand is a major factor ensuring that youth unemployment is much lower in Germany than in many European countries. In Spain, youth unemployment is 54 percent.

Then president-elect of the European Commission, Jean-Claude Juncker, announced on July 15, 2014, a 10-point agenda for jobs, growth, fairness, and democratic change.

Jean-Claude Juncker, President of the European Commission[71]

"As candidate for president of the European Commission, I see it as my key task to rebuild bridges in Europe after the crisis. To restore European citizens' confidence, my agenda will focus on 10 policy areas. My emphasis will be on concrete results in these 10 areas. Beyond that, I will leave other policy areas to the member states where they are more legitimate and better equipped to give effective policy responses at a national, regional, or local level, in line with the principles of subsidiarity and proportionality."

Topic 1 of the 10-Point Agenda: A New Boost For Jobs, Growth, and Investment

"We must make use of public funds available at [European] Union level to stimulate private investment in the real economy. We need smarter investment, more focus, less regulation, and more flexibility when it comes to the use of these public funds. In my view, this should allow us to mobilize up to €300 billion in additional public and private investment in the real economy over the next three years. We must not stifle innovation and competitiveness with too prescriptive and too detailed regulations, notably when it comes to small- and medium-sized enterprises. SMEs are the backbone of our economy, creating more than 85 percent of new jobs in Europe and we have to free them from burdensome regulation."

---

[71]Jean-Claude Juncker, "A New Start for Europe: My Agenda for Jobs, Growth, Fairness, and Democratic Change" (speech, Strasbourg, July 15, 2014).

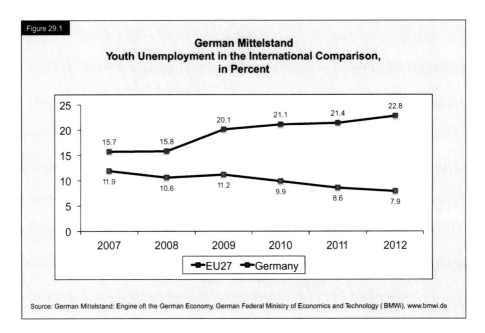

Figure 29.1

German Mittelstand
Youth Unemployment in the International Comparison, in Percent

Source: German Mittelstand: Engine oft the German Economy, German Federal Ministry of Economics and Technology (BMWi), www.bmwi.de

The German Mittelstand is highly innovative and it invests significantly in research and development. Of course, the financing need is significant and depends largely on entrepreneurs' own equity. Additionally, SMEs rely heavily on bank loans, state aids, and other forms of financing, i.e. mezzanine or venture capital, as Figure 29.2 illustrates.

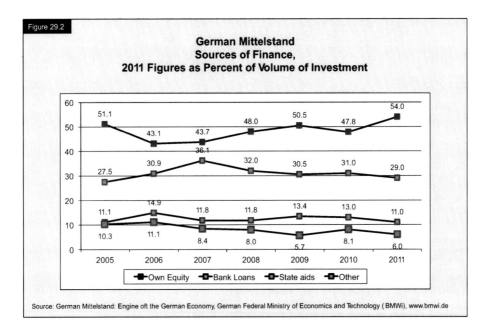

Figure 29.2

German Mittelstand
Sources of Finance,
2011 Figures as Percent of Volume of Investment

Source: German Mittelstand: Engine oft the German Economy, German Federal Ministry of Economics and Technology (BMWi), www.bmwi.de

Number of Firms and Insolvencies in Germany

Figure 29.3 illustrates the importance of SMEs in Germany. In 2011, more than 3.6 million firms existed in Europe's strongest economy, of which 98 percent had less than 50 employees (covered by social security). In 2011, 30,000, or 0.82 percent, of those firms went insolvent.

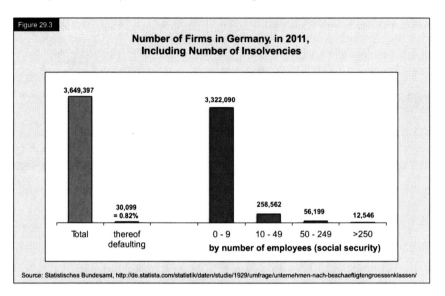

Of course, even in a strong economy like Germany, corporate insolvencies are a major concern for credit risk officers in banks of any size. Figure 29.4 illustrates Germany's corporate insolvencies in the time period from 2000 to 2013.

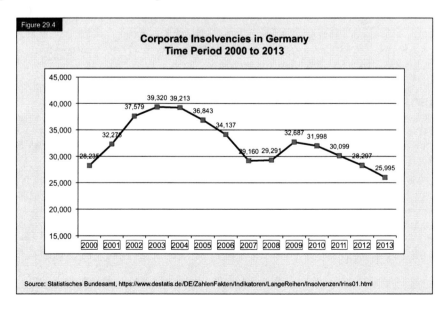

Basel II

Basel II defined regulatory capital requirements in line with the underlying risk of lending and therefore marked a substantial modification from previous regulation. Naturally, this raised regulatory capital requirements for higher-risk asset classes, including SMEs. Basel II introduced risk approaches based on internal ratings and the key credit parameters of exposure at default (EAD), probability of default (PD) and loss given default (LDG). Further, the concept introduced the concept of expected loss (EL) and unexpected loss (UL). All these parameters have been discussed in detail in Chapter 27. Simply speaking and as illustrated in Figure 29.5, banks have higher costs for higher-risk assets.

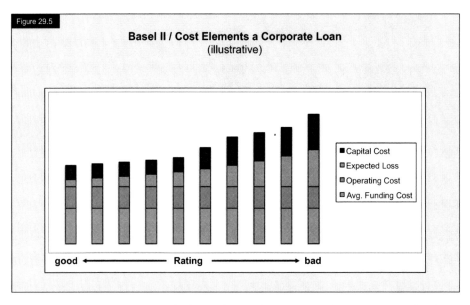

Figure 29.5

Basel II / Cost Elements a Corporate Loan
(illustrative)

- Capital Cost
- Expected Loss
- Operating Cost
- Avg. Funding Cost

good ← Rating → bad

For SMEs, Basel II had installed a preferential treatment of SMEs compared to large corporations, which is still in place under Basel III.

Basel III Impact on SMEs

It was not banks' corporate lending portfolios that caused the big write-downs that led to the financial crisis, so regulators did not explicitly increase the scrutiny for this particular business by imposing, for example, higher risk weights for SMEs.

However, Basel III contains significant implications for SME lending as banks need to optimize capital usage, potentially reduce RWAs, accomplish leverage-ratio requirements, review/adjust their business strategy and efficiency, improve risk-versus-return ratio, and—possibly most importantly for SMEs—their (risk) pricing.

1. Procyclicality

The long history of economic and financial crises shows that procyclicality is an inherent feature of the real and especially the financial sector of an economy. In particular, the recent crisis has been characterized by intense procyclicality of the banking sector and its link with the real sector in a mutually reinforcing manner that may lead to a vicious circle.

The main feature of procyclicality is an underestimation or overestimation of the risks to which the banking sector is exposed, which leads to relatively high growth during the upward phase of the cycle, while downturns are characterized by strong risk aversion that constrains the supply of loans due to banks' concerns about loan portfolio quality and the probability of default. Thus, the banking industry changes from an effective mechanism for allocating funds to one that exacerbates cyclical fluctuations, hindering the efficient allocation of resources in the economy and adversely affecting credit growth and financial stability.

Procyclicality could lead to a potential credit squeeze, i.e., a reduction in the general availability of loans or a sudden tightening of conditions, possibly at a time when SMEs need the loan the most.

2. SMEs Need to Optimize Their Credit Rating

In order to optimize their credit rating—and subsequently the price they pay—SMEs should understand the credit-rating criteria and approaches by their bank(s), and therefore take specific steps to strengthen their company against the competition and enjoy long-term success. Some banks commit to disclosing and explaining the rating result to their corporate clients; thus, the credit-rating process becomes clear, transparent, and understandable. Other banks even offer rating simulation.

In any case, SMEs should thoroughly review all quantitative and qualitative input parameters and run a cost-benefit analysis of how the rating, in order words risk cost, can be improved.

Firms with a non-investment grade rating, or with high levels of debt, should now try to improve their situation. It must be expected that this challenge will even become larger in the future.

Firms must not underestimate the importance of the management factor and other qualitative items in the overall rating process.

3. Funds from Development Banks

As credit pricing will increase, SMEs should look for funding alternatives. Development banks offer interesting programs and aids.

For example, the German government-owned development bank KfW, based in Frankfurt, covers over 90 percent of its borrowing needs in the capital markets, mainly through bonds that are guaranteed by the German government. This allows KfW to raise funds at advantageous conditions. Together with its exemption from corporate taxes due to its legal status as a public agency and unremunerated equity provided by its public shareholders, KfW provides loans for purposes prescribed by the KfW law at lower rates than commercial banks. KfW is not allowed to compete with commercial banks, but it facilitates their business in areas within its mandate. SMEs, start-ups, and import/export companies significantly benefit from this.

4. Long-Term Financings

In many countries around the world, both developed economies and emerging markets, companies—in particular SMEs—traditionally get their financing through a bank loan. Similarly to firms in the United States, SMEs in other countries need to explore the opportunity of issuing corporate bonds, and hence reduce their financing cost. Corporate bonds are long-term debt instruments, generally with a maturity date falling at least a year after their issue date—often even five years and above. From 2011 to 2012, the German market for corporate bonds increased by as much as 25 percent.[72] Naturally, the market is typically tapped by large SMEs.

5. Loan Covenants

As a result of the financial crisis, banks are optimizing their risk management processes from A to Z. Most likely, banks will increase their loan covenant requirements, i.e., the conditions in a bank loan that oblige the borrower to fulfill certain conditions, forbid the borrower from undertaking certain actions, or possibly restrict certain activities to circumstances when other conditions are met. Typically, violation of a covenant results in a default on the loan being declared, penalties being applied, or the loan being called.

6. Collateral

Banks will try to increase their share of collateral loans over unsecured loans. SMEs promise to hand the asset over to the lender if they cannot repay the loan as agreed. By using a collateral loan, the lender takes less risk, and it may be easier for the SME to get funding. Firms need to make sure they know the essentials of collateral loans before they use one.

Collateral loans are used when the lender wants some assurance that it won't lose all its money. If firms pledge an asset as collateral, they can take the asset, sell it, and get their money back. Contrast this with an unsecured loan, where all the bank can do is write the asset off or bring legal action against customers.

When using a collateral loan, firms give the bank the right to take their asset if they can't repay; i.e., automobiles, real estate, cash accounts, investments, insurance policies, valuables and collectibles, and future payments.

Firms should recover their collateral immediately once they have the right to do so after their debt servicing; this process should be very efficient.

7. Checking Accounts

Overdraft facilities on checking accounts are very expensive sources of funding for SMEs. Firms should only utilize this form of financing in special cases.

8. Obtain Loans from Smaller Banks

One of the major criticisms of Basel III is the inconsistent implementation in different legislations. Even within legislations, it is possible that the new banking reforms will be signed into law in different ways for different types of banks. The United States, for example, is applying the Basel III capital standards only to large bank holding companies, i.e., with consolidated balance sheets of $50 billion or above. Smaller banks, typically regional

---

[72]Basel III, die Folgen für den Mittelstand, Bundesverband deutscher Banken, Mai 2013

and community banks, have lower capital ratio requirements, and therefore, lower risk cost. SMEs should simply take advantage of this situation. In the U.S., a corporate or industrial loan should be cheaper when dealing with a smaller bank rather than banking with Citibank or Bank of America.

Key Takeaways

- SMEs are a crucial backbone for the economy; regulations for banks must make this a central concern and focus, and protect SMEs in a particular way.
- Even though Basel III has not been designed to penalize banks' SME lending business, the new reform impacts SMEs implicitly in a significant way.
- Firms need to prepare their discussions with their bank(s) in order to ensure that banks do not overcharge for their expected risk and capital cost.

Appendix

References

Articles/Sources Used

- Ackermann, Joseph, Presentation, Deutsche Bank Investor Day, December 15, 2009.
- *Banking Reform: Delivering Stability and Supporting a Sustainable Economy,* June 2012, https://www.gov.uk/government/uploads/system/uploads/attachment_data/file/32556/whitepaper_banking_reform_140512.pdf.
- Bank of America Corporation Annual Report 2013, pages 16 and 165.
- Barclays Fixed Income Investor Presentation, Q1 2013 Interim Management Statement and 2013 Full Year Results.
- Barclays website.
- *Basel III: A Global Regulatory Framework for More Resilient Banks and Banking Systems,* Basel Committee on Banking Supervision, Bank for International Settlements, December 2010 (revised June 2011).
- Basel III, die Folgen für den Mittelstand, Bundesverband deutscher Banken, Mai 2013.
- *Basel III: International Framework for Liquidity Risk Measurement, Standards, and Monitoring,* Basel Committee on Banking Supervision, Bank for International Settlements, December 2010.
- *Basel III: The Liquidity Coverage Ratio and Liquidity Risk Monitoring Tools,* Basel Committee on Banking Supervision, Bank for International Settlements, August 2013.
- *Basel Committee on Banking Supervision Reforms – Basel III,* http://www.bis.org/bcbs/basel3/b3summarytable.pdf.
- Bazerman, Max and Ann Tenbrunsel, "Ethical Breakdowns," Harvard Business Review, April 2011.
- BIS OTC Derivatives Statistics, 2007 – 2013.
- "Capital Requirements – CRD IV/CRR – Frequently Asked Questions," Bank for International Settlements, July 16, 2013
- CCAR Press Release, Federal Reserve, March 26, 2014.
- *CEBS Guidelines on the Management of Concentration Risk under the Supervisory Review Process,* College of European Supervisors (CEBS), (GL31), September 2, 2010.

- "CoCos: A Primer," Basel Committee on Banking Supervision, Bank for International Settlements; BIS Quarterly Review, September 2013.
- *Comprehensive Capital Analysis and Review 2014 – Summary Instructions and Guidance*, Board of Governors of the Federal Reserve System, November 1, 2013.
- CoreLogic, Press Release, August 26, 2010.
- Deutsche Bank Annual General Meeting, May 22, 2014: Compensation for employees and for members of management bodies of subsidiaries – Increase in the limit for variable compensation components.
- Deutsche Bank Annual Report 2013, Page 72, and Annual Report/Management Report 2013 Page 101.
- Deutsche Bank Investor Relations Website, "Risk Overview" presentation, Stuart Lewis, Deputy Chief Risk Officer, Investor Meeting November 22, 2011.
- Deutsche Bank Research. "Contingent Convertibles." May 23, 2011. http://www.dbresearch.com/PROD/DBR_INTERNET_EN-PROD/PROD0000000000273597.pdf.
- "Deutsche Bank's $4.8 billion CoCo Success Sets Scene for Share Sale," Reuters, May 20, 2014.
- Edelman Trust Barometer, www.edelman.com.
- European Banking Authority Risk Dashboard Q12014 (data of Q42013).
- European Banking Authority, Stress Test Press Release, April 29, 2014.
- European Securities and Markets Authority, Clearing Thresholds for Non-Financial Entities, List of Central Counterparties, Trade Repositories.
- Federal Reserve Data, http://www.federalreserve.gov/monetarypolicy/openmarket.htm#calendars, retrieved 14-Oct-2013.
  - federalreservehistory.org.
- Federal Reserve website, Frequently Asked Questions, http://www.federalreserve.gov/faqs/cat_21427.htm.
- Federal Reserve website, Press Release, "Federal Reserve Proposes to Revise Market Risk Capital Rule," July 2, 2014.
- "The Financial Crisis Inquiry Report, Final Report of the National Commission on the Causes of the Financial and Economic Crisis in the United States," January 2011.
- Financial Services (Banking Reform) Bill, http://www.publications.parliament.uk/pa/bills/lbill/2013-2014/0062/14062.pdf, July 2013.
- First Midwest Bancorp (Itasca, Illinois) Website, Selected Financial Information, December 31, 2013.
- G-20 website, www.g20.org.
- "German Mittelstand: Engine of the German Economy," German Federal Ministry of Economics and Technology (BMWi), www.bmwi.de.
- *Global Risks 2013 / Eighth Edition*, World Economic Forum, www3.weforum.org/docs/WEF_GlobalRisks_Report_2013.pdf.
- *Global Systemically Important Banks: Updated Assessment Methodology and the Higher Loss Absorbency Requirement*, Basel Committee on Banking Supervision, Bank for International Settlements, July 2013.

▓ HSBC Annual Report, Risk Report, Page 136.

▓ HSBC Holdings plc Annual Report and Accounts, 2012.

▓ HSH Nordbank Annual Report 2013, Hamburg, Germany.

▓ JPMorgan Chase & Co. Annual Report 2013, Pages 2 and 223.

▓ Juncker, Jean-Claude, "A New Start for Europe: My Agenda for Jobs, Growth, Fairness and Democratic Change," Speech, Strasbourg, Germany, July 15, 2014.

▓ "A Macro Stress-Testing Framework for Bank Solvency Analysis," ECB Monthly Bulletin, August 2013, http://www.ecb.europa.eu/pub/pdf/other/art2_mb201308en_pp93-111en.pdf.

▓ Merriam Webster, http://www.merriam-webster.com/dictionary/trust.

▓ Morgan Stanley 1Q2014 Fixed Investor Update, May 14, 2014.

▓ Morgan Stanley, 2Q2013 Fixed Investor Conference Call, August 2, 2013.

▓ *Principles for Sound Liquidity Risk Management and Supervision,* Basel Committee on Banking Supervision, Bank for International Settlements, September 2008.

▓ *Principles for Enhancing Corporate Governance,* Basel Committee on Banking Supervision, Bank for International Settlements, October 2010.

▓ *Principles for Sound Stress Testing Practices and Supervision,* Basel Committee on Banking Supervision, Bank for International Settlements, May 2009.

▓ RBS/UBS investor relations website, Investor Presentations / Quarterly Results.

▓ Remarks of Federal Reserve Board Governors Daniel K. Tarullo and Elizabeth A. Duke at the Federal Reserve Open Board Meeting, July 2, 2013, http://www.federalreserve.gov/mediacenter/files/open-board-meeting-transcript-20130702.pdf.

▓ *Report to G-20 Leaders on Basel III Implementation,* Basel Committee on Banking Supervision, Bank for International Settlements, June 2012.

▓ *Report to G-20 Leaders on Monitoring Implementation of Basel III Regulatory Reforms,* Basel Committee on Banking Supervision, Bank for International Settlements, August 2013.

▓ *Revised Basel III Leverage Ratio Framework and Disclosure Requirements,* Basel Committee on Banking Supervision, Bank for International Settlements, June 2013.

▓ *The Run on the Rock,* Fifth Report of Session 2007-08, House of Commons, Treasury Committee, United Kingdom.

▓ "SME Access to External Finance," BIS Economics Paper No. 16, BIS United Kingdom, Department for Business Innovation & Skills, January 2012

▓ Smith, Greg; *Why I Left Goldman Sachs – A Wall Street Story;* Grand Central Publishing, 2012.

▓ *A Sound Capital Planning Process: Fundamental Elements – Sound Practices,* Basel Committee on Banking Supervision, Bank for International Settlements, January 2014.

▓ Statistisches Bundesamt, https://www.destatis.de/DE/.

▓ Stress Test 2014 Press Release, European Banking Authority, April 29, 2014

▓ UBS Annual Report 2013, Risk, Treasury, and Capital Management, Page 217

▓ Wells Fargo, Annual Reports 2008 – 2013.

▓ Wikipedia.

Appendix

Abbreviations

ABS	Asset-Backed Security
AFS	Available for Sale
AII	Alternative Instruments Identifier
ALLL	Allowance for Loan and Lease Losses
AMA	Advanced Measurement Approaches
AOCI	Accumulated Other Comprehensive Income
AQR	Asset Quality Review
ARM (rates)	Adjustable-Rate Mortgage (rates)
ASEAN	Association of Southeast Asian Nations
ASF	Available Stable Funding
BCBS	Basel Committee on Banking Supervision
BIS	Bank for International Settlements, Basel,Switzerland
BHC	Bank Holding Company
BIA	Basic Indicator Approach
CA	Competent (Regulatory) Authorities
CAP	Capital Adequacy Process
CCAR	Comprehensive Capital Analysis and Review
CCASG	Cooperation Council for the Arab States of the Gulf
CCF	Credit Conversion Factor
CCP	Central Counterparty
CCR	Counterparty Credit Risk
CDO	Collateral Debt Obligation
CDS	Credit Default Swap
CE	Conversion to Equity
CEM	Current Exposure Method
CEO	Chief Executive Officer
CET1 (capital)	Common Equity Tier 1 (capital)
CFI (code)	Classification of Financial Instruments (code)
CFO	Chief Financial Officer
CFP	Contingency Funding Plan
CFTC	Commodity Futures Trading Commission
CMBS	Commercial Mortgage-Backed Security
CNY	Chinese Yuan Renminbi

CoCo	Contingent Convertible Capital Instrument
CRD	Capital Requirements Directive
CRE	Capital Requirements Regulation
CRO	Chief Risk Officer
CVA	Credit Value Adjustment
DFA	Dodd-Frank Wall Street Reform and Consumer Protection Act
DFAST	Dodd-Frank Act Supervisory Stress Tests
D-SIB	Domestic Systemically Important Banks
EAD	Exposure at Default
EBA	European Banking Authority
EBIT	Earnings Before Interest and Taxes
EC	European Community
ECB	European Central Bank
EE	Expected Exposure
EEPE	Effective Expected Positive Exposure
EIOPA	European Insurance and Occupational Pensions Authority
EMIR	European Market Infrastructure Regulation
EPE	Expected Positive Exposure
ESMA	European Securities and Markets Authority
ESRB	European Systemic Risk Board
EU	European Union
EUR	Euro
FINMA	Swiss Financial Market Supervisory Authority
FSB	Financial Stability Board
FSF	Financial Stability Forum
FSOC	Financial Stability Oversight Council
FY	Financial Year
G-20	Group of 20 (countries)
GDP	Gross Domestic Product
GIIPS (countries)	Greece, Ireland, Italy, Portugal, Spain
G-SIB	Global Systemically Important Bank
G-SIFI	Global Systemically Important Financial Institution
HNWI	High Net Worth Individual
HQLA	High-Quality Liquid Asset
HTM	Hold to Maturity
IBIT	Income before Interest and Taxes
ICAAP	Internal Capital Adequacy Assessment Process
IMF	International Monetary Fund
IMM	Internal Model Method
IOSCO	International Organization of Securities Commissions
IRB (Approach)	Internal Rating-Based Approach
ISIN	International Securities Identification Number
KYC	Know Your Customer
LCR	Liquidity Coverage Ratio
LEI	Legal Entity Identifier
LGD	Loss Given Default

LLP	Loan Loss Provisions
MaRisk	Minimum Requirements for Risk Management in Germany
MDB	Multilateral Development Bank
MiFID	Markets in Financial Instruments Directive
MPR	Margin Period of Risk
NBFC	Non-Bank Financial Company
NEPAD	New Partnership for Africa's Development
NIM	Net Interest Margin
NPL	Non-Performing Loans
NSFR	Net Stable Funding Ratio
OBS	Off-Balance-Sheet
OECD	Organization for Economic Cooperation and Development
OREO	Other Real Estate Owned
OTC	Over-the-Counter, trading done directly between two parties, without any supervision of an exchange
PD	Probability of Default
PLAC	Primary Loss-Absorbing Capacity
PONV	Point of Non-Viability
PPNR	Pre-Provision Net Revenue
PSE	Public-Sector Entity
PWD	Principal Write-Down
RAROC	Risk-Adjusted Return on Capital
RC	Replacement Cost
RMBS	Residential Mortgage-Backed Security
ROE	Return on Equity
RORAC	Return on Risk-Adjusted Capital
ROSC	Reports on the Observance of Standards and Codes
RSF	Required Stable Funding
RWA	Risk-Weighted Asset
SA	Standardized Approach
SCAP	Supervisory Capital Assessment Program
SEC	Securities and Exchange Commission
SFT	Securities Financing Transaction
SIB	Systemically Important Bank
SIFI	Systemically Important Financial Institution
SLHC	Savings and Loan Holding Companies
SM	Standardized Model
SME	Small- and Medium-Sized Enterprises
SPV	Special Purpose Vehicle
SSM	Single Supervisory Mechanism
TR	Trade Repository
UPI	Unique Product Identifier
USD	United States Dollar
UTI	Unique Trade Identifier
VaR	Value-at-Risk
WWR	Wrong Way Risk

Appendix

About the Author

Peter W. Buerger is Managing Director of Risk & More and specializes in banking- and risk management-related consulting and advisory projects. Within the last three years, he has also provided tailored training services to banks, institutions, and corporations in many financial centers around the world, including North America, Europe, Africa, the Middle East, and Asia. Prior to this Peter worked in banking for 20 years with Commerzbank in Frankfurt and London and UniCredit in Munich. Peter holds an MBA from Long Island University in New York. Visit his website at www.risk-and-more.com.

Contact Details

Peter W. Buerger
Risk & More
Gimbacher Tann 28
65779 Kelkheim (Taunus)
Germany
Phone +49-6195-977610
Mobile +49-151-25678555
E-Mail pb@risk-and-more.com
www.risk-and-more.com